Susan A. Rader

YOU DON'T HAVE TO MOVE THE WASHER TO MAKE TOAST

Religious Autobiography

Susan A. Rader

Copyright © 2016 Susan A. Rader.

All rights reserved. No part of this book may be used or reproduced by any means, graphic, electronic, or mechanical, including photocopying, recording, taping or by any information storage retrieval system without the written permission of the author except in the case of brief quotations embodied in critical articles and reviews.

Scripture taken from the New King James Version. Copyright © 1979, 1980, 1982 by Thomas Nelson, Inc. Used by permission. All rights reserved.

WestBow Press books may be ordered through booksellers or by contacting:

WestBow Press
A Division of Thomas Nelson & Zondervan
1663 Liberty Drive
Bloomington, IN 47403
www.westbowpress.com
1 (866) 928-1240

Because of the dynamic nature of the Internet, any web addresses or links contained in this book may have changed since publication and may no longer be valid. The views expressed in this work are solely those of the author and do not necessarily reflect the views of the publisher, and the publisher hereby disclaims any responsibility for them.

Any people depicted in stock imagery provided by Thinkstock are models, and such images are being used for illustrative purposes only. Certain stock imagery © Thinkstock.

ISBN: 978-1-5127-2734-0 (sc)
ISBN: 978-1-5127-2735-7 (hc)
ISBN: 978-1-5127-2733-3 (e)

Library of Congress Control Number: 2016900727

Print information available on the last page.

WestBow Press rev. date: 01/21/2016

CHAPTER 1

Lasagna at Breakfast, Veteran's Day WAC, Sgt. Rock

"Heat oven to 375. Use center shelf. Do NOT tear film." It was 6:35 a.m. and I was reading aloud because my eyes weren't yet awake.

My husband put his chin on my shoulder to look down at the frozen lasagna box. He noticed I was studying the directions in detail.

"Different directions than last time?"

"Oh, this is the same box but it's got 'new and improved' which means they probably ruined it."

"Hmm. A bit early for lasagna."

"Not if I'm planning supper tonight."

David laughed.

"Oh well, then that makes sense."

I gave him an elbow push.

"Are you insinuating that I'll forget by tonight?"

David put his chin on the top of my head.

"Well, it crossed my mind."

I ignored him and pulled the plastic bowl of frozen lasagna out of the box.

My husband moved his chin to the other side of my neck, then began poking the plastic. He drew an imaginary horizontal line.

"You get this half, and I'll take this half."

I erased his imaginary line and drew a line vertically through the frost.

"Nope. I'll take *this* half. YOU take *that* half."

Silence. I turned my head toward my husband and raised my eyebrows as I leaned back on him.

We both burst out laughing.

"Like I can eat this much in a month! Maybe *you* could eat all this at one meal, but I can't." I poked him in the ribs. "Besides, I want the front half of this lasagna thingy. It's shallow and cooks faster." I examined the plastic container trying to see through the frost.

"Oh, OK. Well, that's the part that always burns," David observed.

"Not if I take it out of the box!" More laughter.

I pointed to the long packaged garlic bread still frozen and glistening on the counter.

"That's enough garlic bread to feed fourteen people. "We exchanged glances, as I waited for his comment.

David pretended to figure some calculations in the air and asked,

"Then you think that's enough for the two of us?"

More laughter.

We were going over the meal plan for this evening, but discussing this over breakfast. When I remembered to plan ahead, then I think it's great to plan ahead. Other wise, I wing it for dinner and no one likes my chicken surprise.

With a kiss goodbye, my husband added, "Don't forget to turn on the oven!"

"Ha, Ha. Very funny, funny man. Just for that your half won't be cooked!"

David left for work just as my cell phone buzzed. It was a text message from our daughter. She was already at work.

"Happy Veteran's Day, Mom. Thanks." November 11, 2013.

The smile on my face for her message began to fade. One little thoughtful moment meant so much, for so many reasons. It feels as if I have lived many lifetimes and I've been many people. A tear ran down my face.

YOU DON'T HAVE TO MOVE THE WASHER TO MAKE TOAST

It was three short years in the 1970's. The timing was just as the Women's Army Corps transitioned from 'WACs', as it was called, into Regular Army. My life was so different then, because I didn't receive my new life until 1981.

My daughter's text message made me feel good. She's old enough to understand more about life in general. I recalled some of my time in service, and not coming up with anything better, I replied: "Thank you. Very thoughtful. I love you."

No wonder so many who are in military service never talk about it. Who can relate to the circumstances? It even goes unspoken between veterans. Sometimes there is little sense to what we experienced. My goal when I enlisted was to have a career in the framework of the military, but it ended unexpectedly as a result of a trip through a cyanide gas chamber. That morning in 1974 changed my life. I should have died.

Thinking about this on the larger scale, this wasn't the only time I should have died. It was as if each stage became *one lifetime*, just enough in one direction for Life Lessons, to suffer loss or to triumph, only to be stopped by near death. Then, immediately after one sequence, my life would take another direction. The pattern is too marked to be coincidence. And, there is a reasonable explanation.

Susan A. Rader

My Compass

Let me start over.

One of the main inspirations in my life was my father's brother. My Uncle Art Strawn. He was a Signalman for the Navy during WW2, and deciphered codes. He had a gift for codes, puzzles and language. With these gifts he was able to translate a message to or from any language, without reading or writing the language.

He went ashore in Borneo with a unit from Australia, running across the dead bodies on a beach. He never told me if he had killed any of the enemy. That was not important—'just do the job you have to do, the best you can do it'. That directive left a lasting impression on me. My father was a chief petty officer on the USS Whitney during WW2. He is different story.

I grew up on Roy Rogers, the Lone Ranger, Superman, comic books, radio shows and war movies. As a small child, I listened to the men talking about life on submarines and battleships or units marching through jungles or forests. I learned what it was like to sit and wait for an enemy to attack, or sneak up in the night. I heard them talk of their experience of battle--to rush into battle from some who had been at Normandy yet lived to continue with the march to free France.

One friend told me he saw the blood pouring from box cars filled with Jews when he charged into Dachau. His unit was sent to liberate that concentration camp. The Germans as they were leaving, sprayed the boxcars with bullets.

I heard of the hardships in Burma and then about Korea. There were diseases from exposure to damp and malnutrition. I heard their words, not as complaints but as sacrifice. It was the price they paid for loving this country and going into battle. I learned that it took courage before you ever entered the battle. Courage not to run away, yes, but when you face battle, charge into it with all you have. Good information in the context of life in or outside the military. I listened carefully and stored it all away. As the comic book hero, Captain America says, "I hate bullies".

Two WAC Jobs

In the Army, I never stormed a beach, but I stormed the rooms of barracks where there were bullies. There were over one hundred female soldiers thrown together in West Germany by commanders who suddenly didn't know what to do with the small groups of females attached to their all male units. So Buildings 62 and 63 Waldstrasse, Furth, West Germany, became the catch-all for women assigned to the Nuremberg area.

Our buildings were barely livable with most toilets and light fixtures out of order. It was a matter of adapting to it, until action could be taken. I arrived the week the 'former barrack's sergeant' was leaving. I had to check in with her to be assigned a room.

She looked me over in my clean pressed dress uniform and spit shined shoes, straight from Women's Army Corp Headquarters in Alabama. *Strack Wac.* Hardly qualifications for the the job as barrack's sergeant, but I was appointed, having no experience, and holding a lower rank than at least 1/3 of the women in the barracks. *This wouldn't go over very well.*

"I'm appointing you as Barrack's Sergeant. I'll fill you in on what little you can do here, and good luck maintaining order. You will be held accountable. This job doesn't come with perks."

My Night Job

There were 110 women assigned, unevenly to building 62 and 63. All sizes. All sorts. Few who even belonged to the same unit. Good soldiers, lazy soldiers, nice women, not nice women, belligerents and bullies.

There will always be people making the most of opportunity, for good or bad. There will always be lazy people looking for a ride. And there will always be bullies.

Dealing with a hundred personality types and trying to manage a role in which I had no training, became my night job. It wasn't a job I enjoyed. There were WAC's leaving for the states or arriving; women wanting to change room mates; bickering, feuding, and those who simply refused to abide by common courtesy, let alone military standards. There was the run down, neglected buildings and the neglected women who's assigned unit provided only a mattress with sheets and two blankets, no furniture. It was a mess.

As I took over 'command', I had a few higher ranking non-coms who encouraged me. They didn't want the job. Others ignored me. With a nudge in how to run a barracks, I selected a young woman to be my assistant who saw the Army as I did--a career opportunity. Super Cooper and I both intended to do the best we could under these circumstances. It was rough going.

We were appreciated by some and hated by a few as we established order. There was no pleasing this group first of all because we were not all from the same unit. How was I going to enforce any rules when we don't have the same commanding officer? Good question with no ready answer.

The rooms held women assigned as medics, clerks, cooks, mechanics and other Army jobs. A huge hodge-podge. I was not provided a complete list of the units represented. My assignment was to maintain some type of military order, based on what I had learned in my short 18 months in the Army.

The departing Sergeant said, "Just wing it. You don't want some company commander coming down on everyone in the building. Oh, and good luck getting maintenance to come fix things."

So my night adventures started.

First off, I learned that offering pastry or the local beer as a gift spurred the German maintenance men to work harder and finish quickly. Fitting into the culture became a necessity.

Then, trying to bring order to chaos, I disarmed a druggy who held a straight razor to another woman's neck; reported a tyrant cadre at a unit known for molestation and suicides of new WACs waiting on their first assignments. I caught a First Sergeant dealing in the black market selling U.S. Government meat, and the same day chased and tackled a drug dealer. The fence collapsed right at the feet of M.P.s.

Timing can be everything—the key is going with the flow. Even sheer dumb luck can help. When I came back to the barracks after tackling the drug dealer, I presented quite a sight. Several women were in the common room and saw the gashes on my forearms from the fence. Since I was in shock, which passed for cool and confident, word spread that I was 'tough'. My 'tough' was mostly bluff. I saw John Wayne movies! Who was I to argue with the rumor that I captured a drug pusher? If Providence hadn't collapsed the fence, with a set of loafing M.P.'s on the other side, that guy could have punched my lights out.

Those 'successes', although causing me physical and emotional pain, resulted in a 'persona' of toughness. *Don't mess with Sergeant Rock.* I put a hand painted sign on my room door. I was fair with those who needed help, and came down hard on bullies, knowing that at some point I might have to tackle someone.

My Day Job

And my day job? My orders read 'Enlisted Personnel Records Clerk' in Merrell Barracks. The "Sud Kasern", or south barracks, were filled with male G I's. Military desks were jammed together in a set of small rooms with barely twenty four inches between them.

Conversation was vulgar, lewd, and obscene. The day I made my debut I was a surprise to everyone. Obviously the Sergeant in charge had failed to discuss appropriate behavior in mixed company. My desk was as far away from the door as it could get without being on the balcony. I was one woman surrounded by 20 men in a cramped space. I think some of them drew lots, and the thought crossed my mind I might be drawn and quartered. This assignment in West Germany was a do or die without being on the front line.

It seemed my aversion to bullies and injustice let me see the worst side of the Army. As for justice? A company sergeant forcing his men to buy drugs from him went free; the first sergeant dealing in stolen government meat moved his operation; but the Army drug dealer I captured by the barracks was sentenced. Win some but watch other victories slip away. Sometimes it's a surprise to realize there are criminal acts committed in the military.

I also learned to side step the chain of command more than once to go straight to the top for help. Corruption isn't confined to civilian life. It wasn't as if I went looking for these things. It must have been my mind set. When there was no one to step up to change something, I simply tackled it. Uncovering corruption, sexual abuse, misuse of military property and embezzlement made the military seem a very dirty place. Then as a patient at a military hospital, I uncovered a psycho psychiatrist. What I was seeing was a micro world within the world of unrestrained human behavior.

These things don't fit into every day conversation. There isn't a lot of humor in those stories, but that was one of my other lives. I'm glad that's over. I remember the day my life changed and this chapter in the Army came to a roaring halt, with cyanide poisoning. When faced with new challenges, I automatically go back to that event. Sometimes it limits what I do in the present.

I looked again at the thoughtful text message from my daughter. Hayley is one of the miracles in my life. Since I was standing in the hallway we call our 'wall of fame', I looked up at family photos. Off to one side is a favorite photo taken at a park. My husband David and our then young daughter were caught in a picture snapped on her first roller coaster ride. With her hair standing up and scream caught forever on film, Hayley hung on to the coaster safety bar next to her Dad. David had a big smile and his arms raised over his head in sheer delight. What a pair of goofs. I love them very much.

Other photos were there, and then my military display. "Certificate of Achievement, US ARMY EUROPE/7th ARMY".

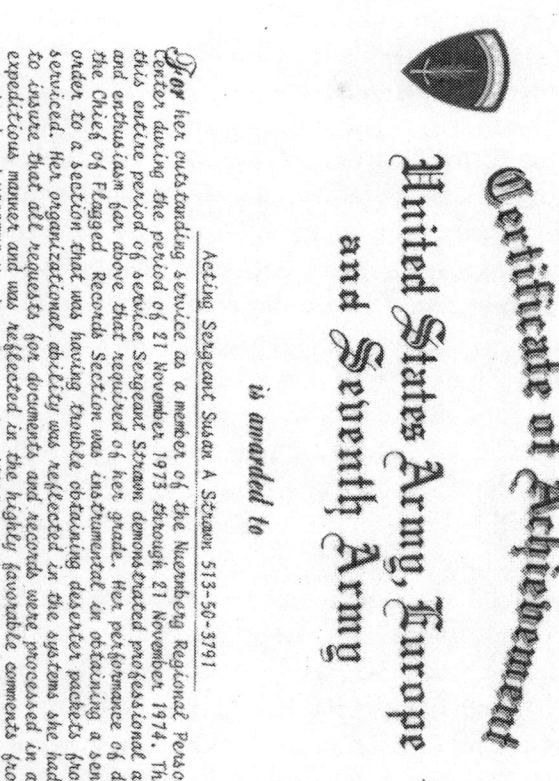

The man who sent me into the cyanide gas chamber with 84 other soldiers in Nuremberg, West Germany was quietly reassigned. No justice. I remember going into that chamber, but don't really recall coming out. My service was not recognized as a barrack's sergeant, since that position "was appointed"--no paper work. There were no details recorded about my being the first female soldier to go before an all male Promotions Board in US Army Europe under the new blending of male and female soldiers. There were many oversights by being a woman in the military in those days. Women did not receive medals for serving overseas. A lot was left undone.

Sitting on a staple

Due to the constant turmoil of my first job in Personnel, causing disruption by being female, I was moved to Flagged Records. This was a smaller office under the control of an E-6 (Staff Sergeant) who respected women and was a great teacher. He was about to rotate back to the states, and wanted me promoted. I was like a sponge soaking up Army Regulations on the Uniformed Code of Military Justice. I didn't realize he was training me to take over Flagged Records. I was simply happy doing a job that needed doing, and a job with challenges.

My new job actually required an E-6 position. I was an E-4. I could run the office since I'd been taught to do the work, but needed to be promoted. In other words, a technicality. I was to be in charge of Flagged Records. Eight hundred twenty five Army criminals from drug possession to murder and every deviate crime in between. Secret clearance and a locked room. It was mind boggling.

At that time in world history, Communist propaganda would have a field day with those records. My job was without formal training because there was no time or place in Europe for a woman to go to school for either position-Flagged Records or Barracks Sergeant. I just did the best I could.

Then I was told I was up for a promotion. I was advised to get my 'dress uniform cleaned and pressed', so I used the Post Exchange Cleaners. I don't know what chemical they used on my uniform, but as I pulled off the clear plastic cover, my unit insignia patch began to let go, then dropped to the floor. I stood in shock. I had 15 minutes to get dressed and be in line to be called before the Promotion Board!

One of the women who worked with the Adjutant General, Maggie, was letting me use her office to change from my olive drab fatigues and boots to hose, blouse, and skirt. I was faster in those days at changing clothes, but didn't expect things to start falling off my uniform.

With her help, using clear tape and staples, we reattached my unit insignia and my rank patch on the left sleeve. When I pulled on my skirt, we realized the hem starting on the left side and half way around the back had no stitching. It probably dissolved in the cleaning solution.

YOU DON'T HAVE TO MOVE THE WASHER TO MAKE TOAST

Whatever happened at the cleaners didn't matter anymore. This was a rush-to-fix it job!

We used three staples at one strategic seam, and then rolled tape along the rest of the hem. *How long will this hold?* My metal insignia was polished so it was just a matter of aligning my two ribbons with my name tag. Improvisation took on a new meaning. Who knew to examine my newly cleaned uniform for anything that needed to be *re*-sewn?

Maggie said. "You look fine. When your name is called, go to the door. Knock firmly but don't sound impatient or wimpy. You are all business today. Answer as best you can. Remember if your insignia falls off, leave it on the floor unless told to pick it up. If you don't know the answer to their question, say so. Don't chatter."

Maggie stepped back and said, "OK. Turn around slowly. Let me see if the staples show."

I obeyed.

"Good. You look good. Now, listen, this is important. Women haven't been promoted in the last year, that I knew of. And those recommendations come through this office. You are the first woman to go before this board. Make a good impression. Oh, and there is one man being interviewed for this same position. Let's hope your Personnel Unit sent over details of all you are doing. Good luck."

As I thanked her and stepped into the hall, Maggie added, "And don't sit down while you're waiting your turn to go in. Stay pressed."

I didn't have to wait long to hear my name called. I dutifully knocked as efficiently as I knew how, and walked boldly into the room. It's called bluffing boldness-acting like I did this every day.

After entering the office, I saluted, then stated my rank and name. My salute was returned by the Colonel in charge. I was told to sit in the solitary straight back chair facing five officers. I sat on some of those staples. *Don't react!* It kept me on the edge of my chair in straight posture.

There were three Major's, a Lieutenant Colonel, and a Colonel sitting at a long table. Behind them were huge glass windows displaying a panoramic view of the city of Nuremberg. Very impressive setting.

After the interview, I left to go back to my job in Flagged Records, with instructions to wait for the posting. Three days later, a tall soldier in dress uniform came into my office with papers in his hands.

He walked up to my desk, looked at me and then laughed.

"Uh, congratulations. You've been promoted to Specialist E-5, with a field promotion of Sergeant." He laughed again.

The paperwork was the Promotion Order, and stapled to one corner were Sergeant strips, made for a man's arm. He snickered.

"I thought this was some joke. You know, some guy named Susan. You're going to have to wrap those stripes around your arm, or you can wait until I order you a set of itty-bitty ones." He left laughing, and I was very glad I didn't work with him. After all, I now out ranked him. I might have to reprimand him and I wasn't in any mood to do it nicely.

It was a special day. I was humbled by the faith of the Staff Sergeant who recommended me for this job. I was going to miss his counsel as he left for a new assignment in the U.S. I wanted to learn leadership in order to serve in the Army for many more years. But that wasn't meant to be.

Within four months, everything changed with the chemical weapons training session. It was just the company commander's whim to have us try out the brand new shipment of gas masks. Three of us succumbed to cyanide skin poisoning. We were not allowed to shower or change clothes, the usual precaution after chemical exposure. I remember making it to my room at the barracks and then I had no memory for nearly six months. Except for words on my transfer orders, I didn't remember being in Germany.

I was dumped onto a Medi-Flight back to Andrews AFB, stacked like sandwiches in a vending machine. Being unconscious at arrival, and addicted to pain medication, I awoke at the Great Lakes Naval Base, mistaken for a woman who lived in the Chicago area. My records were lost while being switched from one plane to another. With my short term memory gone, I had no answers for the doctors at that Naval Hospital as to why I was sent back to the states. It was discouraging.

After five months in the hospital, I started to remember my last assignment was in West Germany. Bits and pieces would cross my mind, and I wondered where they came from. It was a long road to remembering. This was the end of serving in the military, and the beginning of five dark years, I haven't cared to remember. They have a part in my story, too. All of this I recalled as I looked again at my daughter's text message.

"Happy Veteran's day!"

* * *

Leaving the Army, Moving to the Country, Questions about God, Wanting my own home

Now, I want to go back to 1975, before being married or having a daughter when I was Honorably but unceremoniously, discharged from the Army at Fort Sheridan, Illinois. Sort of dumped and homeless. After hanging around Illinois for four years, I took a train back to Oklahoma, coming 'home' to no one. I was basically waiting to die. The cyanide poisoning damaged the right and left temporal lobes, leaving me with seizures. No way to work, not sure what to do with myself, and no way to get around.

Having been put on the Army disabled list with $250 a month pension, medically discharged, but with a one way ticket to Oklahoma, I had few choices. With so little money and no health to hold a job, I needed someone with which to share expenses.

I moved in temporarily with a cousin, and her grumpy Siamese cat. Having just come from the military, I was hardened and no longer shocked by any behavior—mine or others. No one could work in Flagged Records and still be shocked by human behavior. I remember my cousin noticing how gaunt and underweight I looked. It was more than that. Hardened and cynical about life and morality, it was in my mind that there was nothing hopeful for my future. I would just exist one day at a time.

When my days in the Army were filled with prisoners who came to see me under guard or handcuffed, all behavior was open to consideration. I filled out the paperwork to send a great many soldiers to prison in Ft. Leavenworth. I didn't have the opportunity to judge the cases, but simply arranged all the paperwork. I had a hardened military mind filled with situational ethics.

Friends of my cousin had a friend who was moving to the country. Her mom owned property there and she needed a roommate to share expenses. This seemed to be a great way to get out of the city, out into the country and try to re-figure my life. Maybe. I felt I had very little to look forward to as a disabled veteran with Post Traumatic Stress Disorder, seizures, and Meniere's Disease. No way was I going to make more plans.

This just affirmed so much of my life up to this point. My plans didn't work out. I believed I went back to Oklahoma to die. I may as well die in the country on an acreage. There is after all, the old adage--'what can't be cured must be endured'. So I would live or die doing nothing, the way my parents predicted. But Life without dreams or plans is insufficient. Who knew that a landlady with a Bible could break through my now unbelieving shell.

＊＊

My room was the back corner of an addition to a very old house. It was one story with lots of old boards that needed painting and patching. Lots to do to fix up my surroundings. There was an acre of open field to the south of the house, which could be turned into a garden if the weeds were kept down. Heavily forested areas along a small creek behind the property made it a haven for fox, raccoon, other wild animals. Along with stray or abandoned pets.

The former tenants were responsible for the trash filled gully on the north side of the house. The trees hid part of it, but the dump pile covered over thirty yards in length and about fifteen feet wide. The pile of garbage seemed to be the place to start to build up physical strength. I could work at my leisure and rest when feeling ill. I needed something to do.

The house had its own water well with electric pump, inside the back of the house in the bathroom area. It was an addition to the wood frame house built with cinder blocks. The water pump was in the corner, near a cabinet. Beside it was the water heater. Double narrow windows on the north wall let some light in to reflect onto the dark low ceiling. There was a wall sink and a tub with feet. My room walls would sweat in the summer. The homemade back porch just outside the bathroom provided a storage area for cat and dog food, and I added a homemade pet door.

One night, a opossum surprised me. *They don't lay down and play dead*. Who started that rumor? They charge and have teeth. No problem. I just let him finish the dog chow bag, and then the next day I nailed the cat door shut. Adapt or get bitten.

My room mate knew how to sew and to cook but loved the idea of wanting a chicken coop. Oh swell, I never liked that idea, but I loved eggs and eating chicken. So I agreed to help her remodel the abandoned shed at the edge of the woods, dig post holes, and stretch chicken wire. My background supplied me with learning experiences in wood work, post hole digging, fence mending, and elementary carpentry. No expert, but it held together.

While we worked on building a pen, a stray dog came loping into the yard. She was a light yellow and part great Dane, all gangley legs and ribs showing—*Ginger color*. She reminded me of the spice, so that became her name. She was the biggest dog I had ever owned.

Ginger loved everyone and everything. She loved to chase squirrels but she also enjoyed being sprayed by skunks. I gave up washing her in tomato juice to neutralize the smell. After Ginger arrived she adopted a long haired white kitten as her soul mate. That huge great Dane/German shepherd mix and her bright white long haired cat went everywhere together. Before too long we had a lot more cats and a few more stray dogs. It was a place for strays.

While I built up my strength and energy working outside in the dump, or mowing, or learning to fell a tree with a chain saw, I spent some time with my land lady, Ida. Ida Carlisle was a widow of many years who lived at the north end of the acreage on the ten acre family lot. Her second daughter and husband lived next door in their trailer home. Ida's was the largest house. Ida asked me one day if I knew God.

"Well, I have the idea He's there, but He's never been interested in me, not since I was a kid."

"What makes you say that?" Ida asked me.

"When I was 6 or 7, my second sister was born crippled. That same summer, I was forced to go to a vacation bible school. I didn't like it at first. I was a monster that could scare those women teachers. I believed I needed to be that way, because I didn't know how they would treat me. And if they were afraid of me, then that made me powerful, and they wouldn't hurt me. If I had to be there, then I wanted to be able to defend myself."

Ida frowned. "What did you do to scare your teachers."

"Well, I used bad words and shouted. One woman told me that if I color the picture of Jesus, then I could have cookies and milk. I was hungry but I didn't want to tell her. So I picked up the red crayon and used it like a knife to make ugly red marks to ruin the page. The teacher said I should practice more and try a few other colors. Then she let me have cookies and milk. I thought I won."

"While I was drinking the milk, I heard a story about Jesus, and a man named Zacchaeus. The teacher told me that if I prayed, Jesus would come

Susan A. Rader

to my house. Since Zacchaeus was little, and I was little—well you know, it made sense at the time."

Ida smiled. "Yes, that is a easy connection to make".

"I wanted Jesus to come to my house to heal my sister and make things better for all of us. I waited in my cherry tree, like Zacchaeus waited in a sycamore tree. I lived on Sycamore street, but the sycamore tree was too big for me to climb. I sat in my tree everyday for a week after coming home from vacation bible school."

I paused, surprised at the lump in my throat. I didn't want to cry about this. I drank some of the iced tea Ida had made for us. *Why is this bothering me now? This was all a long time ago.*

"But Jesus didn't come. I heard my parents talking about how my little sister might die. I'd already seen my dad try to suffocate her with a pillow. After I listened to stories about Jesus that week, I asked my dad about God. He told me God didn't care about anyone, and as long as I knew about God, that was good enough."

Ida was silent for a long time.

"Susan, I think Jesus did come to your house, or you wouldn't have asked your Dad about God. And even now, you wouldn't keep thinking God has it out for you for some reason. People don't worry about God if they don't believe He exists. I think when you prayed all those years ago Jesus did come. Not physically walking down the street. He accepted you. And your sister didn't die. She can walk now, and you are here after all the things that happened to you as a child. I'd say that God visited you and you have been aware of Him ever since. Don't you think you should check in with Him and see who He really is?"

Well, what an idea. I just thanked her for the homemade chocolate chip cookies and iced tea, paid my rent and went back to my room.

What an idea. I began to think back on how many times I should have died, but didn't. Then memories rushed in on some impossible situations which suddenly resolved themselves without anything I did or didn't do. To Ida, God was real, and was the focus of her day, her thoughts, and her worship. She was happy and healthy for her 60 some years, and managed her money well. I knew she had lost her husband to a brain aneurysm when he was in his 50's and it had been hard to raise her girls alone.

Ida's faith kept her strong but with me, she never pushed the topic again. Perhaps that's one reason why I couldn't stop thinking about it. Ida didn't want to argue or cajole or press me on the subject of God and faith. That was irritating and intriguing to me. Did it really matter? Was there any rush to learn about God in my late twenties? What difference would it make? Ida told me she was praying for me. I didn't know if that would work either. My life had turned into a mess and I was living with consequences of being in the military. I was also living with my poor life choices that came back to haunt me.

A few weeks later, the mail man came to the house and handed me a registered letter. I rarely received mail and when I did, it was addressed "Occupant". There was a check for $3,000 and a letter from the Veterans Administration stating my disabilities were now recorded as service connected, and I would receive a larger monthly income. Fantastic news. I didn't even remember applying for disability. My memory was spotty at best. It was now two years from my awakening in the Naval Hospital wondering where I was and where I had been. That day seemed clearer than ever now.

From visiting at Ida's, I picked up a postcard to send for a free Bible study course. The Bible Study arrived the same week. Money and Bible Study through the mail at the same time. I was more grateful for the money, but within six months, I was hooked on Bible Study.

There were really answers to questions like *why did people suffer*, and *does being alive have any purpose* other than self gratification. There were even answers to *what does God want from you*, and *what happens when you die*. These are basic questions so many struggle with but don't bother asking, and just live as they please. Most people have learned to 'decide for themselves' about everything. I know I had. I remembered I was once curious about life. I didn't realize that dusty Bible actually held answers to every question.

Wanting my own home

After my income stabilized, I was able to consider having a vehicle and maybe my own home. I realized that although my roommate and neighbors were friendly, I was missing something. I bought a used pick up so I could take myself somewhere and not ask for a ride. I really didn't go anywhere or socialize unless a trip to the grocery store counted.

I wasn't going to start house hunting right away, so I bought an old truck. Having been on foot for a long time and with my rental house a

Susan A. Rader

long way from town, I had to re-adjust to driving. I began taking myself out for lunch.

The local BBQ place made beef ribs. It was a roadside stand during the summer so it seemed a good place to start. I needed to try being social. People always love dogs. I could probably start up a conversation by bringing along my giant dog as well as my miniature Chicapoo.

Ginger the giant and Tana Man, my tiny ten inch dog, loved riding in the truck. I pulled up to the front of BBQ Haven and all noses went on alert! I brought the special order in two bags. Ginger who rode in the back of my pickup, stuck her face into the sacks as I reached to open the truck door.

"Wait, greedy." Bad timing. I took out her two ribs, no sauce, and put them in the truck bed.

Now, to get Tana Man away from the door. For a tiny dog it would be a long fall from the front seat if I couldn't get him away from the arm rest. With a shout that moved him back, I managed to open the door and let him sniff the bags as I climbed into the cab.

With Ginger in the back lying contentedly, gnawing on a rib propped between front paws, it was safe to give Tana Man his BBQ rib on the floor mat. They both acted like it was their first meal.

I felt extravagant, but I had not gone anywhere by myself for a long time. Since I was concerned for my dogs about the possibility of cooked bones splintering, I replaced the first rib treat, bones now bare, and gave Ginger my three leftovers.

When Tana Man was down to bare bone on his first rib, I substituted a second one. Why not leave the nearly clean bone for a fresh warm, meat covered bone. That's how you get a bone away from a dog!

Tana Man sighed heavily looking at the rib bone on the truck floor. He struggled to get back up onto the front seat, having stopped before finishing his second rib. He tilted his body side ways to lean against the arm rest. He was stuffed. I picked up the take out box and put it on the seat beside him. He looked at me with sad eyes, letting out another deep sigh. No more tummy room! Next time he only gets one rib.

BBQ Haven was once a month. At the two week mark, I took us all to a Sonic Drive In. It was the perfect break before the heat of a summer day. Get up early, work clearing brush and trash from the gully by the house, and go before the lunch rush. I could still be in my grungy yard clothes, drive my equally old, faded, '70 Chevy' to the drive in, where no one cared what you wore.

I ordered Tana Man to get onto the cab floor, then handed him his kid's cheeseburger. No more doggy noses or noises. As I unwrapped my burger, Ginger's head filled my window. I think I need a better strategy. Perhaps one dog at a time, next time. Thank goodness I didn't bring the cats.

The Red Brick House

The following Spring, I used my VA Loan Guarantee, and bought a house in a quiet neighborhood, ten miles away. It was a red brick home with room for three cats, my chihuahua/poodle mix and a large fenced back yard for Ginger. Out back, past my chain link fence, were 10 acres of woods, wildflowers, and animals including wild turkey, rabbits, raccoon, and hawks. It was like living in the city with the country out back.

Moving my meager furnishings took very little time. The day I moved in, I realized I didn't have a dining table. As I was pitching some boxes out the back door, I saw something on the other side of my chain link fence. It was a card table. There was a stain on one corner but it was perfect for me. By adding an inexpensive table cloth, I had a place to dine. I only owned one chair, which I used at my desk, but it could do double duty.

I located second hand stores to purchased a bed frame, an extra chair, and an out of date heavy couch. The couch had to be big enough for Ginger. With one more purchase of a large end table that doubled for storage, I had a place for my small television. After moving in, it hit me! I had panic attacks for three days thinking about the mortgage I signed.

My move was perfectly timed. On the fourth day in my new house, I came home with plenty of groceries just before a blizzard locked down most of Oklahoma in February 1982. I had plenty of time to work on the Bible Study course. I learned about God, about Creation, about fasting and prayer. I learned that the *'stories'* in the Bible were historical accounts of real, documented people and, that most of the Bible can be corroborated from historical writings and archaeological discoveries. This makes the Bible filled with Facts and Truth. I spent my time praying and studying, but it was now time to find a church.

My friend Ida and her family went to a Sabbath keeping church. God commands we rest. Work 6 days, rest one. I looked it up. Other civilizations have tried 10 day work cycles or 8 day work weeks and they failed as social experiments. History proves there is a rhythm to life, and it's clearly written in the book of Genesis.

It isn't a matter of which day I was to choose, it is a matter of *taking a day* to worship, pray, give offerings, and realign my life for the following week. Logical and simple facts. *Who knew?* Other cultures tried it other ways, and history proved them wrong. So far I didn't have a rhythm of life and one as old as scripture seemed a logical course for me to take.

This church I wanted to join had very strict rules. No smoking or drinking. Well, in the Army I'd learned to do both as regular habits. Oh great. Cigarettes or God? In order to give up smoking which I already tried and failed to do on my own meant I needed help. So, I signed up for a $35 American Cancer Society Hypnotism --Stop Smoking Seminar. I ran out of breath just saying the name out loud. I had to stop smoking. To stop drinking was easy. I didn't go places anymore that had liquor, then it was easy not to buy it or keep it in the house.

The day of the seminar, I went to the restroom to have my last smoke. Seated along one wall were three older women who obviously arrived together. I lit up a cigarette. The closest woman on the bench, her complexion as gray as dust looked up at me. I smiled.

"Last smoke, too huh?"

"Yes, this has to be my last. I just found out I have emphysema."

I put my cigarette out. Message received. I prayed about this hypnosis working. I was a four pack a day smoker. It was habit but it was giving me a cough and I smelled. I still hated my life. I hated being alone and rarely finding work. Secretarial skills opened doors, but once I wrote down 'seizure disorder' on an employment form, I received the 'don't call us, we'll call you' line. I loved Bible study and learning, but I did need a job. Real life outside my house wasn't very inviting. After losing my idea of a career in the military, I no longer had a dream to be anything at all. I had yet to ask God for help with a life plan.

My new neighborhood was really quiet, except for the man and his son who lived next door. He was usually in a temper and his son was a party animal, their yard covered in broken down torn up cars, car parts, and beer cans. The son finally moved out, and the father decided I was 'a lonely single woman who needed a man'.

After Bible Study one Wednesday night, I came home to find my neighbor staggering around on my darkened front porch. *Why didn't I think to turn on the outside light?* I pulled into the driveway and watched for a moment to see who it was. He heard my truck and turned toward the sound.

My neighbor had on grubby overalls and dirty tennis shoes. He reeked of liquor and cigarettes.

"Hey bootiful," he slurred. "I come to visit."

Oh, great. I did not need this scene. I realized I was trying to decide what stage of drunkenness he was in, as my father had been an alcoholic. I could see he was really soused with slow responses. I selected my approach. If this line didn't work, well, I didn't think that far ahead. I wanted in my new home.

"Well, you picked a fine time! I'm tired. I've got a sinus headache and I just came back from a long drive across town. You should just go home and we'll talk another time."

I slammed my truck door with authority I didn't feel and headed to the porch. My directness stunned him. From inside the living room, I could hear my little dog, Tana Man, whining and barking near the door.

I pushed my key into the lock and turned the handle. It wouldn't open! My heart started racing. For some reason, something was blocking the door. It only opened an inch! Adrenaline spurred me to push harder, as I wondered how long it would take for the drunk to get over the shock of my dismissal. *Pray, Susan.*

I threw my weight against the door, realizing something was piled against it. Something rolled away. *I couldn't imagine what could be piled against the door.* I didn't' know how it could have happened but I had to move whatever it was in a hurry to get inside.

The drunk, still about twelve feet away, suddenly angered, turned toward me. "Haaay, I wanna talk to you right now!"

At that moment, the door gave way. I rushed inside, locking the storm door then bolting the front door. I shut off the living room light and ran into the darkened kitchen. My confused neighbor was staggering around on the porch, as I watched through my living room windows. He soon gave up and went home. *Thank you, God.*

What had blocked the door? I cautiously closed my living room curtains, turning on the light. It was an amazing sight. My little ten inch dog had somehow pulled the large sofa cushions from the couch and stacked them on top. On top of that pile was one of my stereo speakers, and it was the second speaker that rolled off when I was trying to push the door open. How my little Wonder Dog did this I will never know, but what a watch dog!

Of course, it didn't cross my mind that I should *not* have stopped. I should have driven past, called the police, and waited for help. That scene could have gone terribly wrong. My pastor overheard my story at church and gave me an ear full. Something about putting myself in danger and tempting God. What an amazing idea. *Don't handle it myself, go get help.* Extraordinary idea. Thankfully, God answers prayers from a foolish woman.

Lighthouse Keeper Wanted

A few weeks later, a woman at church asked me if I did any house cleaning.

"Well, that's relative. If you looked at my place today, you might not think so, but I do know how. Why do you ask?"

"I clean for several very wealthy clients. Finding honest workers who don't steal, who work unsupervised, and keep to a schedule are hard to find. I have one too many jobs right now. I need to let one go. The Galloway's are the newest client, with a huge house that I just can't get to. I have to take a day off now, to keep my granddaughter. Do you think you'd like to do that as a job? The pay is great. You can go anytime, just once a week, and when they ask you to do something extra, they pay extra. You can even house sit when they go out of town and earn $200-$300 for a weekend, if you take care of their dogs."

This wasn't to be believed. Not only answered prayer, but work as Housekeeper. My seizures could occur unexpectedly, and while I'm not sure where I am, I can just sit until they pass. It wouldn't matter for housekeeping. I already knew I was good with dogs.

"I'll take it."

This was the start of a new career. "Lighthouse Keeping" were the words on my blue business card, along with a sketch of a lighthouse and seashore drawing attention to the pun. Below the drawing, I wrote: *Honesty, integrity, dependability. References.* Before the year was up, I had 3 large homes to clean and two businesses. Life was suddenly do-able again.

My work kept me too busy to do socializing. But then again, I remembered the bad days after dropping out of college. I barely escaped a date rape but was molested by a sorority sister. My self esteem dropped to cynical. I left college to travel with two poor choice companions: a pathological liar-thief and another acquaintance who turned out to be a professional prostitute. What a collection of companions. Three years shot doing nothing, working as a waitress and living in a building with fleas in the carpet. To get to the soda machine it was required taking a hammer to protect yourself against the rat that lived in the candy machine. Those days are best put behind me.

Socializing? What did I know about that? I knew now, God had real rules for life, and a lot of those rules I had broken. There were things in my past that needed rethinking. It was time to move on, past my bad choices, and to ask for baptism. Baptism didn't save me. Baptism was just a public confession of repentance, and my covenant to abide by God's rules.

My assignments for the "I want to be baptized class" included memorizing certain passages. It meant looking with clear eyes at my life choices, looking at experiences in my life. Those that were done to me before I ever made it to high school. Then there were the poor choices I made after leaving college and heading to Texas. How I ever got back to Oklahoma in a $400 car I'll never know.

My next choice had been enlisting in the Army to escape not only terrible relationships which I'll always regret, but the idea of making a better life for myself. Regardless of my lifestyle, I was always pro American and having grown up on the idea of serving my country, it wasn't a hard leap. Odd now that I think about this. Honor and integrity in service to my country, but not my personal life. That would have to be given more thought. So, I put my hope in the military. That had gone sour with the cyanide poisoning.

Now my hope had 'eternity guarantees for the right place'. I was sure I liked that better. Rethinking my life promised positive thinking, the right rules, and a brighter future. Living the new way, the new *ME*, let me sleep at night with no regrets. I don't ever remember having had that kind of peacefulness.

***

Susan A. Rader

Baptism

In September, I was baptized along with two other singles the same night. I shall forever remember the elder's garage with the canvas tub. I was first to be baptized.

The pastor spoke with authority that seemed to come from outside of him.

"Susan, do you believe that Jesus Christ was crucified to pay for your sins, was resurrected to life, and now lives?"

"Yes, I do."

"Susan, do you repent of your sins, and accept Jesus Christ as your Lord and Savior?"

"I do."

Then the pastor baptized me in the name of the Father, the Son and the Holy Spirit. When I came up out of the water, I heard the sweetest words I ever heard.

"Susan, I can tell you with the authority of Jesus Christ, your sins are forgiven."

Susan, your sins are forgiven. A Promise written on my soul.

What a night that was. The start of a new life with the new values--those I had been studying. Values that were harder than any I could imagine, yet worth every choice made using them. There would be fewer regrets, and if I did regret something, it was because I made a wrong choice, not because God's rules ever fail. I am always the one that fails in this relationship. But I can mend it in a heartbeat, with a sincere prayer, and know I am forgiven. I had my disability income, a good job, and a home. These were things I never thought I'd ever have. A peace I couldn't explain settled around me.

* * *

CHAPTER 2

Plans for England

What are the odds that a cleaning lady could take a trip for 14 days to England? Well, five years later, that is exactly what I did. The annual Church festival in the fall was held in many cities stateside, and around the world, but I wanted to go to England. I set aside my money faithfully, made installments to pay for lodging. I had a small discount on lodging by pledging to learn the alto parts for the praise and worship. I would serve in the choir for each of the services over the 8 days of the convention. Some of my payments were set aside for a 5 day organized tour of sites around London at the conclusion of the church festival. I had an opportunity to go, and I worked hard to pinch every penny.

Every week, I called an operator in London to ask the time, just to hear the accent. I enlarged and copied detailed maps of London, Surrey, and all the way to the southeast coast of England. These maps were pinned all over my kitchen wall. I located Greenwich (Gren-*itch*) with the intention of standing on the very spot of the Prime Meridian at the Royal Observatory, then go to the Thames to walk through the old, three masted clipper ship, the *Cutty Sark*.

My reservation was finally paid up to share a two bedroom 'caravan", equivalent of a mobile home. I would be staying on the south east coast at small holiday park called Camber Sands at Rye.

Each day as I worked at housekeeping, I sang along to the tape recorder to memorize the words and music as part of my offering. I loved the English accent of the young woman who recorded the alto part. It was easy to pick up the accent and be able to blend in with the choir.

My American money would be cut in half when I traded it for English pounds and coins, but I was in for a trip of my life. Who but God knew this October would be recorded in history. The event was a hurricane the category of a '200 year occurrence' causing severe damage across England into France . The extra-tropical hurricane would come to shore across southern England, and right through the little English coastal village of Rye. The storm would blow flat or uproot trees over 200 years old all the way from the coast to London, then continue on to terrorize ferry boat passengers across the channel into France. Amazingly only killing 22 people.

Forecast missed by the meteorologists and fueled by convergence with a super low off the French coast, the storm produced the worst overnight disaster in England since the blitz in 1945. What an adventure this trip would turn out to be for a great many people. Who but God knew I'd be at just that spot.

* * *

Guardian Angel

As I prepared for my trip, I invested in second hand clothes and a mail order luggage set. Six matching pieces. Yes, I see now I would look like a tourist, but then, I couldn't figure out what things to take with me. Maybe I thought I could take everything. I just didn't give much thought to moving it from place to place by myself once I arrived in England.

One afternoon, I came home from the grocery store on my usual routine. The neighborhood looked nearly vacant during the day with little traffic and no one outside. I carried in several bags of groceries, and was heading back to lock up the full glass storm door, when a nice looking, dark haired young man of about 30 came walking up the driveway. I just stood at the door, not giving it much thought. *It's cold out and he's not wearing a jacket.*

"Hi, is this the house with the transmission for sale? I saw the ad in the paper."

"No, I'm sorry. It's probably the neighbor next door. He always has car stuff for sale."

The nice looking young man's face changed to one of dark rage, so quickly it took my breath away.

With his lowered menacing voice he replied, "Oh, yes, this is the place."

He reached for the handle on the storm door, and in horror I realized there wouldn't be time to lock it. My dogs were out back. *I was alone.* Terror filled me. *Oh God, help me!*

Rage filled the man as he grabbed onto the door. He suddenly stiffened, released the door handle as if it had burned him, and began to stagger backwards. He was looking wide eyed in horror at something over my right shoulder. He stumbled backwards off the porch as he said, "uh, uh, wrong house", fell, rolled back to one knee, and raced off down the driveway.

"What in the world was that?" I locked the storm door and bolted the heavy front door, but began to tremble.

"Oh, My Lord." I dropped to the floor, horrified. "No jacket. It's freezing outside. No car. No witnesses. Just enough conversation to make it appear I was expecting him or going to let him in." *Thank you, Lord.*

I had read about Divine Intervention and guardian angels. I looked timidly toward the kitchen to see if I could see whatever terrified the man who came to the door. Nothing there. That man whose intentions were now obvious, was frightened by something I never saw. God is our rear guard, and ever present. I just had this proved, and for a lot more reasons. I was going to need that protection.

* * *

English Language Barrier, Crossing a London Street, Storm Warning Dream

A few days before my flight to Atlanta to catch the overnight to London, I went into downtown Oklahoma City to exchange a great deal of my trip savings into English paper and coin. I needed the bank to show me how to use and count English money. With the exchange rate the way it was, my $1800 was cut to $900 in a few moments. My Dream Trip to England had been planned and paid for on my small salary so that housing and side tours were already paid. The 14 days was going to be a matter of pinching English money, like my Scottish ancestors, in order to have a dime left when I returned. Each of my clients, surprised me with bonus money for my trip. It amounted to $300. I planned to manage it well. Just a few souvenirs, send some cards, and take eighteen rolls of film.

Susan A. Rader

Before I left for England, I had several nights of odd dreams. Two of them had significance in a way I couldn't have predicted. I did not know *yet* of the impending devastating hurricane.

In the first dream, there was a terrible wind, as I had never heard even near a tornado, but it did not touch me. It was off to the side of where I was. In the second dream, a man was giving a long winded speech in what appeared to be a large cold room with an ocean view through a wall of windows. The man, obviously in authority, was giving a talk while holding a model of a four masted sailing ship. He told a joke, only part of which was audible in the dream yet I seemed to know the answer to his riddle.

"I always say that ships go faster with holes in their sails." Then inaudible on the rest of his words. Wouldn't you know it, I can never remember punch lines anyway. *Yet I did know the punch line*—it just faded when I awoke. The really odd thing about it was looking out the window at a scene I did not recognize.

The other unusual dream took place four months before I left for England. The setting seemed to be the same. I did not know how to recognize my surroundings, but there was a calming message. "We will be all right". *Who is 'we'? And 'all right' about what?* After I puzzled over what seemed weird scenery, and a poor joke in odd dreams, I forgot about them, until these very scenes unfolded in England.

My flight landed at Gatwick outside London. I never knew I could be worn out from trying to sleep on a jetliner. With a stop at a kiosk to buy a reusable bag brightly decorated as a British Union Jack, I boarded Shuttle bus #777 to Victoria Station.

I could hardly contain myself with the excitement. I was in LONDON. *Where is Baker Street?* How about Number 10 Downing Street, home of the excellent world leader, Margaret Thatcher--*The Iron Lady!* Oddly enough, I had the chance to see her years later in Oklahoma City. So nice of her to return the favor of a visit! I was on my way to the Civic Center that summer evening to hear her speak and pulled in behind her limousine as traffic left the interstate. How awesome, to think that this woman I prayed for over the years as the grand Iron Lady, was driving along looking over Oklahoma City, Oklahoma, when I had gone all over London where she lived. There must be something to be said about what a small world it is.

Outside Victoria Station, I just stood, like a tourist with my six suitcases and enjoyed the sounds of the city. The traffic never stopped and they *were* on the wrong side of the street. I saw the famous 'London Taxi' hiring line and approached one to take me to Greenwich.

It is not a good thing to watch a cabby maneuver through London traffic. Amazing skill, even on the wrong side of the street, but the breath taking, paper thin spaces between vehicles near collisions boggled my mind. I was getting close to hyperventilating. Next, I'll take a train. Forget the Underground.

My destination was Stonehall House. A remodeled row of Victorian houses joined together, used for lodging by workers, visiting neighborhood relatives, and few tourists. My choice had been from research, as I wanted to see how the English lived, over hear that delightful language pronunciation, and meet common people.

My room was near the front and I slept peacefully in an old style iron frame bed, with lace curtains on the windows and a comforter on the bed. No television, just an English landscape painting, a dresser, one bedside table, and peace and quiet. Perfect for recovering from eight hours on a plane to a race ahead in time.

I awoke to the sounds of some man with heavy boots stomping down wooden stairs. For just a beautiful moment, I traveled back in memory to a summer at my Grandmother Josephine's house. I could hear the clanking of dishes, pots and pans from a kitchen, and smell breakfast. I expected to see my Uncles at the table and Grandma rushing in and out with platters for those big appetites. It was going to be a great day.

The dining room was the equivalent of a sitting room at the back of this old home. It had an all glass wall giving a grand view through double doors into a beautiful, well manicured English garden. There were roses, unidentifiable colorful small flowers, an herb bed, vines draped over the fences and a bend near the garden shed. Sunlight glistened on the morning dew. Here was a smallish back yard transformed into a lovely, restful, enchanting place.

I asked for the simple breakfast. One egg, with toast and jam (don't say jelly)--tea, and orange juice. When the waitress brought my tea, she placed a short metal contraption beside my water glass. It belonged on an office desk. Four slots. *A toast holder.* What fun. I've never looked at arriving mail the same way.

My goal that morning was to see the wooden ship, *The Cutty Sark*—a

Susan A. Rader

floating historical museum of the English navy. Many times I had made that plastic model and learned over the years how to make the deck look like glistening wood. But nothing in photos or plastic model kits could prepare me for actually walking on the deck.

When I went to the front desk at Stonehall, a quiet young woman readily answered my questions about how to find the Cutty Sark Museum.

"Just a little walk east, at the bottom of the hill, Miss. The Thames (pronounce *Tems*) is not very clean, but you can see a great many barges and dories. Have a nice day, Miss."

A little walk down to the bottom of the hill? My map showed about one half mile, but some fast flying crow must have given out this map information. I started walking down the long steep hill. About ten minutes from Stonehall, it began to pour. No lightning, no thunder, no wind, and no warning like Oklahoma. My felt fedora folded. I did look wilted after this short burst, but I just laughed. After all, I was being rained on in *England*.

My raincoat was a second hand store gem, with the brand "London Fog" inside on the label. Appropriate pun. As my legs were wearing out half way down the hill, I came across a short row of little shops. The Green Grocer sold produce. The other shops sold one or two items—it seemed the English loved to shop. Personally, I'm not that fond of it. Give me a short list and one place to go to get it over with!

When I came to where the map indicated I'd have to cross a street, I stared in amazement at the traffic. It was coming from the wrong direction. Of course *we know* they have road rules opposite the United States, but *to see it* is another thing. Don't step off the curb! And you better look to the RIGHT. Their idea of traffic flow using lights is non-stop, literally! Red, yellow, green, yellow, red......forever in motion. I was wondering how to handle this when I heard a man's deep voice behind me.

"Just go-fer-it." In the doorway of a vegetable and fruit shop was the aproned Green Grocer. A large smiling man. "American?"

"Oh, someone told you! That obvious, right?"

"Bit of a soggy hat there. Showers today."

"Yes, I forgot my umbrella."

"Brolly."

"What?"

"We call it a brolly."

"Oh, thank you." He was still chuckling.

My focus turned back toward the traffic that was 'not stopping on red'. "Just go on yellow at the red."

I tried twice, really, but the cars continued to roll. There was no stopping this traffic.

"You can do it. I'll tell you when to go. Then step lively right across. Nothing to it."

I looked back at him a little skeptical.

"Oh, I won't tell you wrong, Miss. I don't want the tabloids writing the story near my shop."

Smile, Susan. It's British humor and frank speech. Reluctantly I gave in to trusting a stranger. At the oddest moment, it seemed to me, without rhythm to the stop-roll-go traffic flow in three narrow lanes from curb to curb, all one direction, the grocer shouted, "Now!"

I obeyed, moving out in front of the rolling traffic at a fast clip. Safe to the other side.

The grocer nodded. "That'll do. Luck at the next!"

Whatever did he mean? It wasn't really something ominous. I know I left the impression I was very timid. I pulled off my limp fedora to stuff it into my newly purchased carrying bag—the bright Red, White, Blue British Flag design that fairly shouted 'tourist'. That was all right for me. It never crossed my mind to consider the ramifications of a single woman traveling alone in a foreign country. However, I was asked about it over and over. "Are you traveling alone?" I was beginning to think that I was breaking some social custom.

After another fifteen minutes walking the supposed half mile, I found a cross walk with bells, traffic lights and ground markings. Excellent. This was something I understood. Stay in the lines. According to my map, I should be looking right at the Thames and the Cutty Sark Historical Museum. Nope. Just some business on an angled street corner. I stopped in mid sidewalk to study my map, just as a man came around the building. We collided.

"Oh excuse me," I said with a smile. "Can you tell me where to find the Cutty Sark?"

The man looked blank. He replied in a language I'd never heard before. I couldn't even guess its origin.

I looked blank. He looked blank.

I pointed to my map. Then, as if it made language any clearer, I said slowly "Cutty...Sark.""

Susan A. Rader

The man laughed and nodded, then replied in that same strange dialect only this time I made out the last two words: *Cutty Sark*.

We both laughed at the same time, and pointed to each other. Cross culture communication is amazing. He then crooked his finger to indicate to come with him, and used his left hand to point toward the side street nearest the angled office building. Within a few steps, I could see the masts and then the full sailing ship at anchor.

I smiled and said, "Thank you." Which started both of us laughing again. He must have to guess what I said. He said something in reply that could have been anything, but he was on his way and I had found the object of my search.

Within a few yards, the dead end street opened up to show a beautiful view of the Thames. There on the right side of the dock, was the sleek three masted clipper, *Cutty Sark*, still dripping from the rain shower but gleaming in a patch of sunlight. As I lifted my camera to snap this scene, a rainbow appeared over the bow. What a sight. What a gift! I watched the rainbow, and forgot to take the picture. Oh well, my scrap book has only the wet decks and gray overcast skies that replaced that moment of beauty. Just barely in the background were the remnants of the rainbow.

The ship was now waiting in the sunlight so I could always remember it that way. No need for a photo. Providence arranged my trip, financed it, even adding bonus money, knowing I barely had enough for the trip. This moment like so many others since becoming a believer, were hope filled.

The *Cutty Sark*, Irish for the "Short Shift" dress on the figurehead, was more than I expected. I used an entire roll of film just on the rigging and deck. Everything glistened with sunlit raindrops beading on highly polished wooden surfaces. The clouds moved in to gray the scene just as an elderly retired Naval Officer came on deck to give me the topside tour. He answered my questions and let me take my time before going down into 'tween decks', or into the 'hold' to see the museum. It saddens me now to realize just a few short years ago, some electrical wiring set the ship ablaze. It was not salvageable. The *Cutty Sark* is gone, but available in my photographs and memory.

Not far from the *Cutty Sark*, was an old pub, *The Gypsy Moth*. Since I wanted to know about Pub Grub, to savor some English food, I entered innocently. Recognizing my accent as American I was rudely ushered through the Pub to the restaurant in the rear. English people knew not to ask for food in the Pub. After purchasing a sandwich at a counter in the back restaurant area, I sat with two older women at their invitation. I was probably recognized as American. They wanted to chat.

"First time in London, dear?"

"Yes. I arrived yesterday. I just had to come see the *Cutty Sark*."

"Well, you'd do better to find yourself another place to eat. This isn't good food. My sister and I just retired. We lived all our lives on the other side of the Thames. Never crossed the bridge until today, just to see what was on this side. Would have done better to eat on the other side at a place we knew."

What a fun lunch, with my new friends talking about London, the Underground, and what to ask for when it came to good Pub Grub. And, if I 'want a potato that is baked', "deary, ask for a 'jacket'". American is not English.

After lunch and not far from the main thoroughfare, I found the gated park I wanted. This gigantic park held the Royal Observatory. The Prime Meridian. Zero degrees on my little globe at home! *Hot diggity!*

I was strolling through the park, savoring my visit to the Official metal marker announcing Zero degrees longitude, and a little dog came rushing to me, excited, barking, and jumping up, over and over as if he wanted me to pick him up. I reached down carefully to pat his head and from nearby, heard anxious voices. An older couple were hurrying in my direction. Perhaps they were concerned about my touching their dog.

I stood as they arrived. "Oh, excuse me. I love dogs."

"American!" The woman announced with surprise as she stopped.

"Yes. I should wear a sign."

Her husband laughed. "No need, girl. Its plain." His wife poked him in the ribs.

"What I mean to say is, if you were English, you would be telling me to keep my dog close and you would still be brushing off your trousers."

I just laughed. "I have an excitable small dog and a great Dane. I love dogs."

After a short visit of where are you from, how long will you stay and why would you go to a coastal holiday park off season, we parted amicably with the little dog looking back for as long as I was in sight. That was nice, I did miss my dogs.

Susan A. Rader

By train to Rye and Camber Sands

Camber Sands Holiday Park, off season had minimal staff, with some buildings closed until the following Spring. After all, in October, the water temperature is too cold for swimming, but as I told a rude man on the train who obviously didn't like Americans, I did NOT come to England to go swimming. England was home from ancestor's on both sides of my family.

Looking out the window, I was acosted by a 'Mr. Rude'. At first he sounded pleasant but suddenly turned nasty.

"So the holiday park you are attendening is hosting a big beach party for swimming," Mr. Rude laughed. "It must be wonderful to go swimming there."

I sat dumbfounded. After looking at him for a moment, I lashed out. I explained that along the southern coast was the location of the arrival of William the Conqueror. England withstood the Spanish Armada and held together during the blitz in World War 2. They stood alone against Germany for many years. This trip was my exploration of history. Mr. Rude from the train shut up after my enthusiastic rant. Gazing around the car, I noticed all silence. Mr. Rude dipped behind his paper.

In the silence that followed, I was embarrassed for making a public speech, but encouraged as I realized my impromptu speech left other English passengers around me smiling. Mr. Rude was the first off the train with a backward withering look. From others who heard my enthusiasm, I'd receive comments like "Enjoy your holiday' as they exited. I ended up by myself in that cabin with no one going as far as the coast.

* * * *

My train left London from Victoria Station to Ashford, in Sussex, then to Rye on the coast. It was off season for the beach, so the holiday park prices were perfect for the budget minded. The streets were narrow cobbled stone. The small town is in the coastal area known historically as the Cinque Ports—where there were always ships for hire in days gone by. They were small but historically powerful ports that when not in the service of the King, indulged in barbaric piracy and smuggling. What a history!

Rye was once a fortified town surrounded by steep cliffs and walls with four gates. The Town Ditch also added to their defense, so at high tide Rye was almost completely surrounded by the sea, with the only entrance being Landgate. Of the four original gates, only Landgate remains. It looks now to be a simple gate with no wall nearby.

Strong south westerly winds and sea currents filled in the bay over time, and Rye was left with the three rivers which encircle it. While I read about the change to the coast line, it explained how I could be so far away from the sea while standing by the fortified wall. It really did fill the area. I tried to imagine it surrounded by water.

Old world charm is an understatement to describe Rye. I went through a door older than the United States. It provided entry into a famous pub, the Mermaid Inn. Amazing to me was this sense of being out of time. Along the streets were very short doors. I felt tall. Walking the narrow sidewalks in this historic district kept me feeling as if I were somewhere in history, but happy with all the discoveries. It was time travel for me.

Whoever invented the cobblestone streets should have fired the man who designed those near the Mermaid Inn—all the stones stood up on end. I turned my ankle several times just crossing the street. This explained the lack of traffic!

My hired taxi from the train station, carried me outside the town limits to the holiday park. As we left town, we went past sheep pens and listened to the shouting of an auctioneer. The only difference in the usual unintelligible auctioneer language was the British accent! When we turned onto the coast highway, the Cabbie pointed out bunkers at various intervals explaining them as World War 2 leftovers. This was eerie. Looking out along the flat coast with its grassy dunes and pebble rock beaches, seeing only ocean water in the distance made me think of the grassy plains of home. One would be able to see in clear weather the storms approaching, or like here on the coast of England, the coming of war. Camber Sands Holiday Park, off season had minimal staff, with some buildings closed until the following spring. After all, in October, the water temperature is too cold for swimming.

The Church Festival would officially last for 8 days. Every morning, I would sing in the choir and then hear great sermons with lessons from the Bible, but with English flare and humor. I loved the food. Perhaps because my Grandmother Mitchell cooked English style.

Every morning began with rain just as church started, then right after lunch, the sun came out in time to catch the Day Bus for touring. Then the weather held until we returned around 4:30 p.m. and we rode back in the rain. I overheard comments about rain this time of year not being natural, but didn't think to check any news for an official report. There was a very good reason, but no one to put the clues together until it was too late.

Number 59

My 'Summerfield' Caravan was #59, in row three, and capable of tightly housing six people. Thankfully its position in the rows was not far from the Club Building where all activities took place.

I brought a metal specialty sign to be placed in my trailer window: VISITORS WELCOME. It fit beautifully in the bottom of my suitcase. That brought many Scottish, English, Canadian, and American visitors to my door. Someone gave me that idea before I left, as the sign started people talking and then visiting. One of the men from the choir was on holiday from the Meteorology Branch of the English government. Amazing. We could talk clouds, rains, storms, and exchange the information about how is it to live with a continental climate on the high plains as compared to island climate near a warm ocean current with Arctic fronts. The substance of great conversations.

Each day, our bus tours took us to a new castle. Leeds was breathtaking. Most of the bus had vacated when a passing warm shower started emptying a fat cloud with the sun still shining. Several of us rushed toward the port cohere', to take refuge from the downpour. Once inside, we stood in awe as a beautiful rainbow appeared over the majestic castle. The bright full rainbow against the dark clouds, the sound of low rumbling thunder and bright sun on the castle and trees, made a beautiful portrait shot in my camera, and forever on my heart.

When a tour took us to Warwick Castle, I had my first opportunity to have lunch with a Knight in shining armor. When he dismounted, I found I was taller. Disappointing, but he was a fascinating man and sat at the table in the castle restaurant entertaining all of us with how much the horse weighed, how hard it was to move in 72 pounds of armor. The Knight was a member of a reenacting company that worked for castle tours in the off season, and for movie making companies all over the world.

The last of the Church activities was on Thursday, at the Grand Family Dance, 7:30-11:00 p.m. Everyone was looking forward to a good food and family evening. That day, after church and lunch, another bus took us on our last of the daily tours. Destination: Dover Castle.

At last, the beautiful White Cliffs of Dover, shown in so many of the old movies, and such a prominent landmark in historical accounts. We exited the bus and strolled through town for an hour. I felt dwarfed by the towering white cliffs. By contrast against the base of the cliffs, stood tall, dark gray buildings which dotted the rocky beaches. When I asked their use, I was told they were for drying fishing nets. I just eat fish. I never thought about living on an island where fishing meant lots of fish in nets, not one fish at a time on a pole. That makes sense. It's not often I think about life beyond my little house.

We looked at the artificial bay wall extending a good distance out from shore, to keep back the rough seas. These were built to help control wave action to protect the gigantic Ferry boats. By Ferry it was a trip of less than twenty miles to the coast of France. There was enough moisture in the air that we could not see France, but apparently, it was often visible.

Dover castle was surrounded by thick green lawns yet perched at the top of a white cliff. It looked impregnable—both from the beach and up close. However it had perfectly manicured lawns. Someone told me they used sheep to keep the lawn so perfect. But out of a window I saw what clearly were directional markings made by a lawn mower. They were lined up and exactly the same width, so I doubt any sheep performed that cut! Maybe they used lawn mowers along with the sheep. It's one of those questions I should have asked.

We took a tour of some of the guard's quarters, a few long dark tunnels, and weapons displays before going into the main part of the castle where the Curator ahead of us was already leading a tour. Our private tour guide took us through the area we just missed to view amazing figures in Victorian costume. Madam Tussaud's Wax Museum recreated everyday castle scenes showing the wealthy as they entertained, or servants going about their tasks. The room displays were extraordinary in detail. All the figures so life like they could have been actors posing on a set.

When our guide called our attention to the Curator's approach, I was dumbfounded. There was the man from my dream. *No, it couldn't be.* It was. By this point in the tour, there were four of us single women traveling together. To me that explained the 'we' from my dream.

Dream Vision Fulfilled

The Curator at Dover Castle was a stately gentleman, with a small mustache and a shock of gray-white hair. He wore tweed with a white shirt and two toned vest. Like my dream. While he pointed out antiques in the room, I was drawn to the window from my dream. Ocean waves, the retaining wall, and huge Ferry boats coming and going from the peaceful bay. A cold shiver ran down my spine. There was a feeling of dread, a lurking danger and I didn't know why. Again, as in the dream, I was comforted with *'we'll be all right'*. Not a voice, just a message. And, there was something that drew my attention to one specific Ferry discharging passengers far below my window. There was something special about that Ferry.

The Curator began speaking on the museum pieces in the room, dating the tapestries, the glass, the tables, and then he moved to a small table of nick-naks. On it sat the beautifully scaled four masted model ship I saw from my dream.

Instead of puzzling with a dream that still did not make sense, I turned to listen to the Curator who was speaking on the historical importance of the sea and ship building to English history.

"My favorite kind of sailing ships are the Clippers, known for their speed. Captains of these ships designed them to carry men and weapons into battle, counting on the speed of their vessels and their maneuverability. My research into battles at sea taught me a great deal about types of ships. *And one thing I know is that ships go faster with holes in their sails.*" He paused for affect, and there was murmuring from the tour crowd.

I was frozen in place. My dream. I suddenly knew what he would say. The three women with me heard me gasp. Then I said softly, just before the Curator, "Ships with holes in their sails go faster, to the bottom of the sea."

At that point, almost in echo of me, the Curator said, "Yes, Ships with holes in their sails go faster...to the bottom of the sea." Then he laughed at his own joke. He went on to explain that without their sails to move them out of harm's way, they were doomed to be sunk.

This took my breath away. *What could it mean 'we'll be all right'?* Again a sense of dread, and sorrow came over me for a moment and then left me tired for the rest of the day. I wondered what was to come. Since things like this have happened over the course of my lifetime, I learned they were usually FYI dreams: For Your Information. Why? There is an obvious answer. So I will see that God holds this moment in time, and I do not need to be afraid. In scripture, the phrase, "Do not be afraid" occurs 365 times. That's one for every day of the year. Certainly it is one for every occasion!

Agnes, one of my new traveling friends from Connecticut, whispered, "How did you know what he was going to say?"

I tried to brush it off. "A silly dream I had before the trip. So many months ago, I'd nearly forgotten."

Karen, from Montana, said, "You mentioned this place looked familiar, too."

"Well, it must be one of those *de ja vous* things." Not wanting to go to the part of the dream about a storm or the message, 'we'll be all right", I just laughed. There was no way to explain this and I really didn't want to think about what it meant. It wasn't as if I had some divine directive to announce a great storm to everyone I met. Also, being in England, I didn't know what a 'great storm' might be called. It wasn't like Oklahoma where we have super tornadoes. And all the rain since I arrived were mild light showers or heavy rain with occasional thunder. No great storm.

When we left Dover Castle, it began to rain harder than it had all week. Added to it was lightning and thunder. Our driver for the Day Tour Bus was having a difficult time getting us back to Camber Sands. Over the course of the last five days, eighteen inches of rain had fallen in the area. Now, with the routine afternoon rain pouring harder, parts of the narrow highway disappeared in instant rivers pouring from one side of the road to the other. There was not a lot of conversation on the bus. We were all tired from a full week, but we were also old enough to know the driver, usually talkative, needed to concentrate. The festival was about over when someone mentioned the storms were to get worse the next few days. Their information was a little vague, but it reminded me there might be a little time to try to find a weather forecast.

Although we were an extra forty minutes getting back to Camber, the park community center grand room was all ready filling with those who wanted one last night together with friends and family before heading home. Those of us not dressed properly for a formal dinner and dance rushed off to change. The rain had stopped in Rye. It was going to be lovely evening.

Everyone was ready to leave the church festival site to go back home. There were twenty one of us, who were ready to go to London on a continued holiday. I was excited to see more of London for five day extra days, so the idea of storms was not good news. Before I left for Family night festivities, I used one of my English coins to power the 'Tely'. I pushed the coin slide into a box attached to the small twelve inch screen TV. In a moment I had the British Broadcast Corporation, 'Tea Time' weather report.

Being from Oklahoma, a land of storms, and having studied meteorology, I was fascinated by the low pressure-hurricane symbol on display behind the talking suit on the evening news. This hurricane symbol was just west of England in the warm off shore current that tempered the English climate. Since we had dependable as well as accurate weather information in Oklahoma, *I did not* wonder about this British forecaster ignoring the storm symbol off shore. He never mentioned it! So, that must mean it means nothing here. I shut off the broadcast.

Based on what I knew from my books and life experiences, a tropical system meant more rain, in bands, probably with more wind. I had no concerns about us having a tour bus the next day to take us to London. My tour agenda showed the order of historic places to see, starting with Windsor, to tour her majesty Queen Elizabeth's castle, among other bright spots. I was not dwelling on the odd afternoon scene at Dover Castle, so I didn't put the puzzle pieces together. Obviously, I forgot about odd dreams I had before arriving in England.

After the family dinner and dance, many of the people at Camber Sands packed their belongings and headed to all the parts of England they called home. The holiday park was emptying a rapid pace. What a wonderful thing it did. Providence knew what was about to happen.

The air was thick with moisture, and smelled of tropical rain as I left the Grand Hall for my caravan. It was a warm night and the air was invigorating. Caravan #59, third row over and third trailer back, seemed a long way off. With so many gone, there were few of the neighbor's welcoming lights to guide me. The ground squished under my dress shoes and filled with muddy water. No trouble. They'd be dry by morning.

Our bus was to arrive around 10:00 a.m. to carry us to London. Then by tomorrow night I would begin five days of travel to such sights as the Royal Botanical Gardens, Stratford-Upon-Avon and attend the Hatfield House Elizabethan Dinner Theater. The last day would mean back to London for tea at the Waldorf Astoria, plus one performance of my favorite author's play, running continually (1952-1986) for thirty five years: Agatha Christi's *The Mousetrap,* at St. Martin's Theater, London. Oh, I could hardly wait.

Hurricane winds, Miracles, and *The Mousetrap*

It was nearing midnight when I finished packing my belongings. I had used up 15 rolls of film and guarded them with my money and passport. Everything was packed when the thunder began to rumble, the rain began to pound and the winds picked up. I love a good thunderstorm, so I lay down to listen, thinking about how great this trip had been so far and drifted off to sleep.

My sleep was interrupted by pain. My left arm. Why does my left arm feel like a lead weight? Oh, my elbow. It brought back the memory of falling from a runaway horse and shattering my elbow. The bone fragments severed the ulna nerve, leaving my left hand useless for two years when I was eight. My arm felt like that, all over again. By now I was fully awake and realized the caravan was rocking in the wind.

I pulled back the curtain on the window and there was only darkness. No lights at all. A brilliant lightning flash illuminated the grounds. In that brief bright light I saw boards and other flying debris. A Tornado? In England? If it was, it was the biggest thing I had ever seen.

My left elbow had a nagging bone deep ache whenever I was in a Low pressure area near a storm in Oklahoma. Nothing could make it stop hurting except the passing of the storm. This elbow warning system had alerted me to more than one tornado in my lifetime, but this was worse. What is worse than a tornado in a trailer park? A hurricane hitting a trailer park!

Just then, I heard something tumbling past the trailer with a metallic sound. I knew it was the three step iron entry from the trailer next to mine. I heard metal tearing and the sound of glass.

I gathered up my small bag with money, passport and my rolls of film. I began to pray for protection for everyone at the park and readied myself to be blown away. Just then I heard my roommate, Janice from New Hampshire, roaming around the living area of our shared caravan. I rushed into the hallway entry.

"Why are you out here, Janice? Can you hear that storm? You could get hurt out here!"

She was sitting down on the floor near the space heater, and was re-wrapping herself in a blanket.

"I'm cold. I don't like that little room. I want sleep. Leave me alone. You go to your room and be safe. I want to be warm."

Frustrated with her short shortsightedness, I lowered my voice.

"Can you hear that wind?"

"Yes. So WHAT?"

"Janice, I live in Oklahoma, land of tornadoes and severe storms. I'd guess that wind is at least ninety miles per hour and I just heard glass and metal from the trailer next to us."

"SO!"

"Do you see the long glass window right above the cushion seat over your head?"

Janice looked irritated as she glanced up. "It's been there all week."

"I've already heard some big stuff blow by the side window. That wind is strong enough to pick up anything. All it would take would be one gravel sized piece of something to blow that window out, shredding you with glass as it ripped through the trailer. What do you think that would do to you?

You need to be in your room. Now, I'm going back into my little room. I suggest you do the same.

A small space is better if there is debris. Besides, we can't get outside to any other shelter. That window could blow out any minute. At least with your door shut, in your room, you might not be sliced up with flying glass. It's your choice."

As I pulled my room door closed, I heard Janice scrambling and muttering to herself as she moved through the rocking trailer.

"Going to my room, *Mother*. Hope you're happy!"

This attitude was why I had not spent time with her outside choir practice. If I was to die tonight, at least I warned one person, and I could say, I had a great trip to England with no regrets.

The roaring of the storm increased and sounds became distorted. I heard some shouts and more shattering glass and crunching metal. The Caravan swayed, jerked, and rocked.

Later, I was to hear a story from a newly married couple who had been coming by Ferry from France after spending the afternoon. They were aboard when the gale force winds moved into the channel. They watched eighteen to twenty foot waves swallow and spit out their Ferry. Yes, the British Meteorological Center failed to get warnings out for many reasons, but one was the sheer magnitude of this storm, the likes of which few had seen in nearly a generation. It wasn't normal.

As I continued to pray for those who might still be on the road after Family Night, or for those who were in shelter here and down the road at Romney Caravan Park, I thought back to the message of the dream. *"We'll be all right."*

Among the hundreds who had been at Camber Sands, only two college students needed medical help after rescuing an elderly widow from the trailer next to mine. The young men had weighed enough between them to hold her and themselves down. Their Caravan's storm anchors had given way due to the heavy rain. After the trailer went over, they managed to make it outside and then to shelter with only minor cuts. The main building had some exterior wall and roof damage, but had been soundly built. My Caravan trailer stayed intact.

***

About dawn, with just enough light to look around, I could see what appeared to be a hole in the clouds cover overhead. It was the collapsing 'eye' of the hurricane. Dark rain clouds were still to the west. The wind was howling when there was a knock on the west door.

"Anyone in here? Wake up! Security! Come to the door but DON'T OPEN IT!"

I went over to the door as Janice came out of her room.

"Yes. There are two of us."

"All right. We need to get you out of the caravan. The anchors are no longer working. More rain and wind is coming." The man was shouting over the howling winds and still some of his words seemed to fly away.

"You can bring one bag with you, but DON'T OPEN THE DOOR until I tell you. Then, open it very slowly and don't let go of it. The winds are about 60-70 kilometers. You hang on to your small bag or purse, but grab my arm and hang on."

"OK," I shouted through the door. "Janice? You coming? Get your bag."

"No. I'm staying here. I'm not going out in that."

I shouted to the rescuer.

"ONE TO COME OUT. ONE TO STAY. SHE WON'T GO."

"All right, but she stays here at her own risk until these powerful winds let up. Maybe two or three more hours. Tell her that." Janice shrugged and went back to her room.

My signal was to knock on the door. "I'm ready."

"SLOWLY! AND DON'T LET GO!"

Never in my life did I experience anything like the next 10 minutes. My carry on bag was over my shoulder and my purse was around my neck. I had one hand on the door handle, and the other to grab this man's arm. As I stepped out onto the metal platform, locking my hand around his forearm, my feet flew out from under me. I flapped in the wind like a rag doll. My huge rescuer leaned into my weight, then closed and fastened the Caravan door, as he hung on tightly with me still flying in the air. He turned toward the Caravan then pulled me down out of the air. I was floating with only my toes touching the ground as my rescuer led me to a heavy truck parked only ten feet away.

With effort he managed to open the truck door against the wind while still holding onto me. Seated inside was a small frail man, as wide eyed as I was. This must be what its like to be rescued by a Giant. I was being saved from becoming a human kite, and very grateful to God for sparing me.

The Rescue truck stopped three more times in just that third row. This was now the front row of Caravans as the first two rows of trailers were gone or piles of twisted metal. Most of the rest of the park buildings were severely damaged or obliterated. The brick wall that kept the trash containers had been hit by something and reduced to a pile of rubble.

We exited the truck near the Club Building entry just as the wind died a little. A man stood pointing to the shattered glass of the barometer.

"953 millibars. Never seen it that low." Back home in Oklahoma, it would have been 28.14 and the glass would have broken on my barometer too.

When we entered the foyer, our noses were assaulted with fumes from sewage. All the toilets backed up in the Club Building, from too many people, too much rain, and no power to pump the sewage away. Thankfully, in the restaurant area, there were high windows, propped open to act as a vent, with the smell of tea, coffee, and baked goods masking it well.

Groups of people milled around wondering what to do. With the power off, there was no petrol for automobiles. Reports came in from the local authorities that most roads through town and in all directions were blocked and dangerous. We still didn't' have the answer of what exactly had hit England.

I purchased a hot tea and came to sit down at a table with a few other familiar faces and a family of four. A father, mother, young son and young daughter, all as quiet as could be. They had homemade snacks and bottled drinks with them. The others at the table regaled everyone with their tales of the storm. Word came that everyone had vacated Romney Holiday Park just down the road from Camber before the storm. Now, there was not a building, wall, or caravan left. The property was swept clean. Half of the choir and the music director had stayed at Romney. Thank God, everyone headed home ahead of the storm. I was again reminded of the message from my dream. *"We'll all be all right."*

I looked at the family sitting quietly opposite me. The man's hands were shaking as he took a drink from his water bottle.

"Are all of you all right? You don't look well." I asked quietly.

They looked at me at the same time. I realized they were in shock. The man gave me a wan smile and said, "We have witnessed a miracle."

All conversation at the table stopped. The wife nudged him and nodded.

"We have only a very small trailer. I live in it most of the year. I travel with my work. It holds the four of us, but we have just about everything we own in it. We couldn't pay to hire a lot here at Camber so we were able to get a spot at the road crossing in Rye. There is a brick building used sometimes by the town. Trucks or Caravans can park overnight there."

His wife spoke up, softly. "We were there last night for a very long time."

A tear ran down the man's face. "When we realized the winds would blow our trailer over, we prayed for God to take care of it. We drove into town to find shelter by the houses. We watched a bit of everything fly by us, but we stopped on a side street where the wind wasn't so bad. We prayed we could be safe in the car." He took another drink of water.

"As the storm became worse, a woman came rushing out of a house next to where we were parked. She insisted we come inside. She was alone and wanted company, and couldn't bear that we had no place to go in the storm."

His wife spoke up. "The power had gone out but her home had a grand fireplace. We cooked a meal and prayed and played cards. Then we slept."

The man looked at his wife and children and smiled.

"We went back this morning to where we left our trailer." His voice caught. Tears welled up in all of their eyes.

"When we were near the curve, we saw clothing all over the road. Power poles were down. The brick building at the cross road was destroyed. We had little hope for our trailer, but when we went on around the curve, we could see it. Our trailer had been pushed sideways across the lot, up against part of a pole, and not a scratch on it. Those clothes weren't ours. God protected what little we have, and we don't know how to thank Him."

A kindly woman with a tray of baked goods was standing behind me. "Then we will all share your story of God answering your prayers! Let's celebrate with some baked rolls."

"Oh, we have no money left, except for fuel to get home, if the petrol stations can provide it. Thank you."

"No charge for this. It is free. We have all been spared, and we will tell your family's story every place we go."

And, so now, I have told it one more time. The power of prayer. The protection for those who are faithful. *"We'll be all right"*.

With most of Rye closed down, it was left to a few brave souls to go out scouting for petrol and to find open roads. Four single men did just that, each taking a direction. Only two of the directions had working fuel stations along open road. All other roads were shut down. The report for traveling North was mixed. The British Army moved in to clear huge trees from the highway. All buses and trains were halted.

This wasn't good news as we had to evacuate this holiday park due to the damage and unsanitary conditions. Our bus wasn't going to arrive to take twenty one of us to London to catch up with a tour group. Those of us without personal transportation sat there most of the day waiting for news.

Around 3:30 p.m., a tour bus arrived. It wasn't the one we expected. It was a double Decker with the same company name, but a different number.

The driver explained he was traveling to Dover the night before and had been stranded in Rye. His bus was unharmed and he learned from the manager of Camber Sands there were twenty one people waiting for a bus to London which never arrived. The driver said he needed to get to London full or empty, so we might as well come along. Providence, again. *"We'll be alright".*

As we left town, what met our eyes was surrealistic. Grand old houses with roofs damaged, historic buildings in partial rubble, huge trees that were uprooted in lines, with markings on the ground showing wind directions from the night before. It looked like a pick-up-sticks game only the sizes of the trees were unbelievable. What power it took to uproot, toss, scramble, and flatten so many things.

We had to drive out of the way to go around streets and roads still blocked, so we ended up near the beach. Amazing two to four feet walls of the large stone pebbles that make up English beaches paralleled the road, like brown snow drifts. There were rock deposits from the storm surge. These stones had been pushed by a sea swell from the beach over the highway. One row after another as the storm surges rolled in, the new rock drifts lay as testimony to the fury of the storm. Several houses closest to the road had small drifts of pebbles across their yard and all the way to front doors. When we were on the main highway toward London, we moved along with no oncoming traffic, which was eerie. Nothing was moving south. As we drove, I noticed the familiar shaped zigzag lines on the ground and through the forested areas.

As usual, my voice carried beyond my own surprise at what I saw. "Hey, that was made by a tornado. Or more than one tornado."

A few non-Plains Americans on the bus thought I was exaggerating.

"Tornadoes occur with super storms, and in odd places. Look to

Susan A. Rader

the left at that batch of trees. See the zigzag lines, at the edge of the woods? The grass and bushes have been sucked out of the ground in the direction of the rows of missing or splintered trees. More than one tornado went through that area ."

"How can you know that?" one woman said.

"I live in Oklahoma. Before that I lived in Texas and Kansas. We see this all the time but not on this scale. We don't have all these trees to lose, except in cities or along streams. Outside of cities, there are few trees. This is terrible."

All were silent now as we came to a road blocked with a gigantic tree trunk. British military with heavy equipment were everywhere. A giant tree had been thrown onto the highway. I have only seen tree trunks this big in the Redwoods of California.

The military had obviously been working many hours to cut a hole through the giant trunk. Our double-Decker bus was waved through. With the tree lying on its side, the trunk covered the bottom row of windows creating an eerie darkness inside the bus as we inched along through the narrow opening. I pressed my face onto the window glass to look up. The trunk extended upward so only a tiny bit of sunlight came in at edge of the trunk along the lower portion of glass windows on the upper section. It was an amazing moment—to drive through a tree.

At the other side of the trunk, we could see flares and a small line of cars waiting their turn to go south. Only one lane was open on this highway. Looking back at that tree was unbelievable, yet there it was. Silence on the bus continued as we saw mile after mile of destruction. England was recording this historical event, and we were trying to come to grips with what our host county endured. Our jolly holiday reminded me that unexpected things happen in life. Again, it was a moment of realizing how small people are in the scheme of time and events.

The damage extended all the way into London. A park I saw my first day on the way to Stonehall House, was now reduced to a fenced squre, every tree was down, crushing sidewalks, with roots uplifted. It broke my heart. Those trees had lived and grown a long time, to be reduced overnight to rubage. I could only imagine what happened at the Royal Observatory, and the lovely park I saw my first full day in England.

The tour trip was canceled to the Royal Botanical Gardens as it was devastated by the storm. A terrible loss. Having only seen a few majestic sycamores, pines and oaks in Kansas, Texas and Oklahoma, I was always delighted with their magnificent, rhythmic swaying in the prevailing south winds of the Plains. To see one fall was a loss, and now all around me trees that were nearly as old as the United States were uprooted.

Our bus driver took us to our hotel destination, across from the British Museum. It was an older hotel, dimly lit with the atmosphere reminding me of the business in a cattle yard—masses of people and luggage moving non-stop day and night. I was given a shared room with a woman not in our group. It had a small half bath, one dingy window, and two twin beds. We were simply paired together. She was Canadian and to go on her way to France when transportation would again became available. This tour required prepay for all the side trips around London, or none of us would have had a room after the storm stranded so many people.

We went downstairs for a meeting with our new tour guide, Campbell Stuart, a transplanted American man in his forty's. When one of our group complained about the poor quality hotel, the tour guide bristled.

"You need a room to sleep in and change your clothes. We eat out for breakfast and dinner. Everyone is responsible for their own lunches. You want to see great landmarks and experience an Elizabethan Dinner Theater at a good price or have a big, luxury hotel room for sleeping?" Case closed.

One of our group went out and purchased all the leading papers to distribute. The headlines were strictly tabloid, but after what we had seen, they fit. I purchased two for my scrapbook, just to keep the headlines from this historic storm.

"THE NIGHT WE NEARLY BLEW AWAY!" *"THE WORST STORM EVER!"* "SMASHED TO BITS!" "WHY WEREN'T WE WARNED?" "POWER BLACKOUT CRIPPLES SOUTH!" "DISASTER STRIKES WITHOUT WARNING...13 DIE!"

Actually there were 18 deaths in England and 4 in France, mostly from lack of warning. Camber Sands and Romney Holiday Parks had their miracles—minor injuries, but materially, incredible damage. Neither place would be open by spring.

On page three of *The Daily Mirror*, under the headline, 'The Night We Nearly Blew Away', was the Sealink Ferry I had seen from the window of Dover castle. It was abandoned. Its hull stove in from being driven onto a concrete apron. Of course, since we heard the story of the young couple who were on a Ferry in 18 foot' plus waves, we could see how this happened. After all, living in Oklahoma I know more about storms on the plains, than about living on an island. But I have seen entire towns destroyed in the blink of an eye. Devastation happens, and we are left to wonder but always conclude we are no match for the forces of Nature. With all our power and inventions, there is something very humbling about storm damage.

Thinking about surviving hurricane winds, I was amazed to have lasted the night. Then an interesting thought crossed my mind. *How do you hold down a trailer in 110 mph winds?* The answer: *on your knees.* Why? *With God, you weigh more.*

Finally the sun came out with only occasional quick showers. Our tour of London was fascinating, and I saluted when our bus passed 10 Downing Street. The tour guide pointed out Buckingham Palace and we had the opportunity to watch a platoon of mounted guardsmen leave the Palace grounds, on our way to the town of Windsor.

The docents at Windsor castle were fascinating, and we had lunch in town across the street from a large statue of Queen Victoria. The restaurant on the corner prepared our tour menu in the upper dining room. Above the double door was an oil painting of the royal family. Supposedly, the Royals ate in this upper dinning room when in residence at Windsor Castle. Everything was special. It was certainly a trip of a lifetime.

***

Perhaps I was wearing down from the trip. It seemed everywhere I went, I felt more and more alone, wishing for someone to share my adventures. I didn't dwell on it, but the thought crept in more often than other times in my life. I enjoyed the company of my new tour friends, but more than ever in my life, I seemed irritated with thoughts of traveling alone. Part of me had elected to live alone, but somehow this resolution was fading. Oh, well, no time to give that more thought. There was more to see and do in London.

There were four of us with reservations to see *The Mousetrap*. The three women who exited the bus at the same time as I did were older, and also American. They joined me because having decided by my confident stride, I knew where I was going. It didn't take long for me to realize I was being followed. As I discovered I was not seeing a theater, I stopped to meet the group behind me.

"Hello there. You *are* going to St. Martin's theater for *The Mousetrap*, correct?"

The taller white haired woman smiled. "I'm Edna, from Maryland. These are my friends, Alice and Carol."

"Oh, yes, from the bus. I'm Susan from Oklahoma. I want to see this play, but I'm not sure I've gone the right direction."

"Well, we're following you because you walk like you know where you're going."

I just laughed. "Oh, that's a good one. I was sure a few minutes ago that I was going the right way, but now I'm not. It was supposed to be in this direction, two blocks and a left."

"Let's go on down two blocks more. Maybe they count blocks differently," Carol said.

"OK with me. We still have thirty minutes before the door closes."

Two more blocks went by, more closed stores but no theater. We stepped into a mini-China Town.

Agnes whispered. "I don't think those red lights over the doors on the left is a good sign."

Carol and I laughed. "So, you still think I know where we're going, right?"

Alice remarked, "Well, since none of us know, we are at least together."

We moved together, reminding me of a flock of Guinea Hens. The Chinese pretended not to speak American or English. We just smiled, and continued walking in the direction in which we started. *Voila'*--there was the theater. After that night, the four of us traveled everywhere together.

St. Martin's Theater was wonderfully old, but well kept. It had what I call 'atmosphere'. We went into the vestibule to a ticket window, then were allowed to enter the theater. There was a Pub at the back of the room! Snacks, wine, beer, or ice cream. And here I'd been chewed out by a the barkeeper for trying to buy food in the Pub! The ladies I met at the Gypsy Moth were right. So much for life on the other side of the Thames.

The Mousetrap was wonderfully preformed. I knew the plot by heart but seeing it played as if it were the first time the plot unfolded, was memorable. During intermission, we each enjoyed ice cream from a small paper cup. It came with a disposable spoon-shaped wooden stick, and reminded me of ice cream I had as a child. I didn't think anyone served ice cream this way anymore.

Since the four of us were the last for the bus, our driver was waiting out front. Very thoughtful. He kept track of who got on and off, and knew the entertainment events first to last. No more getting lost for an evening.

After a free day, one I spent at Harrods, I headed back to the hotel to rest and change for the last evening, an Elizabethan Dinner Theater at Hatfield House. The setting was the great hall dining room, with a Lord and Lady on thrones as hosts, a Court Jester, and a Villainous Knight who battled another Knight. There was the sampling of Mead, a strange drink with the odor of rose petals. One sip was enough for a lifetime. The meal was plain, but entertainment kept up with a troop of wandering Minstrels singing. My last night in England. The plane home would be uneventful. What a gift—to travel. My eyes were full as well as my heart.

* * *

Jet lag is totally under rated and under stated. Oh! I couldn't understand what hit me half way across the Atlantic on the return trip home. A stewardess just laughed at my description, then kindly helped me to a row of empty seats so I could lay out flat to sleep.

"I'm one of those who can travel west without jet lag. A majority have only minor affects from hours of travel over great distances. Don't worry, it isn't fatal. It just feels like it for a few days."

I marveled now that I had very little fatigue *going* to England, but returning home felt like I'd never recover!

After a week of jet lag, where I missed most of the reports on the storm and investigations into the missed warnings by the British Meteorological Office, I returned to my housekeeping business. It was fun to share my adventures. But things at work had changed. It wasn't my clients attitude toward me, but the jobs were ending. Two of the three wealthy, successful couples were getting divorces and the other was dealing with a spouse going to prison for tax evasion. The business I cleaned for twice a month was sold, so I was without work. How odd, that once again, the Hand of Providence changed my life's direction. God gave me a trip to England, a dream come true, providing the means to go, and keeping me safe in a trailer on a beach during a hurricane. Another era was closing, but for once I wasn't afraid of another life change in direction.

With the friendships of those who employed me fondly remembered, I paused for thought. We choose our life styles. Life isn't about money or property, but values and decisions. But I have lived that way. When the values of 'self' take forefront, it falls apart. We live with what we do, and with what we fail to do. Added to this is crossing paths with other's choices. We intersect lives everyday. At any given point things happen, like having a purse stolen, a loved one killed by a drunk driver, or being in a hurricane in England. Our lives cross others for a reason, and a season, for good or bad. It is just one of the rhythms of life. We learn something from it, or we miss the lesson, but either way, we are changed.

* * *

CHAPTER 3

Single female, Church Socials, Man in the Brown Suit

Over the weeks following the church festival, everyone took turns sharing adventure stories, or lessons learned. It was a bonding time as we settled in for the upcoming Thanksgiving holiday. Everyone had plans, but me. No family. Well, there was always a restaurant buffet, but for some reason this year, I felt more melancholy.

After the disappointment of ending my cleaning business, I spent the remaining winter months in study, and making more friends at church. When March rolled around, I was offered a job at a greenhouse for three days a week. Perfect timing. I settled into a routine and enjoyed the work.

Early mornings in the greenhouse were filled with the earthy rich smell of fertile soil. Humming birds were everywhere as I moved flats of spring flowers to display for customers. As the day progressed, butterflies joined the colorful arrays with soft sunlight coming through the greenhouse glass. Another perk was the opportunity to learn more about plants. From college botany there was little useful information! College just wasn't real life.

My days were satisfying. I had the work at the greenhouse, and walks with my dogs in the untamed area behind my house. Evenings I spent in Bible study, letter writing to the friends I made in England. Life settled down. Something was missing, and I realized it was a lack of social activity except at church twice a week. This made me decide to fit more people into my life. Singles have a tendency to just live narrow lives, which isn't always bad, but for me, it had become empty.

By now, I had been a Christian for 5 years, and decided to start going to the family friendly Church Socials. Church socials meant lots of people, all ages, attending from our church and other churches. There would be potluck dinners and snacks, games for all ages, and nice dancing, as in ball room, bunny hop or polka. No heavy metal with strobe lights.

We had all ages at any given activity. Singles, elderly, young couples with or with out kids, old couples, visitors, married and widowed. It always reminded me that I arrived alone, and lived alone, with no family. At 38, I was still single, never married.

When the Spring Social rolled around, I made a beeline for the singles group. This sounds really odd, but I was still learning how to live with my ear disease and the seizures. My absence seizures caused me to sit and stare, then left me confused. That doesn't go well in social settings. The ear disease caused staggering and slurred speech. To people who did not know about the sudden onset of a Meniere's attack, it looks like drunkenness. The associate pastor never heard of Meniere's and didn't believe me. Of course, he never looked up the disease or asked a doctor to see what happens. It's one of the myriad mind sets in human behavior, whether a follower of Christ, or a non-believer.

I often felt awkward, as there were some people who were not friendly simply because I had been in the military. Some were not friendly at church because I was single. Prejudice abounds in all walks of life and for all kinds of reasons. My choice was the all single female table next to the dance floor.

"Woo-hoo! Coming to front row central, finally, hmm?" Paula teased. "I'm hoping for a dance this evening," she said wistfully. "I don't think I ever told you, but I go to the men's section of department stores just so I won't forget how good a man can smell." Paula at fortyish, never married, witty, charming, but at over six feet tall, she appeared as total intimidation.

"Men's department. Hmm, I should go there. I live with two dogs and three cats." I replied.

Melba, over 50, leaned forward. "Any new faces on your way in?"

"A few," I said. "I couldn't see everyone. I just got here."

A young man, under 40 came to one side of the table. "Hi, I'm Matt. Which one of you lovely ladies is Melody?" He smiled hopefully.

Melody, shy and 26, beamed. "That's me!"

"How 'bout a dance?" Matt asked. "I'm from Duncan. Quite a drive." Matt and Melody blended into the milling dance floor.

Beside me, a voice spoke conspiratorially. "Do you see the guy in the corner over there?" Anna nodded to our right indicating a man in a faded green suit. Betty was the resident cynic. "That guy's deodorant wore off before he got here."

Patty, thirtyish, quipped, "Oh! He always smells like that. He was in Dallas two months ago—same green suit. That smell *is* his cologne!" Some laughter to break the tension.

As we watched the dance, conversation died at our table. Not exactly uplifting or encouraging. I hoped all the socials weren't like this one where the main group attended the dance. It was nice for married couples, but disheartening for singles.

Thinking about this merry-go-round, I started to wonder about this "single" thing. Common sense as well as scriptures show us rules for being with people who hold the same values. And it was never a good idea to date someone from your job. If that went bad, it could mess up your work day. These sensible principles relegated social activity, and with good reason. However, we didn't have an official Singles Ministry, so it was merely a matter of getting together if someone held an event. Not wanting to seek company in bars, the church social was at least safe.

My favorite place at family socials was the buffet table. Cooking is not my strong point. I liked to glance around the room as I put 'what I call the extra's' on my plate. That would be stuffed eggs, homemade coleslaw, olives—these things there were luxury on my salary.

In the next room, there was a group watching an 8mm projector of an old Bowery Boys movie, domino and board games, with a volunteer handing out small bags of popcorn. All ages, lots of activities, but I was missing something. I didn't seem to connect. It no longer seemed enough for me to be around the noise of fellowship. I returned to the non excitement at the singles table. Three of my women friends just sat down.

"Well, those three guys are finished for the evening." Paula quipped.

"How do you know?"

"Look," Paula, tilted her head toward the doorway. "See, they're moving into the game area. They each have three dances, then move on. It's their set routine. My dad told me. I can't stand predictable."

Just then, a tall, well built man in a custom cut brown suit walked up to the table. *Where did he come from?* Regal bearing and broad shoulders. Striking.

Looking straight at me, he asked, "May I have this dance?"

Shocked, I replied, "Aaa, yes." And popped up from my chair like a jack in the box.

"Are you enjoying the social?" he asked.

"So far," I replied. "My name is Susan."

He looked at me seriously. "I know."

What an odd thing to say. Of course, it didn't occur to me until later he might have asked someone about me. But why would he do that?

We danced without any more conversation. The band was too loud for conversation, although I tried to ask his name. He just smiled. Maybe his hearing was as bad as mine.

As the music selection faded, he nodded to me and said, "Thank you." He turned us to escort me toward the singles table. When I turned to ask if he would like to sit down, he was gone. Vanished.

Maybe I made him up! With a visual sweep, I located him in a far corner. How he managed to get away that fast I didn't know. Maybe he was a one dance guy. Oh, NO! It was probably me. *Gone in twenty seconds.*

Mysterious. Stoic. He had a cleft in his chin and a small, unusual scar on his right cheek. Rugged looking, and tall. Suddenly I felt shallow because I certainly did like the way he walked. *Is the way a man walks important to notice?*

My friends took turns with "oohs" and "ahs" over my dance with the stranger. What a stir, with rapid fire questions.

"Oooo—ee, Who is Brown Suit?"

"Where's he from?"

"What's he do for a living," Anna demanded. "You've gotta' watch out for unemployed!"

"Has he been in the church for very long?" Patty asked.

"Prob'ly a headhunter at the meat market," Anna quipped. "Ya' know the type. Popping in and out of churches looking for single women." *Why did Anna come to these things?*

My replies were lame.

"I don't know anything. The music was too loud."

Paula drew an invisible line in the air to mark her imaginary scoreboard.

"One chance-- down". She leaned up with narrowed eyes. "Girl, you've GOT to get his name. Who knows, a door may have opened for you."

Melody piped in, "Even *I know* to ask for a name. It's hard to find eligible men with values and not secret agendas. Look around. Things aren't any better than the last time we came."

Anna snorted. "Better than re-runs on TV."

Susan A. Rader

A sudden overpowering wave of burned popcorn swept the room.

"Ooh, I wish somebody knew how to run that machine!" Patty waved her hand in front of her face.

"Air. I need fresh air!"

"It kills the chance of any man noticing my perfume," Paula sighed.

But my thoughts were on tall, regal, Mr. Brown Suit. I was trying to recall if he had on any cologne. Then with a jolt, I realized I forgot to put on perfume. *Who cares, Susan! What are we, bees?* But it didn't matter now. There is no way to over come toxic levels of burned popcorn with cologne or after shave. I only wore perfume occasionally because it was suggested in a conversation at church or some one was selling it. In the military, I didn't wear perfume.

My mind wondered back to all the male attention I received in England. An English meteorologist, a Scottish banker, and a Canadian lawyer all took great care to see that I had company everywhere. It was a fun experience, since being in the Army where the men I saw each day were mostly criminal, or draftees getting ready to leave the military. Almost everyone with foul language and lewd remarks. I had closed myself off for a long time to male attention, and for several reasons. Now it seemed the new female friends I made spent most of their time longing for male companionship. Perhaps it's like a virus.

When I looked around, I saw Tall Mr. Brown Suit talking with a few of the casual friends I had met from other singles activities. He was laughing and talking. It made me wonder why he said so little to me. Some time would pass before I found the answer to that question.

When my mystery man came back to ask me to dance again, my friends hooted wildly. Brown Suit frowned, but it was too late for him to withdraw the invitation. What happened to my quiet, critical companions?

I hoped I didn't appear too eager to escape the table. No wonder we were all still single—sitting there like vultures or ravenous she-wolves! It is one thing to sit with girl friends who can 'catch the signal', but it was not an advantage for a shy man who wanted to ask one of us to dance. I'm thinking I should have caught on sooner.

However, Brown Suit was back. This time I shouted over the music. "Thanks for the dance invitation. I didn't catch your name last time."

"David," he replied.

David. Okay, so it wasn't Nick, or Cary, or some name from a novel.

At least I was away from the *all girl* table, and determined to get more information out of him. Not just to save face, but because he piqued my curiosity.

I couldn't think of anything else to say so I blurted out, "Have we met before tonight? You didn't have to ask my name."

David smiled. "We were both at a single's retreat a few months ago at the lake lodge. You were with Jill, Melody, and Jody."

"Oh," I replied. I didn't remember seeing him there, but then he did seem to prefer being inconspicuous. I also wasn't looking for a date. I went to hear the Bible Study sessions, and enjoy fellowship. Tall, with broad shoulders and that distinctive walk, how had I missed seeing him?

Suddenly, David decided on conversation.

"You know, there are a lot of single girls in the Church." (*Who argues with that?*)

"One of the ministers said, at a men's retreat, that we single men should attend the dance at the socials so we can dance with single women of all ages. It's a way to learn to dance better, and a way to serve."

"Wow," I thought, *"I'm a service project!"* I kept his remarks to myself, feeling embarrassed. It killed any ideas I had of more conversation. Great. He was only doing what a minister directed him to do, so this wasn't personal. After the dance, he smiled, said "Goodbye," and left. I knew nothing more about him or even where he lived. I didn't see him again until the next wave of socials. *Better luck next year...* I decided on more at home Bible study and less of these social non-events. If God chose to answer my prayers about a male friend or even a husband, I just wanted Him to drop the guy on my front porch. I didn't want to go out on my own. My taste in men had been disastrous before becoming a Christian. I already knew the way *NOT* to go. It was time to try T*he Way* to go.

* * *

Dance for Charity, Crib notes and dating toward marriage

Thirty-nine and unmarried. It wasn't like I was desperate to be dating or engaged or married. Well, not exactly. I longed for companionship but I was fearful of it too. My wonderful dogs didn't reply to conversation. The topic of marriage was one everyone else seemed to be discussing, and I kept being drawn into those conversations. From the sermons and Bible

Susan A. Rader

Study topics, it appeared that marriage and how to treat your spouse took a lot of work. Then, after a sermon, all conversation dissected the pastor's talking points. The subject of marriage seemed to be something everyone needed to study. It was easy to be on the outside, looking at someone's marriage and seeing plainly how the couple treated each other. I wondered if it was easy to see how to treat your spouse from inside a marriage.

I was pretty sure I would never marry, for many reasons. My family background and how I lived before becoming a Christian. I didn't see first hand that marriage ever made anyone happy. My family tree sure didn't find happiness that way. I was sure I had 'dysfunctional' written all over me.

My friends at church were always looking for Mr. Right to show up at church and pick them out. It must be the 'Pollyanna' syndrome, some idea leftover from long ago about not being alone. Sometimes I felt "forever-hopeful". Sometimes "forever cynical". Perhaps promises from the scriptures, now so dear to me were helping me lean toward 'hopeful'.

After a rough week at work, I was feeling more discouraged than usual, wanting conversation at church to cheer me up. Instead, one of the well-meaning widows patted my arm after another sermon on marriage.

"Well, honey," she said, "I *'magine '*t*if*'in you hain't been married 'ba now, you might as well 'a- quit tryin'." Note: For future reference-- if I I live to be 70, *don't* say something like that to a single person!

One year later, I found a message on my answering machine.

"Would you like to go with me to the Men's Spokesman's Club dinner in Ada? I'll call you back at 9:00 p.m. David."

Wow! David. Brown Suit. I'd heard a great deal about the Men's Spokesman's Club, and I would be with a live date. I didn't mind being a service project if it meant dinner. I didn't want to spend another night alone with my two cats and two dogs.

If David Brown Suit wasn't destined to be THE man for me, I'd still be in a room with lots of other people. *What IS his last name?*

I began imagining the evening. I wouldn't be sitting with a tight little group of women huddled together against the "cold" of a specific place in society. Pegged is one term. The other is selected. Alone appears to be the worst title. Maybe, just maybe, this was where the tide turned for me. Oh well, things were at least looking up. I called to accept his invitation. David didn't have anything else to say on the phone except when he would arrive. It seemed awkward, but I tried to overlook this since I would be glad to get out of the house. He was certainly hard to read.

For over a week, I tried on everything in my closet. I invited a young, fashionable, married friend over to help me select something.

After looking over everything in my closet, Betty sat down on the edge of my bed, put her face in her hands, and said, "Susan, dear, none of this even goes together!" News to me, but suddenly embarrassing. I went to a boarding school with a uniform and then the Army. *I just discovered I'm fashion handicapped.*

Betty was able to find me something that would go together for this date, and recommended I buy pastels for my wardrobe. She was a little vague about what pastels meant, but at least I had a outfit for the dinner. After all, I worked at a greenhouse—I only needed church clothes for Wednesday and Sunday until now. I hadn't even stepped out in faith to purchase something so I would 'be prepared' if a date happened.

***

David arrived in his fire engine red '78 Mustang, cleaned and polished. I mean, his car was cleaned and polished. He gallantly escorted me from the house, dutifully opening the car door. He was clean, smelled good, too, and, oh, I still loved the way he walked! I could tell how much he loved his car. I read somewhere that admiring his car was a good start to conversatin this warm spring evening.

"This is a great looking car, David," I said, as I ran my hand along the edge of the sunroof. "But don't you get sunburned with this hole in the roof?" Good thing I smiled just then as David looked extremely serious. Maybe I insulted his car.

"No," he replied. "I like the air rushing in, especially on long rides. I've been driving for three hours to get here, so we'd better get going."

Three hours to reach my house? Where did he live? That should have been a clue as to his interest, but on a regular basis, I miss obvious things. Soon we were on the interstate for another two-hour drive, and this time he talked, a little.

David pulled a small square of paper from his shirt pocket, looked at it and put it back.

"Where did you grow up?"

"Kansas," I replied. "Born in Texas, raised in Kansas, and since I couldn't make up my mind, I chose Oklahoma. How about you?"

"Aaaa...born in Texas," David replied. His words and body language were stiff, as if I had pried top-secret information from him. I couldn't figure him out. He again pulled the small square of paper from his shirt pocket, glanced at it and then at the road ahead.

"Did you go to college?" David asked.

"Yes, here in Oklahoma. I studied Geography and Geology. My head is full of maps and rocks," I added with a laugh. He didn't respond to my joke and I was beginning to feel interrogated.

Another glance at his square of paper.

"Do you have any hobbies? I mean, what do you like to do in your free time?" David asked.

"Oh, television, reading, especially action or mysteries. I also like to paint and put models together. I just finished the U.S.S. Constitution," I replied. "What about you?"

"Yes, I built that model," David answered as he glanced down at the tiny square of paper.

"How many different places have you lived?" he asked.

Suddenly a light went on in my head! *Crib notes!* What a nice idea! He had given a great deal of thought to good conversation. Little did he know I never needed notes to make conversation! I can talk about nothing. I can talk until the phone goes dead, just ask around. David let me talk for the entire two hours enroute. That's probably why I was so quiet at dinner.

Years later, I thought about our first date and asked him about that little square of paper.

"Oh, that. It had **HELP** written on it."

"Help?"

"'**H**' for hometown or own your own home. '**E**' for education. '**L**' for leisure, hobbies or recreation, and '**P**' for places you've been. A little formula the minister gave me."

Simple but effective! HELP-he needed help to talk to a woman. *Help?* At this point on our first date, I was going to need help talking to him.

After the spokesman's club dinner, David and I talked a little about the night sky, the topics and jokes from the dinner meeting, and just enjoyed the cool night drive. We arrived back at my home by 1:00 a.m.

After David came around to open my car door, he went to his trunk, and pulled out a long thick wooden box he placed on the porch steps. It was his telescope!

"Saturn is pretty close tonight. I thought you might like to take a look. This telescope is strong enough we should be able to see the rings."

Wow! I love telescopes. I had one as a kid and always used it. I loved looking at the moon and identifying planets and stars. Amazing! David obviously did too. Many facets to this man.

After we looked at Saturn, he turned the telescope toward the moon.

"If you look carefully, you can see the place that was the site of the first moon landing."

"Oh, I loved watching that on television! Did you watch it live?"

"Yes," was all he replied. I could tell he wanted to say more, but something held him back.

After pointing out the area, he began putting up the telescope.

"I'd better get started. I have a three hour drive. It has been a great evening."

"Where do you live?" *Finally I ask.*

"Altus. It's in the southwest corner of the state." David extended his hand.

"Thank you for coming with me. Goodnight."

I watched him drive away, wondering if I would see him again. So quiet. Was he shy or was I so intimidating that he was overwhelmed. *Why do I have to talk so much ? For Pete's sake I babble.* Oh well, there was no way I knew to find out.

A Proposal of sorts

A few weeks later, at a single's seminar weekend, I saw David with another woman. I didn't know what that meant. Maybe he was still 'serving single women' by getting them out of their homes.

I wasn't sure if I was feeling disappointment, or slightly jealous. *Oh, this is confusing.* I just tried to put David out of my thoughts. Easier said than done. His chiseled profile and intense hazel eyes kept coming to mind. He was too mysterious and interesting to forget.

A few months later, I found another message on my answering machine. David had moved right here to the city. Now, instead of being three hours away, he was only twenty minutes from my house. David invited me out for Mexican food. What I didn't know was how much interest he really had in me, or that he called the local church pastor to ask for my phone number and character reference. Wow! I was in for a shock.

David arrived exactly on time, to head for the restaurant before taking us to Bible Study. Destination: Mexican food at the Mall. I had never been to this restaurant but enjoyed the atmosphere. When warm tortilla's arrived with butter and vegetables, I dove right in. *Such a ladylike thing to do!* Just after I bit into a jalapeno pepper slice, he said, slowly and carefully, "Susan, I'd like to date toward marriage."

Gasp! I couldn't breathe. Was it the hot pepper? No! I was about to turn 40, and this man I'd only dated two times said the words 'date toward marriage'? *What do I do now?* I needed time to think. Was this related to my prayers about being lonely? How did he jump to this level? From a date to dating toward marriage? And *What does THAT mean? I had overload with questions and choking on the hot pepper wasn't helping.*

I stalled my reply by drinking an entire glass of water. David look amused. I sputtered, then coughed to postpone my reply. *What do I say?* I've had many prayers answered, but this topic of a husband finally appeared on my prayer list three years ago. I didn't really want to spend my life alone with dogs and cats.

Just because a man asked to "date toward marriage" didn't automatically make that "answered prayer". Perhaps this was a test. Maybe it wasn't anything at all. Maybe God knew I needed basic education in relationships and a chance to think in this direction. Maybe this wouldn't work out but I could learn something. I believe God gives us many choices on many issues. After all, He knows us better than we know ourselves and He has our welfare in mind. He wants to lead us, not force us.

I sat frozen in place. David waited patiently, that smile on his face and a twinkle in his eyes. Was he teasing me? I must have skipped this part of day dreaming since I never got to the part in a day dream where a man actually wanted to get to know me well enough to marry me!

"Aaaa...ME?" I asked. *Let's clear this up.*

"Yes," David smiled. "Don't look so shocked."

"Oh. I don't mean to," I replied after gulping down some iced tea to kill the burning jalapeno.

"You really mean--*me*?"

"Yes, I really do." David stated firmly. "What you don't know is that I had narrowed my search for a possible wife down to three women. I saw you at church functions and socials. You are outgoing, always talking with people, laughing, and having a good time. I've kept an eye on you. Two weeks ago, it wasn't coincidence that I offered to chauffeur you and Melody on the singles canoe trip."

I was speechless. A rare event.

He paused. "Of course, you can think about it. Let's eat and then walk around the mall, before Bible Study, and I'll get you home right after. Tomorrow, I've got an early assignment on a job site, out of town. I'm the project architect."

Okay. Be calm. *Oh, he's an architect*. He has a job. Nice. But what about this question? What would any other single woman do with this proposal who was about to turn 40. How would I know? I saw 40th birthday on my calendar, scheduled my first mammogram. Obviously, I should call the minister and ask for emergency counseling! So the next day after work, I raced across town, talking aloud to myself, with an occasional glance heavenward.

What did David *mean*? What kind of commitment is involved here? *Wait, Susan. Your past is checkered. How can you consider dating?* How *do* people date? For Pete's sake, my last date was at a private college a long time ago. There was a fraternity dance and one of my sorority sisters set me up with a date. Not a memorable evening. That guy had never had a date before me let alone danced!

I must have looked peculiar in traffic alone, waving my arms around, speaking aloud and praying. On the subject of dating, thinking back to high school, I didn't have a date for the senior prom! I served punch. *I'm in way over my head. Maybe I was beginning to believe I was a good person.* By the time I reached the pastor's house, I was so distraught I missed the driveway by half a block. Oh well, reverse works.

The pastor told me that as far as he could tell, I was frightened of commitment--any kind! Was that supposed to be "news", a statement of the obvious or comforting? His information was of no help. There must be a practical side to dating. I like having a plan, being the random person I usually am, some sort of plan helps.

The Pastor laughed at my trepidation. "Susan, this is dating. You get to know each other and for the specified time, you don't date anyone else. You try to understand each other. Do activities together at church, go bowling or sight see, or walk through museums. See how you fit into each other's lives. Ask questions that are important for you to know about him, and tell him things that are important to you, about you."

"I haven't had much time in my new life. I've never thought about what things are important to me. I lived day to day. I don't even have a relative I can call for advice."

"That is not all I meant. You must open the topic of how you have lived your life. And I might add, ask him how he has lived his life."

I looked down at the floor.

"You mean tell him about my past?"

The pastor replied. "Yes, Susan. Ask God how to do this. He will help you."

***

I had ten days to think over this serious proposal, while he was off to California because I knew he would ask me again. He told me he wanted to talk to me when he returned. *Why didn't I take him up on going to out there?* I could have met his family, attended all the church activities with him, and had a better chance of getting to know him. *Dumb move, Susan.* Maybe it was supposed to be this way. Maybe God had me face this now so I wouldn't torment myself with thoughts that I could have a normal life. *A normal life.* What an odd phrase. My life had never been normal. I know God didn't want me tormented. He wanted me to look at my life through His eyes, through the Grace and Mercy He extended. That was going to take a while.

Ten days. That's not a great deal of time to look over the idea of a once upon a time dream becoming reality. I prayed a great deal, looking over my favorite narrative examples in the Bible, talking with other singles, and finding some newly weds for sounding boards. *What kinds of things do you face when getting married? What was dating like before marriage? At what point do you know whether or not to finish the dating phase, and get married?*

But there was no one to ask about my problem: what do I tell David about my life before and after I left home? How could I tell him the list of events on a downward spiral when I didn't' even understand them myself. Well, it was a matter of asking for wisdom and understanding I didn't have.

In order to persuade him not to pursue me, I needed to tell him a lot of things. This was just the way it was. There can be no secrets in marriage or there would be trust issues. Who I am now, is *not* who I was. But I needed to look back to see this as good news.

Get real, Susan, once you tell David this mess, he'll run for the hills. I really liked David's company. We seemed to have a great deal in common, from what I could pry out of him. Things like science, photography, astronomy, model making, and travel. Obviously, David 'out talking me' would never happen. Would communication be a problem? At the moment, the communication had to come from me. What did David see in me?

For years, until church socials, picnics, or family days, I didn't bother to leave my house.

Usually I attended some group thing, with other singles. I could not imagine finding a husband without Divine Intervention, and that is why I prayed so often about the subject. Why now, was I so frightened? After all, David just wanted to date so we could get to know one another.

It would be like the old-fashioned idea of "going steady". We weren't sizing rings. I wouldn't really have to share all my sinful past with him unless we were truly meant to be together. Falling in love would be different for us as older singles. We had practical life experiences and had watched so many others in relationships we knew some of the pitfalls. But now, this would be how to get to know someone totally and openly all according to God's ways on how to behave.

I had been alone a long time. My two dogs and two cats didn't care how I dressed or if I used table manners. Thankfully, David had not dated until he was in college, and then only a few times. I was relying on his not expecting much! But that still left finding out about each other. What did we each like? What depth of commitment did we each have to God first then to the idea of marriage? Were all of our personal views in line? I already knew we both believed there is only One authority for truth, wisdom, and right behavior. Our 'feelings and opinions" are secondary to that Truth. That much we had in common.

With all of this running non stop in my head, I felt as if there'd be no end to questions. *Just stop thinking about it right now and pack your things for the fall festival.* With so much to think about I was glad for church every morning, singing worship songs, giving an offering, taking notes on great sermons about how scriptures applied to real life, and then some fun time with old friends and new friends.

I had to tell him I had Post Traumatic Stress Disorder. And what about

Susan A. Rader

my seizures and that I was going deaf. Then, there were things about being in the Army in Europe. I felt pressured. Ten days to examine my life, summarize it, and ask his forgiveness for a litany of sins. How much depth was I to go into? *Don't do this*. You can do this. *NO*. Let it go. Let him go. Oh, what was I thinking when I hoped for another life, free of my past?

* * * *

CHAPTER 4

Firetruck Towing, Let's Make A Deal, Reggie Regal, Dining Bucket Debut, Horror Flashbacks

After I returned from the Church Festival, I went back to work as did David. He called me for a date to Bible Study which would start up the following week. I agreed and we each shared a bit about our trips. I was eager to see him again, but the list of things we needed to discuss was growing and I avoided setting aside a time to talk seriously. I wanted things to stay the same. That way I didn't have to face my list.

In the meantime, I brushed up at the library on national news and new movie lists. I wanted to have some general topics to discuss and then maybe see how much I could ask him about his life, hoping to postpone my confessions. Oh, I wanted this way to work because I found I really loved being around him.

On my way home from the library, in rush hour, at a busy intersection, my '70 Chevy pickup coughed and the engine caught fire. I grabbed my purse, jumped out onto the grassy area next to the street just as the signal light turned red. The lanes around me were filled. I was worried my truck might explode and injure someone. *Hurry, Susan—pray*! I didn't know that much smoke could come out from under the hood, except in movies. I prayed for help.

Suddenly, a man with a fire extinguisher came running across the street out of nowhere, over the center island, popped open my hood, sprayed it down, and ran off before I could say anything. I heard sirens, the traffic light changed, and the cars moved safely away. *Thank you Lord*.

There was a hook and ladder unit arriving. *Oh great*. Not a regular sized firetruck which is still loud and bright red. What a scene! I never thought about the size of those ladder trucks! Before I realized it, I was surrounded with firefighters all holding fire extinguishers.

"Looks like it's already out," the first firefighter said. "Just steaming."

"Oh, good," I stuttered. "Some man ran out of no where, squirted it down and vanished."

Another firefighter smiled, knowingly. "Guardian Angel, right?"

"I guess so, thanks." I hadn't thought of that—my guardian angel must be worn out after years of watching over me. No wonder the man with the extinguisher, said nothing to me, and looked annoyed.

"How 'bout we push your truck out of the traffic, over to the other corner 'til you get a tow?"

"Yes, please."

"Miss," the first fireman said, "You look a little pale, like you need to call someone. Have you called for a tow truck? I recommend Jacks' Towing Service. I have his number."

"Sure, thanks," I replied gratefully. I think the shock of this was beginning to hit me hard. I couldn't think straight. What a headache! *Oh, please Lord, that I don't have a seizure and get confused.*

"I wish all our calls were this easy," said the driver as he maneuvered in behind my pickup.

The hook and ladder unit pushed me across the traffic, with lights flashing. There's nothing like being MORE conspicuous, so I just concentrated on steering into the driveway of a closed muffler shop. With a loud horn blast and a wave, the firefighters left. I dug out some change and headed for a payphone to call for a tow.

As I waited, I sat looking at the bubbled paint on the truck hood, barely aware of the rush of traffic past me. A new vehicle was going to be needed if this fire was as bad as it looked. I knew more prayer was needed, more divine intervention with my budget, and suddenly I remembered an answered prayer a few weeks back. It was about my truck.

We had a sermon about "being content" with what we have—not getting into debt or keeping up with the latest and greatest things. After that sermon, I had prayed that I wasn't being covetous, but would it hurt if I could have some hubcaps for my rust bucket—something I could afford. My prayers were simple on the subject.

That very next afternoon at a shopping mall, I was getting out of my pickup on the way to a grocery store, when I saw an elderly man standing a few vehicles away with an odd look on his face.

"Excuse me, Miss," the elderly man said. "I just wanted new wheel covers and I don't want to throw away the old ones". He hesitated. "I couldn't help but notice that you don't have any at all...and would you like to have these. You know, so I don't have to throw these away?"

Dumbfounded, I just nodded. "Sure. And thanks."

After only a few minutes, the elderly man had pushed on all four "used" but shiney hubcaps that exactly fit my old truck tires. What a difference!

"God bless you," I said, truthfully. "I really don't know what to say."

"Nothing, Missy," he replied. "Now, I can go home, watch TV and not worry that I threw something away that I could give away. Frugal, you know."

Wow, was that fast. I totally forgot why I went to the shopping center, having to return later for bread and milk. Simple is good. Now, months later, my rusty, trusty truck with new wheel covers had a brownish bubbly place on the hood.

But, there was still the trouble with a car payment fitting into my small income. I was disabled, as far as regular work was concerned. My memory moved vividly into a small round chamber made of layers of concrete with a window. My last memories in Nuremberg, West Germany. I could now see the pedestal that stood off- center in the small low chamber, and the thick glass on an outside window. We were at a German military base to 'try out the new gas masks'. *Flash back*. I was there, but I didn't leave. Cyanide. It looked the same as the tear gas used in basic training, except outside that window in full view were German tanks and armaments. Skin poisoning that I didn't remember for nearly a year after that fateful day. Brain damage from cyanide. That's why my jobs have to be office and only three days a week. *Come around Susan. You're in a truck. Think.*

I was thinking about my limited budget. Yes, I'm in my truck, and what else? Oh, a fire in the engine. I looked at the remaining change in my hand. Oh, call a tow truck. The world seemed bleak at the moment, in the fading light of the afternoon, as I stood by my broken down truck in the drive of a closed business. All alone. I think part of this was shock, which could easily set off a bad seizure—the kind that could last for hours. I would hate to be at the mercy of a stranger with a tow truck when I was in the confusion of a seizure. *Please Lord, protect me.*

Just then, Jack with no last name arrived in his tow truck. I climbed into the dirty cab, and glanced back at my '70 Chevy in tow. We began the trip to the garage to see my regular mechanic.

"Fire, huh?" Jack with no last name asked as he spit chewing tobacco into a cup. I turned my head to hide a gag.

"Yes, and lots of smoke." I rolled down the cab window for air, trying to ignore the slobbers and drips on the dashboard and the sloshing sound from his nearly full spit cup.

"Too bad. Nice old truck. Real collector's fixer-upper." Jack spit again into that disgusting cup.

"Do you collect trucks?" I asked, hoping he would talk and stop spitting.

"Nah. Got one older'n yors," Jack spit again and laughed, his yellow teeth and dribble on his chin making me want to ride on the outside.

"Besides, I'm always pickin' up somethin' at the side of the road—if 'ya get my drift! It's ma'job!" Jack roared with laughter. Tow truck humor. *The seventeen miles to the garage is going to be a long trip!* At least Darren's Garage was my safe haven for truck trouble. When Jack with no last name and I arrived, Kendall the mechanic rolled out from under a car propped up in the work bay. He recognized my truck, since he'd seen it often enough.

"Well, kiddo, what'ya do to it this time?" Kendall wiped his greasy hands on a ubiquitous red cloth. Glancing at the hood of the Chevy, he grunted, "Aah! A little hot under the hood tonight, huh?" *Don't we love garage humor?*

The sun was setting. I had a monster headache, and wondered how much this little adventure was going to cost. It wasn't as if I made loads of money working at the greenhouse.

Kendall popped the hood, and began looking at the engine, mumbling to himself.

"Unbelievable!" he finally said. "Would you look at this? I can't believe it. All you need are a few new wires and a fuel pump. That's what caused the fire. A broken hose. This'll cost 'ya about eighty-five bucks, and labor. Unbelievable, lady. You sure got someone looking out for you!"

"You have no idea!" I replied. *Thank you Lord*.

"Will it take long to fix?" I asked, wondering about getting to work.

"I'll have it tomorrow afternoon, but what you really need is a new truck or a newer something. Every seal on this buggy is leakin'. It's a wonder you haven't had some other kind of fire or breakdown before now...not counting all the times I've seen you for used tires and rims. Someone sure keeps a watchin' over you!"

I smiled. "God is good to me. I can't complain."

God gives me hubcaps and saves my old truck. That made me pause to think. I can trust Him to help me out with new learning experiences. Like my getting another vehicle or dating toward marriage. Hmm, maybe this is a message.

Kendall looked at me with his older, wiser eyes, and said, "Woman, not that you ain't got some grit, but get yourself a husband that knows how to fix trucks, or get a great used car!" He slammed down the truck's hood. "Or get the great used car, and then get a husband to take you places. But start by going to see your banker for a loan as soon as you can. I'm fond of seein' you, but tired of workin' on this old heap. Get me something new to look at will ya, kid?"

Kendall's boss gave me a ride home with no conversation, which suited me. Get a new vehicle? Would this look good on my "resume'" with David? How do I go about getting another vehicle? Do I ask David for advice or be self-sufficient? Maybe being self-sufficient was what David liked about me. Okay. Keep this to myself. I had a problem, and being on my own at least if I embarrassed myself, I was alone at the time. So I set about helping myself out of another mess, as usual, the hard way. How does the old saying go? "A day late and a dollar short." Maybe this time, I should pray about all of this first. The answers are quite often surprising, and always, right on time!

* * *

Lets Make A Deal

Be a single female, without any male family members, and try to *buy a used car in Middle America in the 1980's*! Ha! Around here, a woman needed written permission to even *look* at a power tool, let alone buy a car without being totally scammed, ridiculed, or bamboozled. For all I know it's still a state sport!

When I went in to ask for the loan, I added that I might have *some* trade in value in my '70 Chevy pickup, but what I really meant was the value of the newly donated hubcaps plus the cost of the fire extinguisher I kept under the seat. That's not a lot to work with, is it? But my bank

Susan A. Rader

approved a loan for me based on my Veteran's pay at a very low rate of interest.

My garage mechanic and I were still in awe that the fire had only melted a few wires. Of course, my view was Divine Intervention, given the condition of my truck. The fire looked so bad at the time because it was gasoline burning on top of a greasy engine. *Do men really wash their engines?* I thought water flooded something and kept it from starting. Oh well, this detail is not in my 'need to know that' file. Flames and heavy smoke just made it *look* like a disaster.

Face it, Girl! It truly was time for another vehicle. I made copies of my insurance and inspection forms just in case the truck caught fire again on the way to the used car lot. I didn't want anything important to be lost! Surely, this was the way to handle things.

I scoured the newspapers, drove past the "repossessed" lots at local banks, watched those "siren song" car commercials on television, and prayed until I felt ready to jump into the deep waters of the Used Car Lot.

My banker gave me the names of three lots he felt would give me a reasonable deal. So, in faith I started out. I found myself in a Buick dealership surrounded by four sales representatives. I made the mistake of pausing to look over a car on the way to the sales office. Reference Note: *don't do that. There really is someone watching!*

These four men were determined to cover every possible argument I could think of for NOT buying that light blue Le Sabre that captured my attention on the way to the sales office. I was told that I *needed* to buy it right now because someone else looked it over that very morning!

Now what could I do when they were blocking the exit? I sat down with my back to the wall, pun intended, and reached for a phone. The desk, cluttered with empty pop cans, crumpled papers, and cigarette packs, was complete with a full ashtray. I had never purchased a car by myself from *someone I didn't know*. Here I was, trapped inside a car dealership. *(Is there a book by that title?)*

Maybe I could just throw a chair through the plate glass window like the movies and jump out. No, cancel the thought. My truck wouldn't start the first time, and they'd catch me. I did not realize until after arriving that I should have prepared for movie stunts. How do other people buy cars? Why couldn't I have thought to bring help or at least taken time for more prayer when I arrived?

I decided to call a friend for help and thankfully, my friend's father was home. I'm sure a remark like that isn't politically correct or very impressive, but I don't like to be rude, even to used car salesmen!

When my friend's father answered the phone, I said, "Hi, Mr. Bailey, I'm at this car dealer looking over a used Buick Le Sabre. What do you think?" To my surprise, I heard laughter.

"So, you're surrounded by salesmen, and they come back with every reason in the world for you to NOT to leave without *that car, today*?"

I felt stupid. Does everyone know how to do everything except me? I was relieved that he understood, but feeling just plain stupid for learning so late in life what other people know. Let's be cool here.

"Rii-ight! How'd you guess?"

"Okay. Just repeat after me and watch the vultures fade away!"

I listened carefully and followed instructions, repeating what he said:

"I want to think this over. (Pause for effect.) I have to get approval on this, and I need some more opinions. (Pause for effect.) I can't afford this car right now because the bank gave me a strict limit..."

As predicted, one by one, the "Slick Sam's" faded into the dusty background of the Used Car complex. I slipped out with a look towards heaven in thanks for the lesson. I hugged my pickup. It wasn't much, but it was mine, and it still ran. There was only a little melted paint on the hood to tell that anything major had happened recently, and by now I was used to the burned oil smell. What more could a woman want?

My one wish at that moment was to get home. I left rubber tire tracks at the car lot exit. "There's no place like home...there's no place like home...."

* * *

Reggie Regal

Perhaps there are few people left in the world who pray before going into car dealerships, but I highly recommend it. My first stop had taught me great lessons. After another five used car dealers tried to wear me down to buy something, I came across a very nice man named Mike.

It was late, and the car dealership was about to close for the evening. I was weary, leery, and frustrated. I said a short prayer for wisdom as I got out of my pickup and saw the *sports jacket* approaching.

I smiled and said firmly, "I have this old truck and $2500. That's it.

Nothing else. And I can't find an honest man in the area!" I suddenly remembered a quote from scripture. "I have no brother, no father, and no husband. It's just me. Tell me the truth or don't talk to me at all." *My, I wasn't very lamb-like right there and it surprised me.*

The strangest look passed across the man's face. "Come inside, you look tired. I am a Christian man, and I'll tell you right now, I don't have anything on this lot that I could sell you for $2500 and that very old truck. But, if you will trust me, I'll hunt around for you and call you within two days. Is it a deal?"

I felt grateful, even if it might be too good to be true. There are times things happen that can't be explained, and this was obviously one of them. It is true that God moves in mysterious ways! I certainly find it more than coincidence that I used that particular Biblical phrase on that car salesman! I had not intended on beginning a conversation with a Bible quote.

Mike offered me some coffee and we talked for a short while. I explained I was a disabled veteran with fixed income, and he filled out a form including information from my loan officer at the bank.

Two days later, when I came in from work, the phone rang. It was Mike at the dealership.

"Bring your title and your truck. I've got *the car* for you, and your banker already approves. I still have to convince my boss, but I *am* a salesman! It's what I do best. Can you be here inside 15 minutes?"

"Yes. What's the deal?"

Mike replied, "I can only hope that someone will do the same for my sister or my mom someday." *Wow. That was a lovely thought.*

When I arrived, I saw a beautiful steel gray Buick Regal with a landau roof.

"That can't be it--there's no rust," I thought, *but it was*.

There was Mike, the salesman, standing with the owner of the dealership. I didn't make a very good impression getting out of my '70 Chevy with a fire extinguisher. But, think about it. I couldn't very well leave it there to roll around under their feet while they did the test drive!

The look on the dealer's face was incredulous, and I watched Mike waving his arms as they drove off. It must have been his hardest sell! I went inside Mike's office to wait for the verdict. Three other salesmen peered down the hallway and I felt like an exhibit at the fair.

One stepped forward and asked, "Are you the one getting that great deal on the Buick?" When I shrugged, he said, "Well, Mike is giving up most of his commission to let you have this. What did you say to him?"

I just smiled. "Mike is a good guy. And God answers prayers in ways I can't explain."

I drove away with a very satisfied used car salesman who has set the standard in my book for generosity, his puzzled peers all shaking their heads. I came home in the most beautiful car I have ever owned! Some prayers are *just answered*. "Reggie Regal" was all mine!

Now I could tell David about the car since he wasn't thrilled with trucks, and I wouldn't have to go into very many details--like the truck fire and calling Mr. Bailey. I didn't *have* to tell David everything yet, did I? After all, I wasn't sure I would marry him, let alone be a very good date. I suddenly realized that I was beginning to think about David a great deal more.

I couldn't believe how much room there was in my two car garage with just a regular sized car and not a truck. The other thing about a new, even a used car was all the little gadgets I learned to live without on the truck. Now, I had high beams at night. Oh, my new found luxuries!

This is how it used to work. In my '70 Chevy pickup, heating was gloves, extra socks, boots, and a blanket. Summer meant leaving the windows down and wearing as little as possible or the alternative—don't go anywhere from July until October. Tuning the radio was by hand with a dial, and now, I was sitting in a 1982 Buick Regal, the newest I'd ever owned! Where I could set the radio stations I wanted with push buttons. *Wow! Classy.*

My new blue Buick had tinted windows, a blue light thingy that came on for high beams and two maps lights. I could lock all the doors electrically, and roll *all* the windows up and down with the push of a button. I discovered a light in the glove box, adjustable electric seat, reclining bucket passenger seat, a center island for my coffee cup, and a cool brake light in the back window. *Style, Baby, with some class!* And, no, I didn't spend the night in my new car, but I did thank God a lot.

The next morning I was up early and ran through the house to check to see if it was still in the garage. This was definitely a step up. Funny how the washing solution and car wax actually did something on the beautiful surface of my new car. That poor yellow pick up could only look better with the dirt still on it! God was upgrading me a little at a time.

Susan A. Rader

***

Dining Bucket Debut, Horror Flashback

David and I had been to church and to Bible Study every week through October. David never pressed me for an answer. He did ask me if I was still considering dating just him and I said yes, but let's just keep it to church activities for a while. I was still processing information. He smiled, with a nod, and said, "All the time you need."

November rolled around and David asked me to Thanksgiving at his parents' house. I only gave this request a little thought since David rarely mentioned family. I thought they were out in California. Actually, I would find most of them lived in Oklahoma or Texas. It was the sister and her husband who lived in Oregon where the family gathered to be together at the fall church festival in Pasadena. I just didn't know anything about them. I should have asked more questions before we arrived. I had so little to do with my family, it was just as well to *not* mention them at all. His parents knew I would be coming to dinner—I just didn't realize what an event it was going to be. I never thought of myself as an event.

We arrived at a neat white ranch style home in Altus complete with trimmed hedges, trees and a beautiful flower garden near the door. Before we walked inside I could hear lots of voices, and laughter. We walked inside and someone shouted, "Hey, David brought home a girl!" Nearly all voices died at once.

Heads popped out of every doorway. Suddenly, I was surrounded and swept aside before I learned anyone's name. *David had not brought a girl home in years?* Oh, was I nervous! Later, a sister in law would tell me the family had to take reservations, since there was so much interest in the girl David was bringing home. It is a good thing I didn't know that bit of trivia at the time. I was already close to a panic attack.

The group surrounding me were to be three sisters'-in-law, David's two aunts, and my soon to be mother-in-law.

"What do you do?" Mother-in-Law

"Where did you meet?" Oldest sister-in-law...still younger than me.

"What kind of things do you like?" Youngest brother's wife....a lot younger than me.

"Did you know he pulled off the heads of my "Barbie" dolls when I was a kid, and buried them in the backyard?" Youngest sister-in law....a whole lot younger than me.

"Do you attend church?" Mother-in-Law.

"You mean you really *like* him?" asked the younger sister still miffed over the missing doll's heads.

All of these women were Amazons--5'6" to 5'8". I felt like a child—granted, an *old* child, but about the same size of most of the children in the house, except for the ones crawling. Later, when we were taking group pictures, I was relegated to the front row with the little kids—in that tall crowd that meant any child under ten. I was in a house full of giants.

One of the women said, "Look, she's got little tiny feet." Everyone looked. *Now my feet are on exhibit*! My size 6 ½'s were pretty small next to their nines, tens, and elevens. Great. Hobbit size. *Oh, I'll never fit in! Am I answering any of their questions? I must sound like an idiot. Don't be cute or make quips—give straight answers.*

Questions popped from everywhere. I tried to answer as quickly as possible because David had obviously timed our arrival as close to mealtime as he could. I should have expected that since he isn't long on conversation. I had the opportunity to watch the family put the table together, set it, and make it work. It was like a well-oiled machine—one crew on tables and table cloths, one crew putting out dishes of steaming food—enough to feed this battalion. *Oh no, all of them can cook!* I'm doomed.

Shrinking Susan

The entire day seemed like one extended movie, and a comedy, to be sure. While I sat at the counter by the kitchen watching this well organized team put together the last food items, I saw something off to the side. It looked like a stream of liquid shooting into the dining room in short bursts. Oh, one of the little boys with a squirt gun. There was menagerie of children running through the house in groups trailed by a small poodle. The cacophony included voices, screams, toy noises, phones ringing, dishes clanging, laughter—a family. Wow!

Since there were so many of us to feed, there was a seating problem. Between David and his father's ingenuity came makeshift benches. I was offered one end of a plank that was resting on the bottom of an overturned plastic bucket. My hostess had planted me near the center of the table, on display, I think, but at the end of that long board.

After prayer, the voices began again with the clatter of flatware, dishes, and passing food trays. As we ate, I listened and laughed with this eclectic group as if we had known each other for years. Then the strangest thing began to happen. Very slowly, I began to sink lower and lower. At first, I thought it was my vision going from stuffing myself with so much food, or a trick of how everyone was seated. The food was so good it was hard to be concerned about my plate getting closer to my mouth! Suddenly, the bucket collapsed under me and I ended up on the floor. The combined weight of the people on the plank crushed the bucket.

As I went down, I saw eyebrows go up along the opposite side of the table. Conversation halted and laughter started.

"Save my plate!" I shouted.

"Bucket failure!" announced David as he helped me from the floor.

"How much food was on your plate?" someone asked me.

"Too much food on that whole side of the table!" someone added.

A male voice shouted, "Use a metal bucket next time, or get some real chairs!"

The comments kept up until the four of us from the collapsed bench were re-seated. Actually I was the only one who slid off onto the floor. The "unaware of my surroundings gambit", or the perfect description of "dumb blonde" explained my being the only one on the floor.

As it was happening I couldn't think of any rational explanation for my shrinking sensation. Adapt is my motto. I just accepted it, even when I began to tilt, trying to act as if nothing was wrong. Embarrassing myself was not what I wanted to do, on display, at center table. The addition to this hilarious scene was the others who calmly stood up as they began to slide. Me? I stayed. Hmm, late again.

Since the bucket gave us all a rare adventure, it is mentioned every year, like a holiday tradition. If this was a humor test, I guess I passed. For all I knew, they did this to every new comer! After dinner, while everyone else settled in for football, David took me for a drive to a nearby lake. On the way, he talked about how much it meant to him to find someone like me.

David pulled into a lake view turn out and parked. I sighed, afraid. I didn't want our fun relationship to turn into a nightmare. I firmly believed that 'happily ever after' really was only in the movies. I tried one more time to convince him that I wasn't a good catch.

"David, listen to me," I said. "I haven't been a Christian believer my entire life. Yes, I have a tattoo and I don't remember what it stands for. I was with a group of three friends in West Germany at the time. We joined others from our unit to go partying until all hours, and ended up in front of a tattoo parlor."

David replied, calmly. "Doesn't matter now."

"But, David, I eat out of a pan over the sink. Sometimes I eat a TV dinner--that is when the box doesn't catch fire."

"I can cook," David replied.

"David, I don't think you are taking me seriously. I squeeze my toothpaste tube in the middle, and I hate watching sports".

"We don't use the same brand, and I don't like watching sports either."

"David, I kind of like this guy I've been visiting with the prison ministry group".

David hesitated."So, you think you want to wait for him to get out?"

"No. Oh, I don't know. I'm feeling rushed. And...I'm afraid."

He reached over and squeezed my arm. "I'll wait until you are not afraid."

My heart was racing and I couldn't think of anything to say.

"You aren't expecting him to get out of jail very soon then, are you?"

"NO. I don't know why I brought that up." I closed my eyes, took a deep breath and said, "David I haven't lived a pure life. I've only been a Believer for seven years. There are things I've done...."

"Doesn't matter, now," David said.

"Yes, it does! I've got to tell you a few things and it had better be now. I wouldn't want you to run into someone I used to know, in my other life. You'd be in for a real shock."

"Let's let it go for tonight, alright?" David took my hand in his. "You don't really have to tell me everything. If you really feel you have to, then ask God to help you tell me. I hate seeing you this nervous."

"I have...health problems, too, David. I was sent with my unit into a gas chamber filled with cyanide. Three of us got skin poisoning. I have a seizure disorder. I just blank out and lose where I am and forget things."

"OK, I can deal with that. We will have time to get to know each other more, and you can tell me what you need to. Let it go for tonight. I don't want you so upset over this that you run away."

He held my hand gently but firmly in his, comparing how small my hand was to his.

"Let's go look at the lake. The wind will be strong. Let it blow everything away, and just look at the scenery. Let's enjoy our time together."

Lake Altus was full, no beaches in evidence. Gulls over head and other water birds coming across the lake flew against a darkening sky. There would be storms tonight. We said little else, but David continued to smile at me every chance he could. As the sun set, we headed back north to take me home.

***

Nightmares and Flashbacks

That night there was a heavy storm with high winds. I had a flashback I couldn't shake. I didn't have these often, but when I did, they drained me as surely as cutting an artery. There was never any warning as to what time period in my life a trauma would surface. The scene unfolded so realistically it turned me to stone.

The wind is moaning in the tree tops. It 's so cold. There was snow and ice that fell from tree limbs. Overhead the creaking, and groaning tree tops rubbed together masking all other sound. Isolated, cold, and lonely. I can't move.

"Stay still," commanded the Voice. In front of me was a small clearing, with logs and wisps of smoke from a makeshift camp fire. The flames were out. All around the fire pit were the bodies of dead rabbits and squirrels, their blood staining the snow. On a log nearby sat my little sister, Elaine, shivering in her thread bare coat. No hat. Her curly red hair moved with each gust of wind. I saw her bluish fingers. No gloves. No boots. I looked down at my own fingers, so small and white with bluish fingernails. I knew it was her turn.

I heard the gun cock and then the explosion when it fired. Dirt and embers shot up from the ground a few feet from my sister.

Don't move, Sissy. Please don't move. My heart was breaking. I couldn't breathe. Don't say anything. I knew better than to move, but could she stay still?

Another shot rang out closer to her tiny socks, dirty snow flying onto her clothes. Another shot and another. She never moved, staring straight ahead as if imagining the fire could start up again to provide some warmth.

The howling wind grew louder in the tree tops. It was so cold. Another shot rang out and another. Then the silence of the pause. My sister turned to look towards me. Then behind me, over my shoulder.

Softly, very softly she said without inflection. "Can we go home now, daddy?"

I awoke shouting. "Stop it! Stop it!" I was soaked in perspiration and shaking. I could hear the wind outside my house. I was home, not in the woods. It was a memory. Just a memory. Rage and anger filled me again until I screamed in agony. Then sobbing with guilt, I laid back down letting the tears run off my face into my ears.

How could David deal with this when I couldn't? How could he deal with other terrors I experienced? Or the rage?

My little dog whined at the side of the bed. I put my feet over onto the floor, reaching down to scoop up my little companion.

"Come on, Tana-Man, lets get out of here. It's okay, buddy. It's okay."

I wasn't sure who I was trying to reassure. We went to my study. I sat down at the desk, pulling out my Bible, and flipping it open to Psalms. Reading out loud just might push the memories, the guilt and the rage back into the darkness. *Set me free, Lord.*

"You are my Rock, my Deliverer"..... But it began again. That gray fog, that feeling of losing my body and the room disappearing. Again, I had moved into the past.

All I could see was a raging river. It was night with bright moonlight. I shook my head trying to turn away from what was appearing before me. "Oh Lord, this has to stop."

The memory deepened, pulling me into it and a long way from my desk.

It was summer and I could smell the river. It was roaring. The flood. My bare toes in the sand were cold, and I felt the rumble of the river's rage. I was eight years old.

I answered an already shouted order.

"No daddy, I can't."

I knew I couldn't swim the debris filled waters.

Looking away from the memory engulfing me I saw my open Bible as if through a mist.

"O, Lord, heal me, for my bones are troubled, my soul is greatly troubled". O, Lord, how long will this one last? How can I stop this?

As I kept reading, the flashback began to fade. I slumped down in the desk chair, again scooping up my little dog, Tana-Man, who licked at my tears. With a gasp of relief, I realized I was back in my own house, many miles and years from the past. My body ached with left over muscle tightness and my chest hurt from fear. It was suddenly very important to speak out loud.

"Tana-Man, did I tell you how God saved me that night?" He barked and whined.

"It's okay, buddy. It's okay."

"My dad threatened to come back across the river to get me, and throw me in, and that's when I heard another voice. It was my uncle. He shouted at my dad and my dad started swearing. There was a scuffle, and the smack of a fist hitting something. Silence. My uncle shouted over to me and I was so glad to hear his voice tears ran down my face. I wasn't alone anymore, Tana-Man."

"Susan, stay there. I'll come get you." My uncle had hit his brother to save me. He arrived in time to keep me from being swept away by flood waters. I would have died that night, like the other times I should have died. I hugged my little dog who washed my neck with his tongue.

"Hey stinky dog. I'm going to take a shower and go back to bed. Come on, you need a treat."

When I put him down on the floor he ran off to the kitchen, knowing that this episode was over. He always stayed with me through these memories. And when the seizures kept me on the couch for hours, he would lay faithfully beside me. I sighed deeply. Maybe I could sleep now, thinking of these events and others like them, from a new perspective. I could know God already saved me. These things are over. It was done. I was saved. I was alive.

The next day, I made a list of what I needed to tell David, because now I saw my life with new insight. It began to flow together in a story line. Evil done to me, taught to me, accepted by me. One event leading me this way, another event dragging me that way, until I became a reflection of the predator that preyed upon me. It all made sense. The shame of my behavior had been taught to me as a young child, and I didn't try to fight it until my friend, Ida, had asked me if I knew God. Yes, I chose to go the way of my parents in their deviance and vice, but just as surely as I had done those same condemning things, I was now made new. I was forgiven.

Confessions

At the end of the week, I asked David if we could go to a fast food place to find a quiet corner so I could tell him about my life. After a long list of my dirty laundry, there was silence. I told him more about my life before I became a Christian. I grew up in horrible circumstances, but when I was old enough to decide things for myself, I foolishly chose to live as I had when I was a prisoner at home. I made mostly bad choices, with bad people, and lousy activities.

"I had been taught that sex was something to exploit. My parents actions, especially my father...well, use your imagination. Then my mom remarried. Husband number two for her was a lecherous old man who made vulgar remarks to me and my sisters. I got in a fight with my mother about him, and ended up running away, and spent the night dosing in a tree. I had a bleeding ulcer then. I took refuge with a friend and her family who attended the same church. My step dad threatened to get the preacher fired, but the preacher said he would be watching out for me and that I needed to go away to school somewhere to change our circumstances."

David didn't bolt, but he had not said anything while he thought on what I told him. I felt compelled to add some more words to the silence. It was as if I were tying a noose around my own neck yet feeling compelled to finish.

"David, the most beautiful words I ever heard were at my baptism. It was when the Pastor brought me out of the water and said, "Susan, I tell you by the authority of Jesus Christ, your sins are forgiven". David, I'm not that other person anymore, but I'm not sure I'm right for you."

David's eyes filled with tears. He took my hand in both of his and said, very softly, "Since God has forgiven you, how can I not forgive you!"

There was another silent moment as I choked back tears.

Finally he asked me, "Do you love me?"

"I think so."

"Do you trust me?"

"Yes, I think so."

"Well, then, marry me."

Okay. The fear and cynic inside me screamed *"Oh, what are you doing? If you spend more time together, will he still want to marry you?"*

After he took me home, I didn't sleep at all. David's expressions had changed from sad, to shocked, to angry at times about the things I told him, but always kindly at me. I wasn't sure what he thought about all I had told him. Of course, there was more that I was yet to remember.

"I want to keep you safe. I want you to have a better life than you had," was what David said, over and over again.

We went on many dates, and about a month later, he took me downtown for lunch, then for an evening stroll. We walked around, holding hands. It was wonderful to spend quiet time, with no rushing, just looking at scenery as the late afternoon shadows began to soften the day. I was beginning to see I would not be let go—David was pursuing me, as God had. This was beautiful, but the old hurts and mistrust learned at the hands of those who were supposed to protect me kept surfacing.

"David, I have prayed about some more things to tell you. I just need to do this. God let me see my life in a rerun a few nights ago. I could suddenly see the reasons WHY I did some of things I did and then how some things that happened to me when it wasn't my fault, sent me down wrong roads. Or I should say, made it easier to go down wrong roads. Those kinds of things were still my choice, but I can see a reason now. They aren't any less my fault, but I look at it differently."

David just nodded his head, giving me time to talk or not to talk. He was a great listener.

"From the horrid sexual abuse at home, I went off to college. I dated a guy who was older than me--one my mom picked out. I barely escaped date rape, ran into the dorm to one of my sorority sisters and ended up molested by her. It seems to be my lot. Lewd and crude men like my father and step father, and then a woman. It was always going to be that way. I see now, that is a lie but I believed it. That lie kept me making bad choices for a long time. If you don't know there is another way to live, how can you go on the right road?"

"I fell in with a prostitute and a compulsive liar who was also a thief. The three of us stole food, cheated others.....it was a rotten time in my life to be no where, going no where. It was one reason I wanted to get away. I was tired of fighting with the voice in my head about what really is right or wrong. It was easier to ignore it and just try to get through whatever circumstances I found myself in. That's no way to live."

"I received word that a friend of mine from high school had been killed in Vietnam, and it reminded me of the sign I saw on the way to work. 'Join the Army and See the World'. So, I did. I liked the idea of "protect and defend—the two things I had never been able to do very well for myself or my sisters. I could get training, learn to defend myself, be something, and serve my country. I always believed being patriotic was honorable, and I was tired of the life I had been living. I wanted to live honorably."

"In the Army, I could learn how to defend myself. This was the noble influence of my Uncle Art. I was always in band and parades. But in the Army I went through things, too. I seemed to be cognizant of power hungry people, bullies, and predators. When I was waiting to go to clerical school, I came across horrible molesting monster of a sergeant in charge of the Holding Company, resulting in a series of suicides. I stumbled on sexual harassment by both sexes at the mess hall resulting in severe burns to more than one of the female cooks. Then in Germany I reported that my barracks was being used as a pick up point to smuggle US Government meat to the black market. Injustice everywhere. Then I ended up poisoned by cyanide right before I was to re-enlist. My life was over when I got out of the Army."

David looked at me with such compassion, I began to tear up.

"But God changed your life. You aren't like that anymore. You are forgiven. You have new life."

"Yes, but David, what if someone from my past showed up now with something I haven't told you? Or something I've forgotten? You know I have brain damage from the cyanide."

"I would ask you about it, maybe, but it was in the past." David sighed. "I won't force you into anything. You can trust me. Let's just take this slowly. Let's pray together and let God help us both through this. I don't know what to say to you." He paused a moment. "I love you. That's the part I know. I want you to be my wife so we can live life together. I want to make your life better. And, I'll wait on you to decide."

What relief swept over me. I had so expected some change in his facial expression or body language to indicate that I had crossed lines with no return. I expected he would reject me. I was, after all rejected by both parents growing up, so I expected it everywhere I went. But with

David, that didn't happen. Maybe, we could just continue on slowly, becoming better and better friends. Should I try being hopeful?

We both believe that once married, we would stay married. But what would happen when David found out more about me and I found out more about him? Would we still like each other? What was I supposed to know? Is there a book on this somewhere? Why didn't I already know the answers to these questions?

And, what are the exact questions? God knew what He was doing. I just hoped I could live up to what God and David expected.

I think I could describe David and me with a word picture: a large lump of rock with a helium balloon attached. He is a rock, solid, set in his ways, and I am the bouncing balloon in the wind. Maybe tied to him, I could lighten his load, and he could keep me nearer the ground.

We were opposites in so many things—I talk, he does not. I'm excited and enthusiastic about everything. He barely shows emotion. This would be an adventure—I only prayed I'd be up to it!

The next day, the florist delivered a bouquet of roses with a card that read: *The Adventure Begins.*

* * *

CHAPTER 5

Getting to Know You, Having Front Teeth, How to Make Toast

David and I tried to go out once a week but definitely talk on the phone daily. We even sent cards. When the phone rang, I always thought it would be David. I wasn't even rude to telemarketers.

"Sorry, I don't want to listen to anyone but my fiance, have a nice day."

For dates, sometimes we would go sit at a field watching Model Aviation Builders fly scale model planes or crash them. Not much opportunity to talk over the noise of the small gas engines, but flying and building models were two of David's passions. I was open to a new hobby.

It was the "companionable silence" method, which worried me. I love conversation! It wasn't long before I discovered if David didn't have his list of questions, conversation was very difficult for him. He always seemed so tense. One evening all my attempts at conversation failed.

We were going across town to see Teenage Mutant Ninja Turtles. Very sophisticated for an evening at the theater.

"Uh, David?" I asked. "Is everything all right?"

"Yes."

"How was work today?" I asked.

"Fine."

"David, you aren't saying much. Do you just feel like being quiet?" I was concerned.

"Yes."

Well, that answered my question. He is the only man I know who can answer an "essay" question in one-syllable. I wondered if I had offended him, but I found out later he was suffering from shyness. Afraid he would say something to make me run off. We needed an icebreaker. Just something to break the tension. This was when I discovered his wit.

After arriving at the theater, David came around to open my door. As the door opened, we both looked down at a huge wad of freshly deposited bubble gum. It was right where I would step. *Appetite killer!*

David hesitated, then looked up with a serious expression.

"Mine!"

I didn't think we could laugh that hard. This was the discovery of his wonderful sense of humor and from that moment on, he realized I just liked to hear him talk. My casual questions weren't to grill him. This was the break through, of my knowing how painfully shy he was and he realized I really did want to know what he was thinking or planning. He finally *believed* I wouldn't make fun of him on any topic.

Since that evening, it's now routine. Whoever sees the abandoned gum claims it! That night I simply tried to keep my talking to a minimum, just to be sure I didn't annoy him. I must carefully draw him out. At last, this was a glimmer of a plan to keep David talking.

* * *

Our first "dating toward marriage date" together at the movies was unforgettable for one other reason, besides the bubblegum on the street. I had an 'awakening' moment. David had been single for 35 years and suddenly faced with the possibility of sharing his popcorn! He didn't say anything but he kept looking at me as if I was a bottomless pit.

Of course, I was confused. He likes me because I talk, but not well enough to share his popcorn. *Is this a bad sign? Oh, wait. This is that dating thing where we get to know each other.*

I braved reaching into his popcorn bag a few more times before giving up. How do fem-fatales do this and get away with it in the movies? If batting eyelashes and looking poutey-sweet is the ticket, I'll pass. Since I really liked popcorn, I will just buy my own and shock him. However, I was also getting a glimpse of the side of David that was very difficult.

* * *

Weird Cats

Another thing David and I had in common was pets. David is not a dog person. It's a fact that single people are eccentric and tend to pick eccentric pets. His long haired female black cat, Tyne, loved to curl up on my lap, purr, turn over and flirt. Then, when I was distracted talking to David, she would take her claws and rake my arm leaving nasty cuts. Not a nice cat!

Mine on the other hand were odd for a different reason. I didn't really want two cats, but I had to get one cat to take care of the other. Kiwi was the very small, short haired black cat who loved to run across the room, run up the wall, do a flip and run to another wall, repeating this behavior to let me know one of two things: it was going to rain, or Mica, my orange tomcat, needed something. One look at the sky would give me a clue.

Mica, was my 18 pound cat, and an oddball. He routinely checked what might be within reach on the kitchen counter, especially if I was fixing something that smelled good. I would see his paw patting along the edge of the counter, and watch with amazement as he felt his way along the cabinet until he bumped into me. He expected me to move. It was puzzling to see how he walked completely around the counter on his hind legs. I have never seen a cat do that before or since.

Then there were the two dogs. Mica didn't mind them, but my indoor dog, Tana-Man, would go up to Mica and chomp down on his tail. He gnawed little small "chomps" all the way to the base of Mica's tail. Of course this resulted in a cat growl which was Tana Man's cue to hide.

Then Mica would look behind him to see what was going on, get up, move over about six inches, and lay back down. Tana Man reappeared and the game started over. By the third time, Mica stood up as if to give chase, pause as if he had forgotten what he was going to do and turn to leave, usually running into a piece of furniture. At that point, he would give up and go outside.

If Mica went outside, I sent Kiwi with him. Kiwi herded Mica like a faithful seeing-eye companion. If it began to rain, Mica would sit down, look up into the sky and just give long cat howls. He would sit there getting wetter and wetter until I went out to get him. This action, plus his running into doorways and chair legs made me decide to take him to a veterinarian.

The Veterinarian listened to his heart and examined his eyes. Finally, he put Mica on the floor. Mica took the hint, promptly rushing to hide but ran straight into a chair leg. Mica immediately sat down. The Vet kicked his foot out toward Mica, and my cat just looked at him, without blinking. The Vet laughed.

"There isn't anything wrong with his eyes. That cat is just stupid."

This is a fine thing. I paid ten dollars to find out my cat was stupid. What did this say about me? I wondered if David would mind a really stupid cat. After all, we were planning to merge households. David didn't like dogs. My little Tana Man would growl and stand off to one side of the couch while David and I watched a movie. He wanted nothing to do with David. Ginger took anyone in. Mica and Kiwi didn't care one way or the other. David's cat, Tyne, on the other hand, would be a problem. She was used to being the only female in David's life. I had news for her, just as David had news for my little dog.

* * *

How to Make Toast, Teeth in the front

One morning before Church, David came over for breakfast. I made my best omelet, perfectly. It should have been perfect. I practiced every day for a week. *Was I ever sick of eggs?* David offered to make the toast. I motioned toward the open doorway to the laundry area.

"I keep the toaster on the dryer. Not enough counter space."

He dropped the bread in the slots and then helped set the table. We both heard the toaster pop up, but since I was turning the eggs, he volunteered.

"I put in two, but there's only one."

"Oh, the other one's probably behind the washer!"

David peeked around the doorway looking concerned. "What?"

"Oh, the toast sometimes shoots out and bounces off the wall."

He looked and said, "Yep! There's three back there. Would you like me to reach them for you?"

"Sure. Thanks. I always have to move the washer to get them."

"Oh, that's why there are three other pieces of toast here" David said.

"Yes. I'm sorry I forgot to look before you came over. It's like this. If I make toast in the kitchen, it launches upward with such force it crushes the bread. That's ugly toast! It's easier to let it land on top of the washer."

"Then why didn't this one land on the washer?" David asked.

"Oh, that old washer jumps around when I use it. Sometimes I forget to line up the toaster on the dryer with the edge of the washer. Only one out of three slices actually hits the wall. It's one of those physics things."

I glanced at David's puzzled face. "I'm sorry," I added. " We can make more toast. I just forgot to line up everything."

David stared at me, kindly, for a long moment and finally said, "You don't have to move the washer to make toast. Move the toaster to the dining table."

Well, my I.Q. just zeroed out. Why didn't I think of *that*. "Aaaa, thanks," I said. "Wow! I never thought about it. All my life a toaster belonged on a counter but no where near the dining table."

David smiled and shook his head. "Well, you could always get a different toaster."

"Oh, that one hasn't worn out yet." I replied softly. I was now into minus I.Q. "Well, then, let's eat." *Change the topic, Susan—quickly before he decides you're too stupid marry.*

We sat down to breakfast. As I bit into a piece of turkey bacon, there was snapping sound. I stopped chewing. The temporary bridge in the front of my mouth fell off. *Oh, that hurt!* Quickly, I put my hand over my mouth.

"Are you all right?" David asked.

With my hand over my mouth, I replied, "My capsh fell off. I have to cawl duh dentish."

David looked puzzled but finished his breakfast.

I grabbed the telephone directory, and let my unglued front bridge drop into my hand. It was the weekend. Usually this meant a closed dentist's office! No matter what anyone else thought, this qualified as an emergency!

"Hello, this is the Answering Service," a professional female voice announced.

Still holding my hand over my mouth, I turned my back to David.

"Cood you reee-sh Doch-tur Coal-shtun? Mhhy temporrrary casps fell off my fron teefsh."

After two attempts, the operator was able to capture my name and telephone number. In only minutes, I received a return call.

"Sounds like you've developed a lisp!" Dr. Coulston laughed. "Meet me at the office in fifteen minutes, and I'll re-glue you. And, bring along your fiance'. I'd like to meet him."

"Oh-K. Thanksh," I replied.

"What does David think of your smile right now?" Dr. Coulston asked.

"Hhaven't sshown him my shmile, yet."

"Well, this might be a good time to check his response to make sure he loves you for you and not your teeth!" Dr. Coulston just laughed as he hung up. *Dental humor!*

My dentist was curious to meet the man I was going to marry. I didn't care *why* he opened his office, just as long as he re-glued my teeth. It's hard to look charming with two little fangs next to empty holes in front! At 40, little things like teeth matter, especially in the front. It is on the top of the list called 'Asset Advantages'!

* * *

Divine Directives

After David was gone, I took my dogs for walks in the field behind the Red brick house. Ginger was aging and had hip trouble. She loved to lay down against the foundation with her dog bone treat. The warmth of the heated concrete soothed her hip joints.

Usually, I rehearsed the day, talking to God and praying, mentioning people who were having health or family problems. Once, the strangest thing happened. My friends in Mustang, a young married couple were on my mind. I became overwhelmed with the 'Directive' to go buy canned goods at the store. I did not need anything for myself, but I went anyway. I began to purchase cans of vegetables and fruit on sale. Then flour, rice, beans, bullion cubes, boxed menu helpers, and then, as I started toward the meat displays, I was compelled to go back to the canned goods area to review what I had purchased. It was not over my budget or even food for me, but I suddenly had to take these things to my friends Matt and Shelly in Mustang. *Odd.* The more I thought about it, the more I had to hurry.

It didn't take long to get there, but as I drove the urgency was over powering! *I must "drive faster!"* When I arrived, I turned my truck around so I could park in front of the house but facing the highway. Just as I stopped the engine, another vehicle pulled into the driveway at a fast clip, stopping in a cloud of dust.

A woman I knew by sight from church was out of her van and rushed around to the back to open up the rear door. I grabbed my bags of food products and rushed over to her. *We didn't even greet each other! It wasn't necessary to ask her why she was there. At the time that wasn't odd at all, it only seemed odd, AFTER the fact.*

"Do you have meat?" she asked, out of breath. "I tried to go buy other food, but something stopped me! I could only buy meat!"

"No!" I replied. "I don't have meat. Did you get canned goods and beans and potatoes?"

"No! I couldn't buy anything but meat!"

I shook my head. "Same for me. I could only buy canned goods, flour, salt and potatoes!"

As we continued to stare at each other, Shelly came out of the house in surprise at our arrival.

"Thank you for coming!" she said with tears in her eyes as she saw all the groceries. "Matt has been fasting and praying for days since loosing his job. We are just about out of all our food. You two are answers to our prayers."

"Well, that's great," I said. "But next time can you ask him not to pray so hard! We both broke the speed limit trying to get here!"

All the way back to my house, I thought about this odd experience. It felt great now that I thought about it. It was no surprise they needed something, but to have this divided between two people who barely knew each other, to show up with half a grocery list at the exact time can not be anything except Divine Intervention.

* * *

Dating toward Marriage: A Humpty Dumpty at Zero G; The Waterfall Kiss; Sailboats and Pelicans

"How about going to an air show with me?" David asked. "The Thunderbird's Air Force Team will be performing in Altus."

"Sure, but what do I wear?"

"Sunscreen and a hat," David replied.

"Is that *ALL*?" I asked.

"Well...there could be a disturbance if you don't wear some clothes," David laughed.

This would be my first air show and it sounded fun. I saw photos in the local newspaper, and then an ad on television with footage of the

Susan A. Rader

Thunderbird's Team in flight. I didn't know a lot about airplanes other than I enjoyed riding in large ones. I drove to Altus, thinking I was ready for the day.

My directions took me through the Wichita Mountains. They are not really mountains compared to Colorado but out here on the plains, we are use to seeing hundreds of miles in all directions. A little bump or hill obscures the long range view.

On the other side of the small mountain chain, I pulled into what must be the local airport. This wasn't Altus Air Force Base where the air show would be but I saw David's car near a hanger.

"Welcome to Altus International Airport," David announced with a smile. This was a very small airport and my imagination jumped to barn storming and by-wing planes.

"Wow! I hope nothing big or fast lands here!"

"Oh, sometimes it does. Your lucky day. Come over here to see this one, behind the hangar."

I followed David around the Quonset hut and was startled to see a huge green plane that dwarfed the hangars. I wondered how it could have managed to park there.

"A perfect description of the C-130. It's slow, maneuverable but huge." He added, "We won't be going up in that one! What I have in mind is smaller."

David led the way to the open side of the half moon hanger. Inside was a single engine Cessna. With one hand, he pulled it out of the hanger.

"I'm a pilot," David said.

"You are?"

"Yes. And there is plenty of time before the Air Show to do a fly over of the town. I'll show you my house that's for sale, and my parents' house. We can fly over the dam and then fly low over the lake. There's a great canyon to see, too."

David pulled a folded worn paper from his back pocket, and started walking around the airplane.

"Flying instructions?" I was half teasing, but dreading the answer.

"No," David replied. "This is the check list. A pilot always checks the aircraft before take off."

He proceeded to open a small compartment in the nose of the plane, with a tiny engine.

"*That's* the engine? David! That's smaller than the one on my riding mower!"

"This single engine Cessna doesn't take much power. I've been up in this plane many times."

I must not have looked convinced. "Umm, David, this material on the plane feels like paper."

"In a way, it is." David looked up at me with a frown. "Don't worry. It flies."

What could I do now? I really hate heights. This is the smallest plane I've ever seen. Is this a good day to die in a plane crash? Sure, why not? At least I'd be on a date.

The hanger manager signaled David to start the engine. It sputtered, and my heart soared. *Maybe it wouldn't run!*

No such luck. With the second spin of the propeller, the engine came to life, and we taxied onto the runway. David turned into the wind, revving the engine while watching a dial on the console.

"Ready?" He looked delighted.

"Sure. This is cozy." *Not ready.*

The plane moved down the runway, with more speed but less effort than a car. I was starting to enjoy the ride, but I began to wonder why we didn't lift off.

"Welllll?" I said flippantly.

With a twinkle in his eyes and raised eyebrows, David smiled as he pulled sharply on the controls sending us nearly straight up into the bright blue sky. I was speechless, because I couldn't breathe.

David leveled out over the airfield. We soared over the landscape, with cars and fields looking like toys. I picked up my camera to take a photo of our plane's shadow on the ground far below.

"This is great, David."

"I thought you might like it. What about zero gravity?"

"What? You mean like astronauts?"

"Exactly."

David pushed the controls forward, sending the plane into a dive. Suddenly, I felt very strange—as if I were divided into three pieces. My head was floating away from my body. My body came off at the waist, and from waist to my feet fell off by themselves. I came apart! Startled, I looked over at David in time to see his sunglasses come floating out of his shirt pocket.

For a second time in less than five mines, I couldn't say a word! I clamped my hands on top of my head, pushing down to put myself back together. This was a Humpty-Dumpty moment. I actually thought I would feel some drop in the pit of my stomach, like a roller coaster, but it wasn't that way at all. What a strange sensation.

"Well, now I know how to make you speechless!" David laughed. "How did you like that?"

"That was great, but really weird. I think I liked it, but let's not do that again for awhile, until I decide!"

"I love it. At times, I can make it last longer, but I wasn't sure how long you could stand it. Some people don't like this at all and then never go flying again. But for me, after all the hours I've flown, zero-G is still fun."

For the next twenty minutes, we flew over Altus. David pointed out his favorite hobby shop, his favorite restaurants, his high school and his parent's home. We turned to see more of the town, and David dropped a little lower to view neighborhoods.

"Actually, I live on Saturn ...street!" He smiled. "I've planted some almond trees. Over there on the right, the one on the corner."

"Oh, nice."

"OK. More scenery."

David banked steeply, heading back north toward the rugged Wichita's. As we flew over the dam to Lake Altus, we banked again to fly low through a narrow canyon. It was amazing, but stark. Bleached white by the sun, the broken granite gave the impression of gigantic bones scattered between deeply shadowed walls. We were flying very low.

"It's beautiful, but lonely looking. I wouldn't want to crash here."

"Okay. I'll skip that part today," David laughed.

David was mysterious. It seemed like we were flying circles over one area of the moutains, with the air field in sight. We stayed over this same area for another few minutes, and my curiosity was begging to ask why. Before I could open my mouth, I saw David look at his watch.

"Just about *NOW!*" David said.

Suddenly, the roar of jets rocked our little Cessna. The Air Force Thunderbird jets swept by in a flash of light. This was a close call. I sat flabergasted. We could see the preshow off in the distance.

David said with a smile. "Oh, don't worry. They're far enough away. Then we'll go down on the field to see them up close. After they land, they will be introduced and come over to the fenced area where we can meet them."

"Wow! This is exciting," I replied. This was thrilling. But, I still did not understand David was serious about me. Now I see this special event was made to impress me. Of course I was impressed, but it simply didn't register that David might have fallen in love with ME. He was just a nice guy who could fly.

The rest of the day was exciting and exhausting. By the time I returned home, it was late. I dreamed of flying all night, only I didn't need a plane. The day was perfect. David was leaving more and more of an impression on me. I began imagining what it might be like to spend a lot more time together.

The Waterfall Kiss

The following week, David asked me to go out for lunch, and then to The Crystal Bridge Botanical Gardens in downtown Oklahoma City. Of course, I was delighted. This meant he still liked me, and wanted to be around me. In my mind, there was always some doubt about a man wanting to spend time with me.

First, I'm a chatter box, but I actually say nothing. Secondly, I've never been pleased with how I look or dress. Wallflower, nerd, tomboy, and any number of terms come to my mind to describe myself. It is too bad I could not see myself as David did. That has taken 26 years. Always, lurking in the back of my mind at that time, was my past. From being the ugly older sister, when my next sister was the beautiful redhead like mother, and then there was the abuse. That was something I tried not to think about, but didn't realize how much it affected me.

After lunch, we strolled through the Myriad Gardens. Perfectly tailored rolling lawns, ponds with ducks and giant gold fish, along sidewalks and waterfalls. A small footbridge led us to a cave like entry for the glass greenhouse. The Crystal Bridge was a curiously shaped, elongated tube. The ecosystems went from the waterfalls in a tropical rain forest at the south end, to an arid dessert at the opposite side.

Just past the entrance with maps and information, we passed through a small, misty, cool concrete tunnel. It smelled like rain. I was surprised at the size of the greenhouse interior. It opened up to forty-foot palms, bubbling streams, and just to our left, a triple waterfall.

"Let's go up here," David said, as he took my hand.

Oh, wow! Is he going to kiss me today? *Good, maybe my intuition is working.* I know my curiosity was. I hoped my thin hair wasn't getting damp enough to lay like wet string. *Please God, don't let me look wilted.*

We climbed the water splashed stone stairway, under the first waterfall, then past the second waterfall, completely to the top of the glass enclosure. From this height, we looked down on the jungle scene. The only thing missing was Tarzan on a vine. The top waterfall came out of the rock where we stood.

"This is beautiful, and a lot bigger than I thought it would be."

"Look down at the other end," David said, pointing. "That's a desert climate, and has small lizards in the brush. It reminds me of Arizona."

"Oh, I loved Arizona. I went to Tucson once, but I haven't seen the Grand Canyon, except in photos."

"I've been there a few times. I like the Canyon. I took a helicopter flight over it once."

David took me by the arm and led me back down to the second landing. Here the waterfall fell noisily into a gray pool surrounded by a thick growth of tropical plants. The leaves and vines dangled over the edges of the water. By now a few people joined us and I saw David frowning. Hmm, *irritated*. Yes, I too, want us to be alone here.

"Let's stop here for a minute, and let the others pass," David said, still holding my hand. "Want to take a picture?"

I turned to take shots of the waterfall, and then pointed my camera toward the other end of the gardens.

David seemed tense. He had steered me over to the edge of the pool at the base of the waterfall. We were out of sight of anyone above or below. I knew he wanted to kiss me, and I hoped I didn't fall in the pool. *Just be quiet for once, Susan! I told myself.* This is a special moment. *Let him lead.*

We stood there. Forever. Well, not really. There was an awkward moment, as David looked down at me from his height of 6'1. I seemed awfully short just then. As he moved toward me, he said, "I love you, Susan," and bent to kiss me. I stood on tiptoes in response.

The kiss was tentative and sweet, lasting only a moment, as we were suddenly interrupted by noisy people coming up the stairway. David looked flushed. How sweet that kiss was for me. How gentle he was! *Oh, I'll never sleep tonight!*

We held hands all the way through the exhibit, with no need for words. I was speechless again. I was still back at the waterfall so I only remember there was a wooden bridge over a bubbling stream with some goldfish the size of bass. We climbed the stairs at the opposite end of the gardens, and I did see a few lizards in among the cactus plants. What a contrast from the tropical scene. Dry sand and dusty rocks, and little signs giving unpronounceable names of desert succulents. The signs were everywhere, but I didn't read any of them.

I finally concluded. David really likes me. And I really liked David. *But what do I do now?*

* * *

Sailboats and Pelicans

The following weekend, we went sailing. I owned a fourteen-foot, lateen rig Sunfish, sailboat christened *"One Sweet Dream."* David met me at the lake.

"I've always wanted to sail," David said as he looked over my sailboat. "It looks easy. Is it?"

"Yes! Let's get her in the water, and I'll show you."

David helped me untie the mast, and then watched me with amazement as I assembled the boat. After snapping the rudder into place, I asked, "Would you back the trailer into the water for me? I'll shout when you've gone far enough."

With a twinkle in his eyes he replied, "Or you could scream."

"O.K., funny man! Just watch for my signal."

"Aye, Aye, Captain." He saluted.

This could have been a comedy, but the boat launching was uneventful. David was amazed by the boyancy of the sailboat.

"It is light, maneuverable. Or, 'yar' in fancy terms. But I did have to patch a hole in the hull last year. I ran aground at the other lake, not realizing the area was a landfill for chunks of concrete. What a bummer!"

"Oh, so you had it fixed some place?"

"No, I learned how to apply a fiberglass patch."

David looked confused. "YOU patched the boat?"

I laughed. "Ye-sssss! And it floats!"

"Were you near shore when you hit the concrete?"

"No. I had hit it, but the hole in the bottom was just big enough to take on water very slowly. The air pockets in this boat design kept it from filling all at once. I was out in the middle when it filled up inside so it wouldn't move. I promise we won't do that today! This lake doesn't have rocks to threaten the hull."

"And it was this past spring." I continued. "You see my neighbor works at a custom car body shop and showed me how to put on a fiberglass patch. It was a lot of work, the sanding, I mean. But I promise, we won't sink today."

"Hmm, well I'm insured. And I swim well." He paused. "Of course, we are wearing life jackets."

I laughed. "Yes, and just like a seat belt! I don't' take anyone on my boat who won't wear a life jacket. So, don't worry. You're safe! No zero G today! Just the power of the wind, no motor sounds. It's awesome."

David was wearing a t-shirt and faded red shorts. *What bony knees and pale, hairy legs!* It was obvious he didn't go out in the sun without long slacks or jeans. Well he was an architect, in an office, and sometimes at a job site. What was I expecting, tennis legs? I don't know. I hadn't been on a date for a long time and it was to a dance, not swimming.

Do bony, hairy legs matter in a relationship? Probably not. Besides, what must he think of me in my swimsuit, shorts, sailing gloves, sunglasses, and a headband cap to keep the hair out of my eyes? I wasn't exactly glamorous. Who knew? I certainly wasn't going to ask him. I was being efficient today, not glamorous. I haven't ever done glamorous.

David climbed on first, sitting by the mast as I directed. His long legs really filled up the boat. I gave us a push off and climbed aboard. With a tug on the sail I turned the rudder hard to port. The wind was brisk, and this shallow area of the lake, was choppy, but *One Sweet Dream* took off.

"Further out, along the eastern bank, there's a wind break," I shouted over the luffing sail. "Let me give you some pointers on sailing, and you can take a turn."

*One Sweet Dream w*as just that for me! I wanted to sail all my life, but set the dream aside along with many others over the years. When I moved into my little red brick home, I imagined it again since there were so many boaters in the neighborhood. I wasn't fond of motor boats. Bad memories. I wanted a quiet ride with the wind. I prayed about it often as I imagined myself sailing. I wanted to learn another skill, and it seemed to be a good idea. The 'For Sale' ads in the paper sang to me. I even strolled along the boat docks at the lake. Oh well, it didn't seem possible with my tiny income.

One day at Church, during a conversation, I discovered my friend, Christi, had a small sailboat her family no longer wanted. I was disappointed over the price her dad had set. It was fair. But it was out of my price range. Instead of going on about the idea of buying it it, I just listened to Christi talk about her first boat and how much fun she had learning to sail.

Christi went home that weekend and told her dad how much I wanted the boat and then called me from Arkansas.

"Hey, Susan, you can have the Sunfish, by promising to buy a new sail, re-varnish the rudder and dagger board--that's the removable keel. It's a wooden piece that slides through an opening in the bottom of the cockpit.

"You mean, really?" I shouted. "Yes!"

The following weekend, Christi and James, her father, brought the boat with a trailer, and took me for my first sailing lesson. Christi's dad was an expert sailor, showing me how to assemble the boat. Christi demonstrated backing the trailer on a sandy area, to get the boat into the water without sinking the car! Very useful.

With Christi's father James at the tiller, we headed into the wind, basically flying across the water at breath taking speed. Exhilarating. We were racing along after a turn across the wind to show me how the boom on the sail zipped across the boat. "Duck, or you get a headache!"

About then I noticed a water bird wading just off the port bow. Before my brain made the connection, we struck a sandbar, and I flew off.

James laughed as I sputtered to the surface.

"Didn't you see the short legged bird in the water?"

I coughed while climbing back on board. "Yes. I was going to warn you."

"Well that was probably mean of me. I saw the bird and wanted you to get the message that a lake, like a river in Oklahoma can have submerged obstacles. This lake is man made and shallow. There is so much sand and wind, there are constantly shifting sandbars. It's a lot like life. Hang on and watch for obstacles, go around if you can, but always correct your course when you see danger. And remember: Everyone must wear a life jacket! It's the law."

Now that is a life lesson, outside of sail boats. Shortly after my weekend lesson, I signed up for a sailing course with the Red Cross, so by now I was a certified Red Cross Sailor! That is not bad for living in the middle of the plains.

When the wind fills the sail, the boat moves so quietly and smoothly through the water like a chip of ice sliding across a cabinet top. There is a constant soft swishing, with the sound of the wind, water splashing against the hull, and an occasional slap of the sheet against the mast creating a 'pinging" sound. The sail would pop as it filled suddenly in a gust of wind. What a rush! I often think back to that first trip on the sailboat that became mine.

* * *

David and I were enjoying companionable silence, swooshing across the lake in the direction of north shore. Ahead of us, in our path was a floating pelican.

The bird just stared at us, and then, at the last moment, flew off in a squawking flutter.

"I wonder why he didn't get out of the way."

"Must be used to motor boats. No sound to warn him off!"

David laughed. "Sailing is great!"

"I love the near silence. It's just the wind and water. Really relaxing. In a minute, I'll let you take the tiller. Just wait until you feel the pull when that sail fills! It's power without an engine."

"I guess it's a lot like flying. The low pressure caused by the wings actually *pulls* the plane from the topside of the wing, not *lifting* from underneath like you'd think."

"That's interesting. I didn't realize that," I answered. "So, this is the same principal. It was news to me in class that the wind doesn't push the sailboat, it pulls us along by creating a pressure imbalance on the lee of the sail."

"You lost me with 'lee' "but I have the idea!"

"Well, Matey, learn a new word today!"

We both laughed.

"Arrrgh," David said. "That's all I know about sailing."

"That's from a pirate movie!"

David asked, "Was it tough to go from class to doing all of this by yourself?"

"A little, but I had all day for my first solo sailing. I nearly ran out of energy getting the boat back onto the trailer." I paused in thought.

"Funny, though. After reading the lesson books and watching hours of videos, I *really* expected there to be arrows on the water showing me which direction the wind was blowing." David laughed. *At least he didn't think I was stupid.*

"Seriously. I remember coming out for practice sessions, feeling disappointed and then dumb. I really DID expect to see arrows for wind direction. Oh well, nice, simple idea, that would have made it easier!"

We spent a cozy time for a few hours on *One Sweet Dream*, and then pulled the boat out of the water to head for a restaurant. Sailing creates fantastic hunger. I wondered if I would get to sleep tonight. David was really growing on me, bony legs and all.

* * *

CHAPTER 6

Dress Fittings, Microwave Practice, Trousseau, Wedding Day

When we set the wedding date, the real tests began. We were required to communicate more, which was hard for both of us. I talk but seldom listen. He listens and seldom talks. As singles, we were used to doing what we pleased, *when* we pleased. That fault is hard enough to face, much less give up! We read books on marriage and at least half the time didn't have the slightest idea what they meant. So many of the problems in those books weren't problems to us at all.

We looked at six different facilities trying to find "the place" to rent for the ceremony, at just the right price. The first community center we inspected seemed nice, but was booked for the date we had set. Suddenly, the idea of me walking down an aisle in a wedding gown swept over me. It was a lot like the big drop on a roller coaster. Feeling weak, I leaned against David. He pushed me away, frowning and whispered, "Not in public." Well, he wasn't nervous and I just learned he's not a spontaneous hugger.

Fittings for my dress were a nightmare. I put on three pounds then lost five. Every fitting seemed to last forever. I suppose it was the recurring anxiety attacks. My friend Michelle, soon to be matron of honor, checked the differing measurements. When she finished the bodice piece, pinning it for the final seam, I felt claustrophobic! I couldn't breathe.

"Take it off!"

"No, Susan! *Just breathe*. You're hyperventilating! This is *only a fitting*." Great, what could I expect the day of the wedding. I seemed to be rehearsing anxiety.

The dress was nearly finished, patterned after Cinderella's gown, long sleeved with a material that resembled shimmering Aurora Borealis. But I choose a flamboyant, swashbuckling hat. Michelle would attach a short veil on it. The Three Musketeers could count me as one of them. Of course, no sword at the wedding. Too bad.

With all the preparations going on, David seemed a solid rock. Nothing fazed him until we went for the required blood test. He had to lie down. He admitted to feeling quesy and nauseas, but he did not want to tell me. I assured him that I felt queasy, too. We accepted each other, as we were, something others seldom did. Surely this was a good match—one made in Heaven. Or cosmic humor. Did I have doubts then? No. And no one was there to ask me if I had any doubts. We just had plans to make.

The date was set, refreshments taken care of, and floral arrangements purchased. Then a Bridal Shower. I forgot about that--*I hated bridal showers*. I avoided them since I was 15 and had to be in the role of bridesmaid at a cousin's wedding. It seemed like hers was a gathering of females who had very little "good" to say about men in general. I never intended to go to another one, but now I was to be center stage.

The night of the bridal shower, I was so nervous I couldn't find the address where my friends set up the party. Not only was I riding with my soon to be mother-in-law but a sister-in-law that I met that evening. I know I appeared to be an air-head! We drove in circles for a while with no cell phone available! While I fumbled around for the piece of paper where I'd written the address, we arrived. My soon to be mother in law had her own invitation with the address, thankfully.

I hurried inside as they parked the car, wanting to take refuge with long time friends. When I came through the door, all conversation stopped. All eyes were on me. Being my usual self, all I could think to say was, "relatives!" This brought a round of laughter. At least it helped me relax.

It suddenly occurred to me I'd be the target for good natured teasing over the next two hours. Introductions were made, and we settled in to open packages. I was trying my best not to talk too much. It was a nervous habit. Or if I'm hungry, or tired, or grumpy or awake or alive. I talk.

My sister in law handed me a small, 3x3x5 package. Suddenly all conversation stopped. The room became very still. Everyone knew something I didn't! Innocently I unwrapped the tiny package, totally unprepared for the tiny negligee that popped out. Howls of laughter filled the room. *Susan, just look calm and collected.* By then I was three shades of red.

Up to that point, I took time to hold up everything I unwrapped. This time I hesitated only to be met with shouts of "Let's see. Let's see!" Obviously, everyone was waiting for this!

All eyes were on me, watching closely as I held up a very small something made of black lace.

"Okay, I'll bite. What's this for?" Howls of laughter.

Judging by the look of shock on the face of my mother-in-law-to-be, I felt I had better reassure her.

"Cleaning house, right?" *Good, she thinks I'm kidding!* If 'Victoria' didn't keep secrets, maybe I'd be more informed! Oh, what a night! I guess my mother–in-law was looking for some sign from me that meant I was fully aware of the power of a negligee. No, but I found out later.

* * *

The rehearsal dinner was scheduled, buffet style. I picked up a dish of broccoli with cheese, poked David and said, "Remember last Wednesday night's dinner? This is what it was *supposed* to look like." Laughter rang out around the room. I didn't realize everyone was listening to what we said. Well, I never went to a wedding rehearsal before tonight. I had no clue what was to happen.

Most people expect a college educated, ex--military woman my age to know something. *Why is that? Not everything in life is a need to know! Where are the manuals on this?*

When David's mom overheard my broccoli comment, she rolled her eyes. Jean is a fabulous cook, and she knew how particular David was about his food. She also knew he didn't' eat broccoli but it was six months after we were married before he told me!

I'm known in the kitchen for the smoke alarm. It's my favorite feature. Thankfully, David was used to his own cooking, and gave me his weekly menu of what foods on what day of the week. I like knowing ahead of time what he liked, and since I ate nearly the same things just in a different order, this wasn't going to be a problem. No unrealistic expectations in this area. After all, I wanted to please him. Besides, if he didn't like dinner, he shared the blame—it was his choice from his list! I might be blonde, but I'm not completely dumb!

* * *

Microwaves

In anticipation of being married, I decided to purchase a microwave. I thought about another toaster, but instead I considered the idea of learning some quick meals for two. I cleared the last remaining space on my cabinet to locate a spot near a plug-in to set up the microwave. I guess, to sum this up, I could say it was both a blessing and a curse.

Following the instruction book, plus pictures on the side of the oatmeal box, I prepared my first practice microwave breakfast. I knew David liked oatmeal. This is how it worked.

Water. Oats. Bowl. Timer: 51 seconds. Lightning flashes around the rim of the bowl. How curious. 4...3...2...1...PING. As I opened the door to the microwave, the bowl slowly split into three equal pieces with oatmeal oozing across the turntable. The rim of the bowl had mysteriously turned black. *Use Microwave SAFE dish, page 2 of booklet.* Why wasn't that on page one?

Microwave 1. Me, 0.

Let's try a lunch. Microwave SAFE dish, and one can of vegetable soup. One minute twenty seconds on High. Popping and muffled explosions. A

Susan A. Rader

dieter's dream. Whatever is LEFT in the bowl after the explosions is READY TO EAT! Weight loss secret: smaller portions.

Microwave 1 ½. Me, ½. I counted this progress as this bowl didn't break. Take note on page 3 of booklet—cover soup.

Popcorn. "This side up". Instruction book: push "popcorn" button. Lovely humming and popping sounds. Then, no more popping sounds, just humming.

PING! *SMOKE!*

This can't be right, so I rushed the smoking bag to the sink, observing scorch marks. When I opened the bag, smoke billowed into the kitchen. Oh, fire on the inside of the popcorn bag. Good news, the fire's contained! I glanced at the entry way to the kitchen where my small dog and one cat sat patiently. Somehow it seemed the right time for some explanation. After all, I was standing there with smoke billowing up around me despite running cold water into a bag of popcorn.

"New recipe!" The dog waved his nose in the air and the cat left with him. Everyone's a critic!

The purpose of these practice sessions were to get these blunders out of the way before David and I were married. Practice might help. I just guess it is better without an audience. I already knew how good his mom was at cooking, and I could tell by conversation, about the other prepared dishes that my new sisters in law were all excellent cooks. *I'm Doomed.*

I would never be a "kitchen role model", but I'd better at least practice before the marriage or David might run home for a meal! I don't think setting off a smoke alarm can be considered a culinary skill. Maybe emergency cooking lessons would be a gift from some thoughtful person. It probably should have been on a "wish list".

* * *

Trousseau

How does a never fashion conscious single woman, come up with an "after the wedding, travel in a limousine" dress, let alone honeymoon lingerie? Pray hard.

My guardian angel, Artie Martin, was a church friend. A lovely woman with three children, but well known for her beautician's skills in the modeling circles of high priced salons and fashion shows. She styled hair, created and dressed models for shows, as well as cooked great meals. One of those women I have met from time to time that I envied and admired at the same time.

Artie was a tiny, 5'1", petite beauty, who could look elegant in thrift shop clothes. A few weeks before the wedding, she asked, "What about your trousseau?"

"I've heard the word before, but I thought it just meant the wedding dress."

"Girl! You've got to go shopping. You'll need a swimsuit, travel clothes, and negligee," Artie said bluntly. "When you finally get a man—*you keep him!*" I looked blank.

"In the bedroom, dear! Have you planned for your wedding night?" she sounded exasperated.

"Ah, no."

"Where are you from, Susan?" Artie gave me a hug. "Another planet?"

"Ah...the Army...the greenhouse....Kansas?" I replied, lamely.

"I'm off on Friday. Bring your charge card, and I'll pick you up at noon," Artie said, firmly, pointing her finger at me."We're going to Foley's, and we're not leaving until you try on everything that's your size."

I groaned.

***

Friday rolled around, and I was NOT ready to go shopping for intimate apparel. I was 40 years old. Once long ago I embarrassed my self asking for help to buy a better bra at age 22. Oh, I dreaded this outing, but I could see Artie's point of view. She dressed models, styled hair, and created makeup looks for every occasion on a daily basis. I wore jeans and t-shirts to work at a greenhouse. At boarding school, there was a green uniform with white blouse, and the Army only required green clothes, with one-size fits all. She knew my socially handicapped background.

Artie and I arrived at Foley's in pouring rain. The clothing store had more employees than customers that early on a Friday, and the rain was slowing business. A clerk approached.

"May I help you find something?" she asked.

Artie took my charge card and handed it to the girl.

With authority Artie said, "We're going to be awhile, and we're going to start with this rack." She smiled. "Just check on us in about 45 minutes. I may want you to locate some clothes in other sizes for us."

Artie grabbed the rack of swimsuits within her reach and pushed it toward the dressing room door.

"Let's start with swimwear. You'll have a hotel pool, wherever you are going, and I can tell by the look of horror on your face that you're going to need to warm up to stripping."

"Ugh."

"Don't worry. I've seen everything, and I have my own. This trip is to make *you* look the best *you can for* the rest of your life, and for your new husband. You won't forget what I teach you today because this will amount to shock therapy. I plan to teach you a few facts of life you never considered, like seduction."

I turned three shades of red.

"You will look so good when we're finished today, that you will wonder why in the world you never tried to look this good before. David can thank me when you two return from your honeymoon. Consider this my wedding gift. Now, let's get started."

After the first twenty pieces of negligee, I no longer saw a nearly naked 'me'. I began seeing a shape in a garment. I began to see lines, styles, and colors that looked good on me. Artie was a terrific teacher, articulate, and it was like having a private tutor for clothing. I bought a swimsuit cover-up, a travel coat, three dresses, some skirts, slacks, and blouse combinations that traveled well, along with a complete line of elegant negligee from itty-bitty stuff to floor length gowns and robes. It came to just under $1800 worth of clothes, which would last a very long time. Artie not only knew her materials, and how to dress me, she also knew the value of a dollar.

I think I would classify this experience as valuable as fixing my front teeth when the bridge fell out. Now I understood that 3 x 3 x 5 box at the wedding shower.

Artie was pleased and I was now more confident on many levels. I sent lots of prayers of thanksgiving for Artie's skill, her friendship, and that God had put such a caring friend into my life.

* * *

The Wedding Day

The day of the wedding was a bright, crisp, Saturday, March 11, 1989. I hardly slept the night before, as I lay in bed wondering how it would be for the rest of my life as Mrs. David Rader. I decided sometime in the night to buy a personal license plate for my car: "Mrs. Rader." My heart rate went up and I suddenly I couldn't breathe.

Time to get up, shower and be ready for David to pick me up for lunch with his family. *Oh, this was going to be a long day.*

David's sister and her husband arrived from just ten miles away, but his other sister had flown in from Oregon with her youngest son. Then, there was his brother and his wife and one son from Texas, and his parents from southwest Oklahoma. What a menagerie! I really didn't know them very well, but they were all awaiting our arrival at the restaurant. At least, this time, I wouldn't be shrinking at the end of a plank while I ate! The restaurant didn't use plastic buckets.

At the buffet, I was starting to feel overwhelmed. Our pets were boarded for ten days, and church friends from our "decorating committee" had a house key to bring any wedding gifts to my—**our** new home when we left for our honeymoon.

The buffet was loaded with every kind of wonderful food, but I didn't dare fill my plate! My dress was finished, to wear *today. Maybe I better not eat—I can't gain any weight!* An imaginary picture flashed in my mind: Breaking News—*Bride's Gown Splits and Falls!* OK, Salad. I can have salad and cottage cheese.

Once seated at a large table, I displayed my rings and tried not to act nervous. David seemed as steady as ever. He was the eldest, but the last to be married. His sisters and brother had been married for years and some had grandchildren approaching high school age. Here we were, like old teenagers.

At dinner, we both noticed David's brother leaving the table a number of times, but his wife mentioned he wasn't feeling well. We didn't think any more about it, but we should have.

A 'Rite' of Passage

David boasted about not being nervous over the wedding. "Just a ceremony. No big thing." Then he bragged how he had hidden his car

Susan A. Rader

so it couldn't be decorated. "And, since after the wedding we'll leave by limousine, I'm not going to get *my* car decorated!" For some reason this seemed important to him.

What a surprise we had in the parking lot! David saw his car and looked grim. There was shaving cream all over the windows and tires! His brother had done a thorough job while we were dining!

David was stoic and silent. I learned that's his way of being angry. But for me, I was giddy like a child at a birthday party! I was actually giggling when we got in the car.

As we drove off, David said, "That makes me mad. I'm going to wash this off *right now*."

"But, why?" I asked, bewildered. "I think it looks great." I punched him lightly on the arm.

"You're just mad because you didn't think anyone could have a chance to decorate your car!"

"I suppose," David replied.

He took us just around the edge of the parking lot to a drive through car wash. Oh well, at least I got to ride in a "Just Married" car, even if it was only a block. "Just Married" on the window was something I was looking forward too. It was an important rite of passage for someone MY age!

Since there were only a few hours before the ceremony, we went to my home which was soon to be our home, to pick up bags and other last minute items to take to the the wedding.

Once there, I refreshed my makeup, double checked my suitcase and practiced breathing. From the bathroom, I could see into the living room. I expected David to be on the couch flipping channels to wear out the remote, and holding a glass of tea. Instead, I saw him traveling back and forth through the living room with one tall glass of water at a time. One glass. Two glasses. Three glasses. Back empty.

"Nervous?" I called out.

"No."

Shortly, he was back with more glasses of water. This trek through the house and out the front door had to be investigated.

"What are you doing?"

"Washing my car," he replied as he went out again.

I laughed. "Washing your car one glass at a time?"

David stopped at the open gas cover. He poured in water.

"There was shaving cream in here. I thought one glass would do it."

Then he gave me a half smile. "Oh, this probably looks stupid. I lost count after nine glasses."

"But you do look good walking back and forth!" I told him and gave him a kiss. One unique way for a groom to cover over being nervous. Just wash the car in your dress clothes, one glass at a time!

Knock, Knock!

The night of the wedding was beautifully warm for March, with a mild south wind straight from the gulf. There was a tropical feel to the air, and it was invigorating—like right before a storm. Over two hundred guests arrived, including my dentist and my veterinarian.

The motel ballroom was packed. Of course, the management misspelled my maiden name on the marquis...but who cared! I was getting a new one in an hour!

In my dressing room, I had three lovely friends to help me. One to remind me to breathe, one to fix my hair, and one to guard the door so I couldn't run way. It was nearly time for the wedding ceremony when we heard a hurried knock.

"Just a short delay—don't come out yet!" an usher shouted in. "Florist late."

Relief. David had not bolted!

Knock, Knock! The mother of the flower girl rushed in, pushing her tiny daughter in front of her. Jeannie smiled wanly. "Lindsay cut off all her bangs last night. I had a dickens of a time trying to fix her hair. I'm so glad you are running late."

Knock, Knock, Knock! Another usher poked his head in and said, "They've divided off the great room. Half goes to a radio disc jockey seminar. Should I ask them to keep the music down?"

"Yes, please."

The next knock was the photographer. "Did you know there is no picture scheduled for the groom's parents?"

Is this a running gag? We had an entire book of diagrams and plans, which we gave to our volunteer wedding directors. Two friends took the job of overseeing the wedding, and three single friends were in charge of table decorations with our unique specialty cake, designed to be non-traditional. We had been very thorough, we thought, even to favorite song tapes that told our love story.

How could we have missed something? Oh well, just snap pictures of anyone who wants their picture taken. David was to have a lapel microphone so our dialogue could be added to the video. We wanted a complete record of this wedding from every angle. It was to be a once in a lifetime evening, but we like reruns.

When it was time to walk down the aisle, I could hardly breathe. I asked two married friends to stand in as my parents. Jack and his wife, Leta Horner. Jack was waiting for me in the exterior hallway as my escort. He looked great in his tuxedo, and reminded me it was their 47th wedding anniversary--a good day to get married! When I asked his wife, Leta, to tell me the secret of staying married for 47 years, she replied, softly, "Oh, we did so much together, I just couldn't ever get away."

I paused at the door, suddenly terrified, as if I were going to preform on stage.

Jack put his arm around my shoulder. "Steady. Take a deep breath. This is just the beginning of a great life, with a good man who loves you."

"Yes, I think he does. I love him too. I'm just afraid."

"No, you have a serious side you don't show very often and you feel things deeply. You want everyone around you to be happy and for a moment you wondered if it was all right for you to be happy."

I turned to Jack and gave him a hug.

"Thank you. I needed to hear that. Yes, that's true. I really thought happiness deep inside me was something that I could never have."

"Happiness in marriage is not chance, it's choice. First you choose a man who has the same values you have, values worth fighting for. Then, you determine if you trust him to lead you. Then, hardest of all, you let him lead you, Susan, dear. David is a good man. You will be good together."

"Thanks, Dad." I hugged him again, took a deep breath and opened the door.

As I entered the room, all heads turned my way, and then everyone began to stand. *Whoa! All this attention. It's the hat. Maybe it's the dress.* The room smelled of flowers and freshly brewed coffee. Jack held me up as we entered the room.

"Steady," he said, in his deep voice. "You look wonderful."

"I can't breathe," I whispered.

"Yes, you can, Susan, and I'm right here," Jack said softly. "Lean on me. You'll be fine when you turn the corner to the center aisle. Trust me."

I managed to smile at a few friendly faces as everything began to blur. I was acutely aware of my swashbuckling white hat and veil tilted jauntily, pinned in place, and my new shoes cutting into my toes. I nearly bolted at the size of the crowd. My heart was pounding so hard it drowned all other sound.

When I turned the corner behind the last row of chairs, and looked down the center aisle, I caught a glimpse of my handsome David. That's why Jack was so sure I'd have courage when we made the turn.

As long as I looked at David, I didn't care that 245 people were watching me walk. Usually it only took the knowledge of one or two people looking at me to make me stumble.

Jack took me to David, who held out his hands. We stood there for a moment looking at each other as if for the first time. David mouthed the words, "I love you", as the first notes of music began. In my hours of thinking of being married, I wrote an original song for David about our future together. One of the cameras picked up my lip-sync with the song. I knew I couldn't sing to him in front of all those people, but I wanted to! We just stood staring at each other, savoring the moment.

The ceremony went much faster than I could imagine, except the prayer. The prayer was a special part of our wedding, but we picked a very long-winded pastor. When we knelt down on the pillows, my new shoes bit into my big toes. It was torture.

"Oh, Lord, please help me stand up," I prayed, as the circulation went out of my legs.

When we stood up, I was sure everyone could hear the creaking sound of my knees. No wonder people get married when they're younger—it's less physically strenuous. David took the ring and began to put it on my right hand, then on my left, and then just looked at me helplessly.

I whispered, "Pick a finger. Any finger!"

There was snickering from the wedding party on stage which caught the attention of everyone in the room. On the video, it sounds so loud. Very few heard me, but anyone could guess what was taking so long. It was the ring. I took my time putting David's matching ring on his finger.

When the minister said, "You may kiss the bride," David lifted my veil with a smile. It was a wonderful kiss, and I didn't care how many people were there. David's father shouted, "Way to go, Dave!"

Susan A. Rader

    I think one of the most precious moments in my new life was when David and I were introduced to the congregation as <u>Mr. and *Mrs.* David Rader</u>!

    On the video play back tape of our wedding, I saw a funny moment. David and I were on the stage posing for photos, when, for the first time, I glanced around the room. My focus stopped on the cake table. While I held my wedding bouquet to smile for camera shots, I took a second look at the cake table. Without thinking I swung my bouquet, hitting David across the front of his tuxedo to get his attention, then pointed at the table.

    "Wow! It looks better than our drawings!"

    David nodded and we heard laughter from the audience. People just kept watching us even though the wedding part was over. It seems everything is news to me.

    David and I spent hours designing the cakes and table lay out, but had not seen the fully decorated room before this moment. The Groom's chocolate cake was cut in the shape of an airplane. Our simple sapphire blue and sliver colors with white lace trim on the table and the candles were eye appealing. I still get nervous looking at that video. I felt so old to be getting married! But now, approaching 26 years, I see I was still very young.

* * *

CHAPTER 7

Honeymoon, Where's My Stuff, A Woman' Place, Marriage Lumps

Where would two *old* singles go for a honeymoon? Well, since it was us, Disney World, of course! What a blast! All except the seven story, falling in the dark, roller coaster ride called something poetic like "Space Mountain." I would name it, "How to Drop Dead in the Dark!"

Here was my David, married at last, and his new found wife hated roller coasters! I felt so sorry for him, so out of pity for his long face, I agreed to go. What was it anyway, but one little sacrifice for love?

When we reached the bottom, I was still so shaken my legs wouldn't work. The car rolled to a stop, and I couldn't get out. To my left, I heard laughter. It was with great effort I managed to turn my still fear--frozen neck to see a woman sitting on a bench along the nearest wall. She smiled weakly.

"Been there. Just did that," she said. "You'll be able to walk again pretty soon. I made it this far."

David helped me out of the coaster car with my legs still wobbly. I went straight to a restroom. Ah, the price of a ride—one pair of new underwear, trashed.

At the hotel check in, David came back to the car with a broad smile.

"I told them we were Mr. and Mrs. Smith."

"Mr. and Mrs. SMITH," I was indignant. "I finally get a new last name, and you list us as SMITH?" He hadn't changed his name. He hadn't looked forward to the new title. I lost my sense of humor for a moment.

David looked alarmed. "I'm kidding. Just a thought. I'm sorry."

As he closed his car door, he asked seriously, "Well, what about Mr. and Mrs. Clark Kent or Mr. and Mrs. Batman?"

"Are you serious!" I sounded as irritated as I felt. "I'm sorry. I think I'm tired."

"O. K. I'll stop teasing," David said quietly. "Until the next time we check in somewhere!"

I saw the twinkle in his eyes.

"Hmm, I can see it now. Might work. But, there'd be a problem if they wanted identification."

"Oh, that's easy! I'll wear my 'dress' Batman T-shirt underneath. With the snap front design shirt I can rip it open."

"Nope. Superman rips his shirt off, not Batman!"

I paused a moment and added, teasingly, "O. K. let's do that. But wait until I get a Wonder Woman outfit!" Now, there's a thought.

We spent the next day driving to Cape Canaveral and the Kennedy Space Center. We loved the space program, and our arrival in Florida coincided with the 7th Launch of the space shuttle "Columbia". Countdown had begun, and we were in a race to be as close to the event as possible. I didn't realize what that would mean.

We were exactly ten miles from the actual launch site, and the last car to pull in before the guards bolted the gate. This was going to be a great view. People ahead of us jumped out of their cars to join a large milling crowd. There were as many radios as people around us, everyone tuned to the launch site frequency. The launch director's voice came from everywhere. Ultimate in stereo.

"We have lift off."

A cheer went up from the crowd. Then as a bright light appeared near the horizon, I felt as well as heard a strange rumbling sound. It was a roar that shook the ground. My heart started pounding uncontrollably. I hid myself behind David, pressing against his back and clinging to his shirt, as the sound wave approached.

"What are you doing?" he asked.

"What's that sound?"

David was annoyed. I really was an amateur. "It's the sound of the blast. It takes a lot of power to take off."

"Well, I never knew that it could make that kind of noise *ten miles away*."

What my imagination envisioned as the sound wave approached was a giant bowling ball. We were going to be flattened. I think it was my fight or flight mechanism that engaged.

David said, "Look."

Off to our right, we could see the shining silver white trail from the shuttle with the bright white flame of the rocket. The ground trembled and shook as the shock wave passed. What a rush! Thank goodness, we weren't any closer to the launch site. We have a number of great photos of the bright white light in the sky and the smoke trail. There just isn't any way to reproduce that rumbling, roaring noise.

Of course, looking at our early photo albums is fun, especially from our honeymoon. We took each other's picture standing, ALONE, by a rocket at the Space Center Museum. Two married people still *thinking* single. Why didn't we just ask some passer by to take our photo, together? Hmm, time for a "do-over." The only problem is we would be 26 years older.

On the flight back from Florida, I asked David when he had first noticed me.

"Oh, at the singles retreat. But I saw your tattoo and vowed never to date a woman with a tattoo."

"So, what changed your mind?"

Here I was thinking great romantic thoughts about his answer, but he replied, "Well, I guess I forgot about your tattoo when you said you liked the movie *The Last Starfighter*. Nobody I ever dated liked the same kind of movies I did."

Ouch, on the burst bubble! Oh well, I liked the way he walked, and he liked me because I liked the same movie. Those were not the only reasons, but those two things always pop to the top of the list when someone asks. That sounds so shallow, but look how it turned out! Our relationship was not all about what we saw. Our happy marriage is this way because we found the most important things about each other *before* saying "I do". More than just the movies we liked.

＊＊＊

Where's My Stuff

When we returned from our honeymoon, we found the spare room filled with wedding gifts—just about knee high. What a surprise! And what fun to open all those presents like a celebration.

We found two toasters! That was awesome. No more burned toast behind the washer. No more moving the washer! There were also two slow cookers, and two cook books. Everyone knew me better than I thought. At least with two of these cookers, I could always burn out one and use the other as back up. Of course, we had to find room for all these new items plus everything else.

We began settling into our small, three bedroom house, on our quiet street. When I lived here by myself, it seemed I was always looking for furniture to fill up empty spaces. When David moved in we found ourselves in a dilemma. What happened to the space?

Where's my stuff? The answer to this question is found in a concept that single people find foreign: sharing. Every available inch must be used. In the house, every closet, even the linen cabinet, received at least one extra shelf. In the garage, David built floor to ceiling shelves, and then began hanging things from the ceiling! First, it was a mattress set, then a train table, and of course, all his gas powered, scale airplane models. The rafters groaned from time to time.

The attic filled up quickly with "frivolous" things like our favorite books, magazines, seasonal clothing, and keepsakes, until we had to extend the attic flooring to accommodate "stuff." Then, of course, we had to make a map of where things were.

David brought his custom made model display cases from his house, plus boxes of unmade plastic models. I kept knickknacks of every place I've ever traveled, and then I had my large collection of petite decorative boxes. Decisions. Decisions. *Whose stuff gets to stay out?* That's a marriage test. Those first few weeks were really tough on learning to adapt. I guess the alternative was death—you know, 'til death do you part'.

During the first few weeks, I often saw David standing in the hallway looking at our marriage certificate. I finally asked him.

"I'm looking for the fine print!" At first that was a funny remark. We just let things like that pass by without a fight. After all, if we don't settle differences before bedtime, it ruins being together tomorrow by waking up alone. We made it a policy never to argue past bedtime. Besides, who wants to start out the next day going over old stuff. There wasn't any place to put that, either!

I didn't realize how deeply David's old fashioned ideas ran on the subject of 'a woman's place'. It was dawning on me as little things began adding up. His idea was a woman didn't know anything about plumbing, door hinges, tools, cars, hot water tanks, or televisions. It actually took him years to realize how valuable I could be with tools—as the helper, of course, and never in charge of a repair.

"A woman's place" kept cropping up—I'd guess about the first six years of marriage. It still irritates me from time to time. Of course, now, we've been together so long, I just threaten to put starch in all his underwear. Now, I suggest he can continue to roll around on the garage floor, getting up to reach tools, and doing everything himself so I can watch. Or, I can find the tools, hand them to him in the right order, and save him getting up every few minutes. His choice.

For David, my garage was a strange set up. There was a small work table left over from the previous owner, and a great many boxes of used plumbing parts. Having lived so often in old rental places meant something always needed fixing. So, I kept plenty of old spare parts. When I bought my first home, I felt like I had jumped off the deep end of life by taking on a mortgage. It was simply reasonable for me to I have spare parts. I was ready to do the work. But, according to my new husband, this was not what a woman was supposed to do!

David overhauled my poorly built workbench. No trouble, I liked the new one. But then he put up a sign: 'Don't even think about putting anything on this bench'. I'd smile, blow the sign a kiss and promise myself I'd move whatever I put there. Time would get away from me and David kept pointing out his sign. By the end of a week, neither of us could see the top of his workbench. After a few months, David forgot about his 'to do list' anyway. Bonding in marriage is wonderful, but it plays havoc with the memory. This subject of a "woman's place", however, would not got away.

***

A Woman's Place, Pro-Flo Mufflers

As a single woman, I was used to fixing whatever my old rental place needed. Now we owned a home. My expertise fell into categories of guns, chain saws, how to fell a tree, installing plumbing, sewer lines, and electrical outlets. I was great with a shovel to dig up sewer lines. These things were necessary skills, acquired over time—after all, I was 40 now. But this was too strange of a concept for David.

"Why do you have all these tools?" he asked when he began the garage remodel.

"For fixing things. Why?"

"Women can't fix things." David stated, flatly.

"Really." *Chauvinist.*

"My dad fixed everything around our house, and taught my brother and me everything he knew."

"Well, if your dad didn't know women could fix things, then he didn't teach you everything you NEEDED to know!" I snapped.

David looked irritated. "I'm around now. You don't need these old tools. They take up too much room. Some are bent, and besides, I'll be fixing things."

Well, what was I to say. "David. Dear," I stated, as calmly as I could. "I've had to fix a lot of things in my lifetime, so that means I can be of great help if something needs fixing. I not only know what tools to use, I know when you need them. Nobody could ask for a better "fixing" partner than that."

"That's a nice offer. But, I work alone." David's voice closed the subject.

I could see this wasn't going to be up for discussion anytime soon. I grabbed up the tools I wanted saved and moved them to a box I kept in the trunk of my car. David sorted through the collection of "old parts" for gas pipe fittings, electrical boxes and switches, and rubber faucet gaskets. He found a horseshoe shaped silver object. Holding it up and turning it, he looked over at me.

"OK. I give up. What do you have this for?"

I picked up a piece of electrical conduit, inserted it in the groove, and using leverage against the floor, bent the tubing into a beautiful arch.

"Aaa, well. I knew that, but we won't be using that anymore."

"Keep it. I like it," I replied. "Just hang it on the wall for decoration."

"O, All right." David was firmly out of conversation on this subject, and nothing but time would change his mind. He truly believed women knew nothing about repairs. My time would come, and he would change his mind, but that took nearly seven years. At this point in our marriage, I was not going to compete with him. If he wanted to fix it, that suited me just fine.

I think it was a pride issue for both of us. I wanted to prove I wasn't a dumb blond, and he needed to shift his opinion of the "woman's place" in the world. Eve was at Adam's side, not behind him. There would be other challenges ahead, and that meant a new way of doing things as we learned to do life together.

It would be hard for David to have seen us as a repair "team". He finally needed my help one night to hold the drop light when the drive shaft of his Classic Mustang fell onto the driveway. We were lying on opposite sides of his Mustang, on cold concrete driveway, in the dark in a howling north wind.

"Can you hurry?" I was shivering.

"Fast as I can," David replied, blood on his knuckles, grease covering his hands, and smudges on his face.

"Hold the light a little over to your right," he directed. "No the other right." He never has understood the difference. I was about to correct him for the gazillionth time when I saw his eyes widen in surprise.

"Wow!" David gasped, grabbing the drop light from my hand.

I felt alarmed. "What? Is something wrong?" *Anxiety on a dark night.*

"I've got Pro-Flo mufflers!"

"WHAT? We're freezing to death! And you're admiring mufflers?"

"Oh, sorry," David smiled, the grease spot on his cheek wrinkling up. "It's just that I haven't had time to look under here since I bought it. I've been studying about the 351 four barrel enigine. Did I tell you the new parts catalog arrived?"

"NO! Not now!" My teeth were chattering. "David, if I kiss your Pro-Flo mufflers, can we go inside where it's warm?"

He laughed. "OK. Let's go."

Who would ever suspect that Mr. Chauvinist and Miss Independent would have a scene like this!

* * *

Marriage Lumps

Being older and never married, it is hard to know what to expect. For example, I found out we both liked to sleep on the left side of the bed. To accommodate me, David moved to the center of the bed. I fit nicely in the crook of his arm. *Very cozy for sleeping*!

As the days passed, I noticed more and more bumps on the back of my head or sore places on the back of my neck. *Does being married give you lumps? Very puzzling*. And too personal a question to ask friends of mine, so I let it go. I found the answer a few nights later when I awoke with a start. Something just clunked me on the back of the head.

There was an elbow against my neck. With effort I moved his heavy arm and rolled over. David likes to sleep on his back with his hands behind his head. I always thought that position looked as if he was lounging on a beach. What happened? David brought down his arm to roll over and sleep on his side. The blows came from his elbow. *Whack*. Well, it was tempting to wake him up to let him know I solved the problem, but that didn't seem very nice. Wouldn't you know, the headaches and lumps cleared up when I learned to sleep on the other side of him!

An Arizona Trip

In the fall of our first year, David and I planned a long trip to a church convention in Tucson, Arizona. Along the way, we planned to see the Balloon Fest in Albuquerque, the Meteor Crater, a volcano and then travel on to the Grand Canyon. We loaded the cameras and packed for ten days.

It is *TRUE* that men do NOT take rest stops. I think David could wait to use a rest room for an entire day. It became an irritation for him to delay his well planned travel schedule by having to stop so often for me. I was either thirsty or needed a restroom. He didn't mind scenic outlooks or roadside parks. Somehow it was just different finding a restroom.

On the second day of the trip, near sundown, I was able to snap my first photos of cactus against shadowed cliffs and rocky terrain. David and I loved this time together.

"Roadside stop coming up," David said. "The stars out over the desert are breathtaking at night."

He looked at me with a smile. "Want to take a stroll in the dark and look for falling stars?"

"Certainly, Sir" I replied. *Oh, thank you Lord for a trip with David* . This was too perfect.

We parked near a picnic table near two lights at a roadside turnout. We began to stroll hand in hand into the darkness. We were aware the late rising moon would be absent, so we needed to be careful. So far the scenery had been majestic, even dramatic with hills and valleys, so different from the plains.

David pulled out a flashlight to shine on the ground in front of us. The fall night was warm with a light breeze. I was enjoying holding my husband's hand. There were only quiet sounds from the rustle of grasses and a night bird.

At the edge of the flashlight beam, there appeared the base of a white post. Without breaking the mood, or our stroll, David moved the light up to a faded sign.

"WARNING! NO WALKING AFTER DARK:
Rattlesnakes Scorpions Sudden drop off

Without a word, as if rehearsed, we turned, walked back toward the car.

"That was refreshing," David said as he opened my car door.

"Well we know we aren't in Oklahoma any more. The sign read sudden drop off."

"Must be a canyon, but let's not find out tonight."

Agreed.

***

Smoke Alarm Food Prep, Fight, Shock Therapy

Thankfully, our ten days together didn't require cooking. My food groups are canned, boxed, frozen, or take out. I actually owned three cookbooks (two as wedding gifts). I also knew a few simple recipes, like "boiling water", "hard boiled or soft boiled eggs, and homemade beef stew. Yes, I could fry a hamburger or boil a hot dog, but no gourmet. Cook up something from nothing like my mother in law--*NO WAY*! This kitchen thing is not on my talent list. Just because the house came with a kitchen, does not mean I know how to use it!

David did not eat very many vegetables, and those he did eat must come from a can. Peas and green beans were favorites. Fine, but what about broccoli, cauliflower, or lima beans? No way! Absolutely no tomatoes for him, either--not even in a salad. Please, Susan, don't send radishes in his lunch, because he has to talk to clients. This man is impossible to feed!

I thought David solved the problem those first seven months of marriage, when he gave me a menu of what he ate each day of the week. It was the list he compiled while being single, and he said it made everything easier when it came to shopping lists. He was insistent that dinner be at 5:01 p. m., and no talking. Well, I thought, as a new wife, maybe this is how newlyweds worked out the meals and the meal schedule. I did want to please him. By now, eight months together, I was becoming irritated.

Menu items consisted of Monday: Hot dogs and chips; Tuesday: Spaghetti and Ragu sauce; Wednesday: Turkey or Hamburger Meatloaf with iceberg lettuce salad; Thursday: soup or chili with crackers; Friday: Fish sticks, peas, and instant mashed potatoes with butter; Saturday: hamburgers and fries; Sunday: Steak, fries, and coleslaw. Breakfast each morning would alternate between eggs and turkey bacon, or boxed cereal or cooked oatmeal—no toast, unless the egg actually made it through the "over easy" process.

Fish sticks burn easily, and David ate fish *only in sticks*. He did like tuna and salmon from a can. No fresh fish fillets. O.K. Fine. One evening, just as David finished putting the garage door down, the smoke alarm went off in the kitchen. Smoke was billowing out of the oven, and it was hard to see from the hall into the kitchen. He came in with his lunch sack containers, and just stopped to see what was happening.

"Hi, David," I smiled, coughing. "Dinner will be late—(cough)—I set the temperature just a little high on the fish sticks."

"Fine, I'll be at my desk," he replied with irritation.

As I thought about his reply, the rebel, single woman or not appreciated new wife inside me wanted to shout, "Get over it, Buster!" I was not used to fixing fish sticks, and the oven was not self-cleaning. But I thought to myself, *I've got to lighten up...adapt...maybe talk about this situation.*

"When the smoke alarm goes off again, you'll know it's time for dinner!" I shouted as he retreated. Actually that was a sarcastic, but a prophetic statement. It seemed that few days per week found us having a peaceful dinner, without an alarm.

The first Big Fight!

Breakfast was quite often 'one egg, over-easy'. I am used to eating eggs as they turn out. If the edges are crispy, cut them off or eat them. If the yoke breaks, eat it anyway—just hurry. This was the last straw. I could NOT seem to get the eggs to go 'over-easy'—'over-gooey' works for me, and so does cooked 'over-hard'. *Just ignore what it looks like and eat the stupid egg!*

"Sorry, David," I said. "The egg is just not cooperating today. At least the yoke broke on the plate instead of in the pan."

"Umph!" David replied, as he began to eat.

My temper was about to reveal itself. "Now look, Mister, I'm trying the best I know how. If this isn't good enough, fix your own!"

"Umph."

"What does that mean?"

"Nothing. This is fine. Don't worry about it. I have to go to work now." David took his newspaper and keys and headed for the door to the garage.

"Hey! Don't you ever talk in the mornings?" No reply. " I'm not your mother!" I was shouting now to his retreating back. "You can't just leave the house like this!"

David had gone. Now, what do I do? Knowing myself very well, I knew I would stew all day long. I would practice telling him off about mealtimes together, then, revise it at least one thousand two hundred fifty one times before 5:01 p .m. when he would return for dinner.

I decided to talk this over with my little dog, Tana Man. He was a great listener.

"Why won't David talk to me at meals? Why doesn't he like anything I cook? After all, the menu is his idea!"

Montana tilted his head and snorted a tiny little sneeze. I was talking to my dog, and of course, he is on my side! This could be the dog's way of saying "I told you so", since he didn't like David.

"All right, I'll ask David at dinner tonight. There is no way to mess up spaghetti and Ragu sauce in a jar, as long as I don't forget the garlic bread in the oven." Prophetic statement: I set off the smoke alarm again with the garlic bread. This must be David's fault—I never had so much trouble in the kitchen when it was just the dogs and me!

David did not speak again at dinner, but right after I cleared the table, he moved the smoke detector.

"Why don't you talk to me?" I was conversation starved. The dog and cat never said anything to me during the day.

"I do talk to you," David replied. "I just don't have a lot to say."

"Could you tell me about your day?"

"There isn't anything to tell. I dealt with some red-lining on one of the drawings, and worked more on the preliminary sketches for the Library."

What is a 'red-line'--a mistake? A correction made on a drawing? Or is it a train that runs through town in the wee hours of the morning? No, that is the "Red Eye Express." What is this man talking about?

I just couldn't let it alone. "Well, did anything interesting happen at the office, or maybe on the way to work?"

"No," David said. "I'm going in here to read for awhile. I have some specifications to go over."

That was the end of the conversation. Of course, I wasn't licked! I'm part bull-dog. I like conversation, and he used to try to talk to me. I counted on breakfast for one more try. Overnight, I hatched a plan.

Breakfast shock therapy

Breakfast rolled around, and I prepared toast, which I suspected he wouldn't eat. Sometimes he had an egg with toast. Sometimes he didn't. There was no pattern, even if I asked him. Of course, there were the ever-breaking egg yolks. I put a napkin, salt and pepper on the table, and NO utensils. No plate.

When I cooked the egg, this time, the yoke stayed intact! Wouldn't you know—just to ruin my plan! This was the one time I wanted that egg cooked hard. *Too bad, I'm going on with my plan.*

David sat down at the table and looked puzzled. I decided that my sudden change in routine would be the best way to do this "ice-breaker."

"Juice is in the fridge, *IF* you want any," I said as I brought the skillet over with an egg in it. I flipped the egg out onto the table, no plate, and said, "Live. Suck it up and then you can leave without talking to me."

David looked at the egg, then up at me with a stunned expression.

"Am I that bad"?

"Yes. You have the table manners of a hog, and treat me as if I am lower than the kitchen floor. Is this clear enough for you?"

David looked stricken. "I'm sorry. I guess I was used to not talking during meals--both at home and when I lived by myself." He paused. "I didn't know it's that important to you."

I gave him a hug and kiss. "Yes, YOU are important to me. I want to know every detail of your day. Everything you think about, and do during a day—tell me everything!"

David smiled a tiny little smile and softly asked, "Can I have a plate now?" I held out for a promise of conversation before he left for work. All right, this was a start, but his lifetime habit was going to take time to break. *Give it time, Susan!*

After sharing our hurt feelings, it dawned on me why we kept getting in each other's way. It really wasn't that our house was so small, or there were too many "things", or even being newly married. Two old singles moving in together had a great deal to learn. Based on the idea by Fontaine, I counted six people in the house: Who I thought I was. Who David thought I was. Who I really am. Who I thought David was. Who David thought he was, and who he really is! That's a lot of people in the same house, and we are still learning.

***

On the morning of our first anniversary, I threw up. It was just a quiet little breakfast on Saturday morning, no eggs—just cereal.

"Oh, this cereal smells terrible!" I complained. My stomach roiled.

"Are you all right?" David asked, looking at me strangely.

"No! Something isn't right...." I put my hand over my mouth and ran out. There went coffee and two bites of cereal.

I thought to myself, "Is this morning sickness?" After all, we did want children, but the doctor's we each went to see held out very little hope. But, I read about morning sickness. I had a home pregnancy test ready to go, but this had happened before, and I wasn't pregnant. I skipped breakfast and lunch.

In the middle of the afternoon, I took the pregnancy test. Positive! I rushed over to my doctor's office for confirmation. The blood test was positive, too! I could hardly wait to tell David at dinner. The meatloaf turned out great, and the smoke alarm failed to sound!

"Thanks for dinner. Aren't you eating anything?" David asked.

"No. Everything smells funny and tastes awful."

"Are you sick?" David looked concerned.

"No," I replied as I pushed the doctor's report toward him. "Look at this."

David read the sheet and grinned from ear to ear. "Are you serious? You're pregnant!"

"Yes!" I jumped up and grabbed him for a big hug and kiss, then ran for the toilet again, leaving David alone at the table.

"Rinse your mouth, okay?" David was always thinking ahead.

We were about to become parents. And, you, *Mommy*, will turn 42 before your first child is born! Is there a support group for this? Usually women have their first child while their sisters and close friends are all having their own kids, and everyone exchanges stories and good advice.

"I'll be 42 before this baby arrives," I kept repeating to myself. " When my child graduates from college, I can collect Social Security, or be admitted to a rest home."

Was that a family record breaker? Yes. According to David's side of the family genealogy, there wasn't anyone MY age having their first child. Maybe, they were having their fifth or twelfth, but not their first.

David had flowers delivered with the message, "The Adventure Continues." The message he sent was always that reference to the first round of flowers he sent for our engagement: "The Adventure Begins." And so, for each anniversary, he gives me another card written as before: "The Adventure Continues." I've saved the cards, so far. I'm not sure we'll still be alive for our 50th anniversary, or like his parents who have just had their 65th anniversary. After all, we had a late start!

Regardless, it was time to give thanks that Providence smiled on us.

* * *

CHAPTER 8

41 and Pregnant, Nothing to Wear, 17 hours on a bus

"Aaaah," I gasped as I fell with a flop onto the bed. Seven months pregnant, and late for an appointment, I realized the pantyhose only came up to my knees. I lost my balance and found myself lying on the bed, all tied up like a rodeo event! Should I laugh or cry? After all, just because I was 41 did not mean I knew how to handle everything! Maybe I would get smarter when I turned 42. There was still hope.

When I managed to get myself untangled, I called my younger sister. Her swift reply was, "Well, silly, give up pantyhose!" Well I missed the obvious!

There are a number of things to say about being pregnant at 41. I know other women in the world have been 41 and pregnant, *but none of them told me what to expect!* The most important point: keep your sense of humor or you'll never make this a fun adventure.

First on my list is a warning to others: situations, which have not amounted to a thing in life before pregnancy, suddenly became monumental. For example, what is the real nutritional value of oat cereal? Where would I get a question like that? From reading everything I could in parenting magazines and books, and from watching health and baby care programs. Nutrition is important in pregnancy. I began to worry about everything I put in my mouth, as well as what I would feed our baby.

"Do not dye your hair or get a permanent!" advised one book and several friends. I watched a well-known baby shows on television and took notes. I never knew those shows were on television until now! Don't feed babies raisins or carrots until they are old enough. When is 'old enough'? I was never sure during pregnancy what was important to remember.

"Don't stand near the microwave!" a church friend said.

"Get plenty of rest, and watch out for inhaling fumes from household cleaners."

"Be careful of deodorants and skin creams—they may contain harmful ingredients that soak into your skin and then into your blood stream. And, for heaven's sake, don't eat maraschino cherries—do you know what they make that with?" No, but obviously they should be avoided for some reason. There is too much to know to be pregnant!

Oh, why haven't I already looked up all this information? Why didn't pioneer women have to watch out for every little thing—they chopped wood, harvested crops, stopped for a few minutes to have a child, and went back to the fields. I know, I'm not a pioneer woman, but I was surely in a panic.

What do I do about the dust bunnies I just found in the silverware drawer? That was easy enough--I started cleaning like mad, while I could still reach the other side of the counters, and the ledge on the opposite side of the tub, *and* while I could still see the floor.

Has anyone but me ever cried over finding a cat's hairball? Didn't it look sad, just lying there on the floor? I mean the floor I just mopped, so the hairball wasn't supposed to be there!

"Relax," my loving husband told me. "It's just hormones! It does not mean our baby is about to come into the care of a terrible housekeeper!" *What does David know about hormones that I don't?*

So that made me cry! It never occurred to me that David might think I was a terrible house keeper. I was grateful for David's hugs.

Secondly about being 41 and pregnant, there really is NOTHING TO WEAR! Oh sure, I heard my younger friends and sisters say they couldn't find anything to wear, but I thought it was only a figure of speech! WRONG! It was a FIGURE, all right, but not like mine at age 41!

Nightgowns for barrel shaped pregnant women do not exist. Yes, I could find something that looked like my grandmother's housecoat, or something 'cutesy.' Who wants to look "cutesy" at 41? Or like our baby's grandmother!

None of our family lived near us. I went by myself to the thrift store and took my time trying on maternity wear. I cried because I found only three tops and two pair of slacks that would fit. That is when I called my mother-in-law.

"Hi, Mom Jean," I started, hesitantly.

"Well, hello, Susan, how are you?"

"Pregnant, with nothing to wear!"

Jean laughed. "That is easy to remedy! I can make you some comfortable tops to get through the summer, and I know I still have patterns from some of my daughter's clothes. Be sure to call your family and anyone at church that you know. I'm sure there will be plenty of things to choose from."

Five boxes of used maternity clothes from younger sisters, and church friends arrived, and NONE of it fit! They all had their children while they were 15 to 20 years younger than I was, and many pounds lighter. Besides, most of them were taller, with a slender build.

I gave serous thought to tent material, until I recalled how badly I sewed! In addition, I would be the largest size during the hottest part of summer and fall. I had imagined myself ON canvas, just not wearing it. Khaki is a good color.

Finally, boxes arrived from a sister-in-law in Oregon, and the one living ten miles away. They were taller than I am, but obviously, they took the similar shape. I could always roll up the slacks or shorts. Good, this must be normal.

When I had passed the three-month landmark in the pregnancy, David and I watched the ultrasound monitor in amazement as our baby moved.

Oh, Lord, what are we doing?" I prayed. Baby has to come out sometime. Oh! There will be one of the TV scenes where the woman is screaming with lots of strangers hanging around. *Oh goody—a public moment.* I thought about practicing screaming, but then canceled that—I realized of all the things I didn't know right now, *I would truly know the right time to scream!*

One morning, a large, open container of yogurt fell at my feet. You know, the area somewhere past my stomach that I haven't seen in months. The question is, "how do I clean it up?" My little dog hated yogurt!

All right, let's consider this problem. I found the multi-purpose duct tape, and taped the plastic dustpan onto the handle end of the mop. I found the grilling spatula and taped it to the end of the broom. Like a bomb disposal expert from extended robot arms, I shoved the offending pile of yogurt onto the dustpan, and then dumped it into the sink. Then,

I turned the mop over and used it to finish cleaning the floor. First crises solved, but then it was time to rest. I should stop and have something else to eat. Hold on to whatever it is with a better grip.

While I was seated at the kitchen table I looked in horror at the garbage collecting under the edges of the cabinet. There were pieces of carrots and a radish that rolled off the counter yesterday. Just how much can I shove out of sight? How long will it take to fill up that space before stuff shows? And round things like radishes roll off my newly invented 'mop-pan'. I think I finally just swept everything out the back door, much to the amusement of my Great Dane. She didn't eat raw vegetables. At least she didn't ask for the salt shaker.

After a long day of trying to pick things up from the floor in increasingly creative ways, I gave into tears. David came home from work to find a soggy, plump woman, who waddled like a duck when I came over to him for a hug. What a picture! David decided we should eat out, which then compounded my bad day.

David loved to take me out. I know he was showing me off, while I was feeling conspicuous. Surely, there were people looking at my silver white hair that used to be blonde, and wondering why an old woman was pregnant. Was David my husband or did he look like a kindly brother or maybe a son taking his mother out to eat. *Oh, the thoughts that pass through the mind!*

One of our favorite places was a greasy spoon called "The Fifty's Place." Greasy burgers and fries, with golden oldies on the coin operated jukebox. David led me toward our favorite booth.

"David," I whispered.

He slid effortlessly along the leather seat. "What?" David looked up at me, puzzled.

"I can't fit in here." My face turned beet red. There was a couple sitting in the corner booth, staring at me, forks raised, and mouths open.

"What?"

"I can't fit in here," I said a little louder. The couple smiled at me as the waiter arrived, out of breath.

"Can I show you to a table?" he suggested, kindly.

"We always eat here," David said.

"Yes, David, let's sit at a table." I leaned over the booth and whispered, "I don't fit!"

David jumped up in surprise. "Oh sure, let's go over there."

The restaurant which had become strangely quiet, began to twitter with giggling. I was mortified. Maybe I should have just worn a "wide load" sign. It would have been simpler, or at least, the laughter would have been under my control!

* * *

Adventures in Travel!

All right, here is the set up. It is your in-laws fortieth wedding anniversary and they are leasing a bus to take all 23 members of the immediate family to a small gathering in Biggs, Wyoming. The doctor says I can go, but who told me to make sure I will fit in the bus rest room for the return trip? Then there are all those hours riding on a bus, bouncing up and down. Staring out the bus window for hours gave me time to think such deep thoughts as: I will be 64 by the time my baby graduates college!

The trip through the Rocky Mountains was lovely, even though my ankles were swelling. I made a trip to the bus toilet and squeezed into the little box. *This is a tight fit for me now. We will be gone a week. What happens on the way home?* It would be a tighter fit, and I am very glad we weren't gone longer! I managed to get the baby side of me in the door, then, squeezed my backside through the opening. I filled up the entire bus restroom.

David watched this entrance with a twinkle in his eyes. "Next time, back in," he suggested.

I looked at him with narrowed eyes. "Thanks, David. And, you can make the 'backing up—beeping noise' that big trucks use!"

"Good idea," he quipped. "That way, everyone will know when you have to use the toilet!" He just smiled and went to sit down—out of reach!

There was one, two-year-old niece aboard, who screamed and cried for the entire trip. Thankfully, there was an overnight break from her and from traveling after our first ten-hour day. We had some teenage nieces who listened to music the entire time, and some elementary school age nephew that ran up and down the aisle. It was a long journey. Our overnight stay is when I found out about in-laws and practical jokes.

Susan A. Rader

Practical Jokers

Our bus pulled into Denver, Colorado around dinnertime to stop at a restaurant. There was a lovely buffet, so I could eat whatever looked good. On the journey, I had brought an ice chest with some whole cow's milk from a farm near our home. I wanted to eat and drink the very best things for this growing baby, and of course, this included chocolate cake.

For dessert, I chose the chocolate cake in a take out carton, so I could have it with the last of the whole milk at bedtime. I knew I would be going to bed before everyone else! What I did not expect was a prank from the sister-in-law who had flown in with her husband and four children to meet the family bus. My husband was involved in this prank, too.

I was extremely tired when we climbed back on board the bus to go to the hotel. All I could think of was getting to the hotel room, which was NOT bumping, or screaming, or moving back and forth. It would be quiet and cool. As I was getting on the bus, my sister-in-law, Brenda, took my chocolate cake and handed it to David. I did not think much about it until I was in the hotel room by myself. I was ready for bed, and everyone else had gone down to the pool.

What a shock to open the carton and find a baked potato! I cried and cried, out of an over dramatic response at the loss of the cake. Then, when that little disappointment was under control, I was furious. I put my swollen feet back into my extra large new shoes and headed to the pool area. I was carrying the carton with the baked potato, and obviously, the look on my face was clear for everyone to read. All conversation stopped, even the splashing in the pool! It was very quiet except for my echoing footsteps.

"David Rader," I said firmly, as I narrowed my eyes. "Very funny! YOU eat it!" I threw the potato at him, turned around, and stomped back toward the elevator. My sister-in-law Brenda came running after me.

"Oh, Susan, please don't be angry with David. I thought this one up, and honestly, it was just supposed to be funny."

"Well, it wasn't," I replied as I pushed the elevator button again.

"Please, you've got to let me take blame for this. David and I were always pulling pranks on each other when we were growing up." Brenda was pleading with me and I felt like a heel.

"All right, I appreciate you explaining this. I'm just tired and I'm sure I will be over this by tomorrow."

Around two o'clock in the morning, I woke up and started laughing. I finally thought it was funny, probably because I felt rested. I regret to say that after discovering how funny this was, and how exactly to pull a practical joke, I did not call Brenda, wake up her entire room filled with husband and kids, to tell her I got the joke! She deserved that prank. I hate missed opportunities! Then again, I'm not used to practical jokes. Oh well.

The second day of the trip took us over the continental divide, above the tree line in the Rockies, where snow still lingered in August. It was beautiful, but the air was too thin for me. I didn't walk far when we stopped to visit a bubbling mountain stream, or the glacier. I was glad to reach Wyoming, although I was in for another surprise from my in-laws.

* * *

Garbage Bag Baby Shower!

Only Brenda and David's other sister, Denise, could have dreamed up an unbelievable party prank like this one. Since I was 41 with one month to go to age 42, and didn't have a baby shower planned, they decided to throw me one in Wyoming. I was uncomfortable at seven months pregnant and certainly not well acquainted with my in-laws. It was hard sometimes to tell when they were kidding. Brenda announced that David and I were to stay in Aunt Mary's living room area, while the others helped Aunt Mary with some chores. I should have suspected a plot.

Suddenly, the door to the basement burst open. In came my mother-in-law, my three sisters-in-law, and a niece, all wearing garbage bags, shower caps, face masks, and yellow kitchen gloves. They grabbed me and sat me down in a comfortable chair, and Patti, a surgical nurse, (my sister-in-law from Texas), took charge to help me prepare for labor and delivery!

They had the biggest hedge clippers I had ever seen for an episiotomy. Also available was a carpet needle with orange yarn to sew me up, and smaller hedge clippers for cutting an umbilical cord. There was an egg timer to time contractions; clothespins to clamp the baby's cord; a plunger (safer than forceps) for getting baby out. Then they explained the turkey-basting syringe was for suction; a paddle (for baby's new bottom); a 'nursing bra' with holes in it; and a catcher's mitt! I laughed until I cried.

Susan A. Rader

This joke I understood! Afterward, when we all caught our breath from laughing, we had cake, (chocolate!) and I opened some beautiful gifts for our baby, who would come sooner than planned.

Food Cravings?

Everyone has seen a television episode or a movie portrayal of pregnancy and food cravings. But, how many shows put in the flip side of this--*sensitivity to smells*. I was sure I was the most sensitive pregnant woman ever.

David would eat M&M's with a glass of milk. Then I would gag, thinking there was a sewer backup!

"What are you eating?" I demanded. David looked confused.

"M&M's."

"Oh, tell me when you're finished!" I left the room, gagging all the way.

"Sorry 'bout that?" David just went on watching the movie, but was nice enough to tell me when the candy and milk routine was over, and then he used mouthwash. The mouthwash smelled like cleaning solution for hospital floors.

One morning I woke up, rushed into the kitchen, and yelled, "What are you fixing that smells so horrible?"

Very softly, David replied, "...a bowl of Cheerios." Oh, well, David adapted better than I did. I told him if there was going to be another pregnancy in this house he gets the job!

When Brenda, Denise and I spent more time together on the bus trip, they both decided that David had met his match, and I just might be able to get back at him for his being the unbearable older brother. David has an easygoing nature. He also has those two fun loving sisters who tried and tested him long before I arrived in his life. I decided that it was not David's fault that smells overwhelmed me. He decided to eat M&M's by himself after I went to bed. I love compromise and courtesy, so I made a conscious effort to stop complaining about everything and just gag—it is quieter.

Since I was an "older" woman, with gray around the temples, blending into the rest of my silver white UN-dyed hair, I endured some strange encounters with the public. People stare. Perfect strangers came up and asked deeply personal questions such as, "are you pregnant or just fat?"

On top of this, every woman I met had to regale me with how she was in agonizing labor for three weeks, or tales of friends who had complications. Great! I hated hearing those things when I tried everyday NOT to worry over an endless list of what could go wrong! Who needs to hear that when they are eight months pregnant? *Toughen up, honey.* Only one month more. David and I prayed everyday for our baby, and for the guidance we would need to be proper parents.

When it was time to enroll in the natural childbirth class, yes, I was the oldest woman there! As I came into the room at the hospital, the nurse in charge of the class asked if I was signing up for myself, or my daughter. I patted my abdomen and said, "Both of us."

Pregnancy does other strange things to a body. As I turned 42, I found an entirely new view in the mirror. I was so big I couldn't keep my feet on the floor when I sat in a chair. From the side, I looked like someone wearing a pillow under my clothes for a stage play. I always looked twice when I went past my reflection. Maybe it was the incongruity of my new body with the silver white hair. It just didn't seem to go together. It was a family trait anyway. My Aunt Dorothy and my grandmother Genevieve turned white-silver haired at 30.

Then I caught a glimpse of a reflection in a mall window of this large mass moving awkwardly along. It was me! The bulky, slow moving mass in the reflection reminded me of the old 1950's movie with Steve McQueen called *"The Blob."* Thankfully, I was not an elephant--they are pregnant for years!

* * *

Laboring at 42

Oh, what was I thinking? Eight months and counting. With all the hormones and changes, I forgot my previous existence.

Pregnant and older isn't easy. However, I remembered one important thing when I began wondering if my arches could take another pound. When I hold that baby in my arms, everything I have experienced will fade into the background! So, I told myself, "You can do it!"

Susan A. Rader

Baby's In Back?

On a Monday, nine days after I turned 42, around noon, I started having back pains. David called to check on me after his lunch, as always.

"How are you feeling?"

"I keep getting tired and have back pains. What else is there when I'm shaped like a balloon. I'm just uncomfortable," I replied with a groan for emphasis.

"Is this labor?" David asked in a concerned voice.

"No, I don't think so. It's just low back pain, kind of like having lifted something too heavy for me. Besides, that would mean our baby is coming three weeks early."

David told me "Time these back pains and call me back, okay?"

"Oh, nonsense. I just have back trouble!"

"Call me back, after you have timed them, OK?" David repeated.

I called him back. "It hurts every fifteen minutes."

"It's labor."

I was skeptical. "If the baby's in the front, who's this in the back?"

David laughed a little and then asked, "When did this start?"

"Around noon, I think. It has just been getting worse all afternoon."

"If it gets worse, or something else happens, call me back."

That wasn't very comforting but I fell asleep for about an hour, and then had to get up to move around. I fixed David's dinner—something frozen, because I didn't want to stand for a long time. I personally think he was lucky to have me thaw it, let alone heat it up!

David arrived as usual, five o'clock, kissed me on his way to the kitchen, and had dinner while I sat stoically on the couch. From time to time, David would glance at me from the kitchen. When he took his dishes to the sink, this wise guy got out the camera and took my picture.

"Underneath this photo, we can write: Not a happy camper." He seemed delighted by everything. Next time, he is going to have the baby!

"Ha. Ha. Funny man."

"It's for the scrapbook, Susan," David reminded me.

We had all ready taken pictures of the doctor, the hospital, the clinic sign, and the suitcase packed for the hospital, why not a picture of me at my worst! We even practice timing the hospital trip--exactly fifteen minutes, on three alternate routes! We were prepared. *Well, David was!*

At the fifth month, David and I had gone in for an ultrasound. Lying on a cold table with an abdomen like an overripe watermelon, I thought about beached whales. It kept my mind off the cold table.

"Well, Susan," said Dr. Motz. "Let's take a look and see if you have a boy or a girl."

What were we going to do, throw one or the other back if we didn't like the outcome? No, I argued with myself, this ultrasound is necessary so we can properly decorate, and gather "nesting" supplies—like birds. David and I were old enough to be extinct!

"Hmm, no extra equipment," the doctor said. "I believe it's a girl."

David and I wanted a boy AND a girl. Couldn't we have twins and get this all over at once? Twins ran in his family, and I was big enough for three or four people. That night, I had a panic attack.

With the horror of my childhood as fresh as if I was still living in the tar paper shack at the edge of the river, I was not a little girl holding onto my younger sister's hand, but holding a baby who was in danger.

I seemed only half awake and couldn't clear my head. *Oh Lord, protect this little baby from me, from my past. Set your angels around her and guide me as her mother.* God knew a great many things would transpire that would thankfully teach our daughter, and change me.

I began thinking that when our little girl arrived, we would be required to fill out papers to start her new life. This reminded me of our discussions of baby names. I focused on the name we chose for our little girl, instead of the sick feeling and strange sensations in my lower back as we zoomed along the interstate toward the hospital.

David and I decided the afternoon, after the ultrasound, to make a list of girl's names. We are both fans of Hayley Mills, the British actress, and especially fond of Disney's Hayley Mills version of *The Parent Trap*. I was such a fan when I was young, my bedroom walls were covered with magazine cut outs of her, pictures and interviews from each of her movies as she grew up in the camera's eye. David and I chose Hayley for that reason. Of course, Hayley had to have a middle name.

One of the names I have always loved is Elizabeth—after Elizabeth II, Queen of England. I read everything I could about her, her mother, the Queen Mum, and the Windsor family. I admired Queen Elizabeth's leadership qualities and ambassadorial skills, as the young queen who took over at age 18. This was long before I was married or considered having a daughter.

Also, the meanings of names intrigues me. Hayley means "ingenious

Susan A. Rader

or clever," and Elizabeth means, "consecrated to God." It seemed a perfect fit—a clever, inventive girl, who belongs to God. With her last name in place: Rader—German, meaning "maker of wheels," her initials became an anagram: H. E. R. In addition, following my interest in the British, H.R. stood for the royalty of England. Hayley was to be our little princess. David liked the idea of an anagram name—that way, when she went off to school, we could mark everything H. E. R., and not very many people have those initials.

My thoughts about names dissipated as David drove us into the emergency parking lot of the hospital. It was dark, and I felt so sick I didn't want to get out of the car.

"I'm too sick to be here."

"What does that mean?" David asked.

"When I go to hospitals, it's usually to visit someone else. I have to work up being cheerful and energetic, so I can cheer up someone who needs it. Well, I don't feel cheerful or energetic or very conversational."

"Let's go inside," David replied firmly. "You need to be seen."

Wouldn't you know, I had one last Childbirth Preparation Class left-- the one on relaxing, but baby wouldn't wait. And NO, I did not volunteer to have my class come for "Show and Tell." As I doubled over on the way to the door, the cheerful voice of one of my classmates shouted, "Well, I guess you're skipping class tonight, huh?"

With a groan, through half clenched teeth, I replied, "Ask the teacher about relaxing. She didn't tell us how to relax when it feels like this!"

News traveled fast. The teacher for the Childbirth Class came down to the delivery area and gave David our 'Certificate of Completion'. I just looked at her as an irritation on top of my misery.

"Doing finals, are we?" she asked with a laugh.

"Uh, I'd like to skip this part. Go away."

David spoke up, "Sorry. Susan isn't feeling very friendly right now."

"No problem," the teacher replied with a knowing smile. "I have heard a lot of really harsh things said by women in labor, both in the emergency room and the delivery room." She glanced at me again and added, "I'm going back up to class to remind them to relax, and how to deal that with back labor!" *Fine for those who were not experiencing finals!*

David was very helpful and stayed by my side. Suddenly, I grabbed his arm because a wave of nausea and dizziness swept over me. Suddenly I was very afraid. David reached up to touch my face and I promptly threw up into his hand. Unforgettable. Was it too late to tell the hospital I didn't feel well enough to do this? Wasn't there another way? Who invented LABOR? Can't we "beam" this baby out like Star Trek?

My wonderful husband just used a nearby towel, wiped his hands, and then picked up a clean, damp cloth to wipe my face.

"Life happens," David said to no one in particular. Later, when I remembered this incident, I asked him how he felt. "It just happens. No problem. I wished there was more I could do to help you at the time." Is this man real? Did I invent him? No, I just received a husband whose character surpassed the requests in my prayers. Our God is great.

All totaled, I was in labor for seven hours before events took a sudden turn.

Being older did not have an advantage.

"Your baby is three weeks early. Her heart is beating too fast, and there are other signs of fetal distress."

I couldn't grasp what the doctor said, but the urgency in his voice was apparent.

"I advise an emergency Cesarean Section, immediately." I watched the color drain out of David's face, and reached for his hand.

"Whatever you decide. I can't help," I mumbled. As I studied his face, some of the fear went away. "I love you, David."

David leaned down and kissed my forehead. "I love you both."

David and I had talked about this possibility. I told him that I would not be mentally capable of making serious decisions during labor. We talked about the worse case scenarios from everything we thought might or could occur. We read everything we could about childbirth. I told him that however he had to choose, I would back him up. We had done everything we knew to do to insure my health and the health of our unborn baby girl. Everything else was in God's hands. And, what a gift God gave us.

One Rude Dude!

When the nurses shifted me to a rolling gurney, I moaned. The pain in my back was unbearable. One sympathetic nurse murmured, "It will pass soon. Try to keep breathing deeply when it hurts."

In the operating room, the anesthesiologist came over to introduce himself.

"Hello, I'm Eddie," he said as he pulled on gloves. "Hmm, not doing too well, huh?" he said with a smirk. "You're just a bit older than I usually see in here."

I wasn't feeling very charitable. "You should try this, and then we'll compare notes!"

Other people in the operating room laughed. He didn't laugh.

"Well, maybe next time you won't wait until you're 42 to have a child!" Eddie laughed arrogantly. "Accident, huh?"

That did it for my tolerance.

"Maybe next time I won't have a puffed up, presumptuous egomaniac for an anesthesiologist!"

There was laughter all around the room, except from Eddie. A nurse spoke up.

"Oh, Eddie. She reads you like a book and hasn't known you longer than five minutes! Go girl!"

Eddie's eyes narrowed. "You don't know me well enough to say something like that."

"Really? It doesn't take long to read personality disorders." Another wave of pain hit me.

"Do something! I can't stand this pain!"

"Well, now, why should I hurry?"

One of the nurses cautioned him. "She doesn't realize what she saying, Eddie, give her a break."

Eddie looked over at the nurse, then back at me. "She can wait for the doctor."

I was in too much pain to think of anymore to say. Besides, it is NOT a good idea to insult a person who is there to aid you, regardless of how obnoxious. It is easy enough to make sharp comebacks, but that's not what God would have me say. It was better to turn my thoughts to prayer. God would assist us. It was time to trust Him.

Thankfully, the doctor arrived and ordered anesthesia right away. The next thing I knew, I heard a nurse announce, "It's a girl!"

This was not an OOPS!—This was a miracle. A wonderful gift from God. We have an angel for the two of us to love, together.

YOU DON'T HAVE TO MOVE THE WASHER TO MAKE TOAST

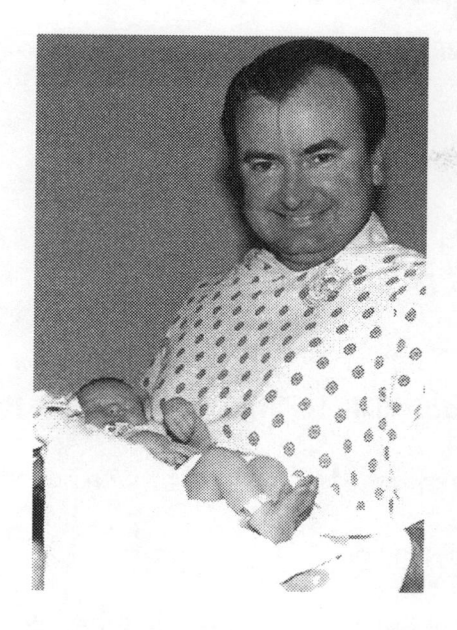

* * *

CHAPTER 9

Baby Comes Home, Diapering 101, Pecan Pie Bandit

How nervous were we the first night home with our beautiful new baby girl?

"What's she doing now?"

David replied, "Breathing."

Two college degrees between us, and we don't know anything useful! One tiny little helpless person changes everything.

Among the first to arrive, after a long drive were David's proud parents. Hayley was grandchild number 11, but the first born of *their first born*.

"Hi, Mom. Hi Dad," I said happily as I met them at the door.

ZOOM. I didn't know they moved that fast. It was a race to see who could see Hayley first!

"Ooooooo," Mom said with a beaming smile. "She looks just like David!"

"Beautiful," Dad said, proudly. By then, they each had a turn holding her, and Hayley was mesmerized.

My mother in law looked up and said, "Oh, Susan, she's beautiful."

For me, this was a "forever moment", for two reasons. It was wonderful to see David's parents so excited about one more grandchild, as if she were their first. And, David met my eyes with a smile. One glance of "validation". Both of us weren't sure we'd ever find a mate, let alone have a child. What a day to remember!

Then came the tour of the nursery. It took six months to prepare. Shelves, changing table, handmade quilts, handmade wall pillows in the shapes of animals, an "ABC" border at crib level. Baby equipment list took up half the room: stroller, walker, highchair, and food processor. Hayley's crib was filled with toys.

"Any room for the baby in here?" Dad asked with his usual teasing voice.

"The toys are for David and me," I replied. "We're just using them to save Hayley's spot in the crib."

My mother in law said, "Cloth diapers? They're a lot of work. Trust me, I know".

"Well, just to start out with," I replied, very sure of this decision.

"Probably the first year," David added with authority.

"Good luck with pins," Dad said knowingly.

"Good luck with the washer," Mom added.

Ah, the voice of wisdom and experience we didn't *heed*.

The old washing machine didn't like baby diapers or the soap we used. That was never cleared up. There was often a trail of bubbles over flowing from the top, making a long foamy trail down the front of the washer. Why? An unanswered question for the cosmos.

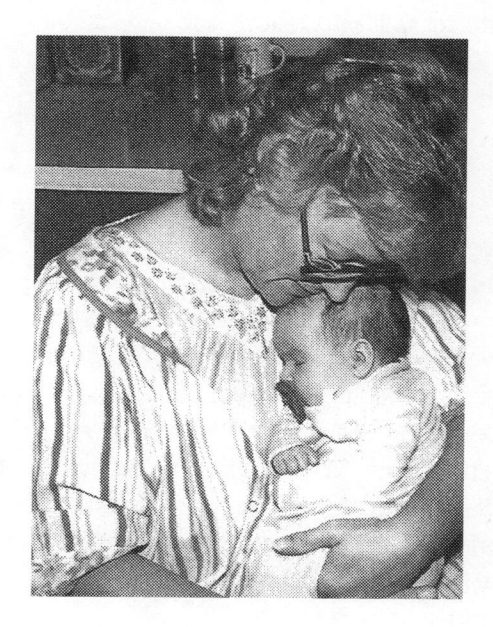

Diapering 101

I loved to watch David on diaper duty. This was his "Creative Diapering, 101." After he'd pinned on the cloth diaper, he would pick up

Susan A. Rader

Hayley and gently move her up and down, to see if the diaper fell off. If it did, he would slip it back on, and adjust a pin. Hayley loved this ritual, and we loved baby giggles.

I realize parents of newborns dote on their baby, but I don't understand why people take the fun out of baby smiles. There are TOO many sightings by parents of babies reporting "smiles". Some people believe in UFO's, and they aren't as common!

We were the object of laughter at family gatherings. David's sisters and brother had three to four children each, and had long since given up being particular about details for a baby. Whenever we made the three-hour journey to a family get together, we would have things packed to the ceiling in the car, and strapped on the outside of the trunk.

"Ice chest with bottles," David read from his list.

"Check."

"Swing, diaper bag, wipes, pacifier, rattle".

"Check".

"Baby blanket, comforter, bassinet with sheets, trash bag, trash can, and replacement sacks," David read.

"Check".

Silence. We both looked at the empty car seat.

"Where's Hayley?" David asked.

I jumped out of the car and ran back into the house. Just where we left her, gurgling along happily waiting for one of us. No need to take all that stuff if we weren't going to bring baby!

Recalling our first outing to Church, David wrapped her with a blanket, picked her up, and started for the door. I brought up the rear with all the baby paraphernalia when I noticed something on his suit.

"David, there's a white streak down your back!?"

Upon close examination, it was obvious our new baby had spit up. Wow! Let's write this down! We were journaling every event! *"Today, first spit up on David's suit instead of her mother's blouse"*. (Well, it looks cute in the baby memories' book.)

I took Hayley from David and said, "Oh, and by the way, change your coat!" I didn't mind waiting a few minutes before heading out the door. Holding Hayley was more fun than holding stuff! I was fast becoming a pack horse!

At church, everyone "ooo-aahed" over the new baby, which we

expected and truly enjoyed. However there were two friends whose comments were unexpected.

A barber friend checked Hayley's scalp. "Cowlicks. Three of 'em. Gonna' be hard to cut."

Right behind him came a beautician.

"Hmm, cowlicks," Arty said. "She'll hate her hair in front, and this left side is going to flip up all her life. Good luck when she's a teenager." This seemed like mixed reviews at a reception line.

Hayley is only three weeks old and this was just another reminder that everyone our age had grown children at various stages. We resolved to enjoy Hayley's cowlicks because it made her look wind blown.

This first church service for us as a family was another "forever moment". This was a chance to worship God, thank Him for our beautiful baby girl, and be a three-some—a family! Then we discovered how hard it is to keep a baby quiet. Why is it that a baby gets her first hiccups during the prayer? And, of course, no one told us that when babies want to gurgle, coo or sing, they just can't be stopped.

Breast-feeding

Breast-feeding was a real experience. At first, the only time I was truly

Susan A. Rader

relaxed was after a hot shower. I really didn't want to keep the baby in the bathroom!

The most interesting part about night-feedings were the late movies. I'd stumble out to the living room, turn on a movie, watch part of it, and go back to bed without seeing the ending. I saw portions of a great many movies.

Breast feeding only lasted 6 months. It was my habit to save breast milk in the refrigerator for short time periods, to be used on car trips or during church. Once Hayley discovered it was easier to drink from a bottle, I lost my job. We slowly moved her to a Soy formula and she gradually began sleeping through the night. However, there was one night adventure totally unique to our house.

Pecan Pie Bandit

It was time for the 2 a.m. feeding. As usual, I switched on the TV. It was then I noticed, through blurry eyes, some "things" on the floor. I didn't care what they were at the moment. It was odd because the floor had been the same brown carpet when I went to bed. So, I just stepped over the things on the way to the couch. When my vision cleared, I realized they were pieces of pie crust. Pie crust in the living room? Just then, I heard a low moaning sound from the kitchen, but it didn't sound threatening. I put Hayley back to bed and went to investigate. What a sight. There was my small dog leaning against the kitchen cabinet next to a pie pan, so bloated he couldn't walk! My mouth dropped open. David's pie was gone.

How did that little tiny dog get the pie from the counter? Suddenly there was a movement near the back door. A skinny yellow cat shot outside through the "doggy door." We didn't own a small skinny yellow cat.

I looked at my dog. "Well, that's what you get for taking food from strangers." He suffered most of the night, but I went back to bed. I learned my lesson. Lock up the doggy door, or he'd be inviting all his other friends for leftovers!

***

Musical Furniture

With the arrival of Hayley, we were, once again, space strapped. To use the baby swing, we needed to move the love seat, one end table with lamp, and the coffee table. For using the playpen we moved the large plant stand out to the kitchen, shifted the love seat, the recliner, and the end table all to the left.

The high chair required taking a leaf out of the dining table. Since things would be this way for awhile, we removed all the dining chairs, replacing them with two brown metal folding chairs. Of course, we had to move the microwave cart to the garage--not handy, but more space in the kitchen. After all this, we could sit down together for a meal! Other options? Eat in shifts. I think that's the reason that our teenage daughter liked to regularly rearrange her room.

When Hayley was about a month old, we made a business trip to Kansas City to stay at a friend's home while they were away. It was a split level home in a Kansas City suburb. Most of the houses on the block looked alike. The front entrance was at street level but the backs and sides had two levels.

The Sullinger home was beautifully landscaped in this quiet neighborhood. There was a basement entrance at the side of the house that went straight into a garage. On that bottom floor was a game room, laundry area, and small workshop next to the garage, with steps up to the main floor. It was a lovely home to use for a week while our friends were out of town.

The third morning my husband made a quick trip to the store but neglected to see if the automatic garage door closed. In our small town that wouldn't be a problem. But, Kansas City had a different view of open garage doors.

Armed Officer Draws Gun on Laundry-News at 10!

Since baby and I were at the opposite end of the house from the garage, I didn't hear much from the street or front of the house. I was recovering at my advanced age from the C-section and Hayley was sleeping. Nearly finished with folding the laundry in the upper hall, I heard an eerie creaking sound from the hallway door. It was very slowly opening on its own. David never came in like that. Suddenly, I saw the barrel of a service revolver. I stopped in mid fold. A police officer moved quickly into the hall.

"Who are you?" His gun was level.

"Um. Susan Rader."

"What are you doing here?"

"Um, the Sullingers let us stay here for this next week while they are traveling."

He visibly relaxed and, thankfully, lowered his gun. "Well, I've never caught a burglar folding sheets." He wiped his forehead. "You'd better go out front to explain to the neighbors before they break in the front door."

When I stepped out onto the porch, I just stood wide-eyed. Nine people were glaring at the house as a mob armed with rakes, shovels, hoes, one golf club and a baseball bat. What a sight! A movie scene right before the lynching.

"I'm sorry we frightened you. The Sullingers are letting us stay here for the week," I said as calmly as possible.

A big man with a rake shouted, "How come you didn't answer the door?"

"I'm sorry, I didn't hear a thing. I have a new baby, and we're in the far back bedroom. I have to sleep when she does."

A woman in the front with a golf club stepped forward. "We've had a lot of vandalism and burglaries around here lately. Don't be leaving the garage door open!"

"No, Mam, we won't. I'm sure my husband just forgot to see if it was closed. We're not used to a garage door. I'm really sorry."

Mr. Gruff lowered his rake. "Well, seeing how you have baby, I can see you needing some sleep. But remember—PUT DOWN THAT GARAGE DOOR, or we'll be back!"

Oh, the difference between small towns and the big city is monumental. It's unforgettable looking down the barrel of a revolver while I wondered if our hostess liked the sheets folded the way I did! At gunpoint doing laundry! When we left the thank you note, we mentioned the laundry police. *My, they are strict in this town!* And, it isn't every day you see an armed mob in the front yard. What a story to tell our hosts when they returned.

***

Baby Grows Up, Co-Ed Backyard, Infant of Days

Someone said that babies grow slowly. That is so parents have a little time to read books to find out what they're supposed to be doing! *Who started that rumor?* And the dumb advice about reading books on baby's stages of life? Absurd. Baby grows too fast, skips chapters in development to head straight for crawling, then walking, and skipping shoe sizes. Where did the time go?

Potty Training?

We had just mastered diapering when a well meaning friend gave me a book: *Potty Training in Less than a Day*. Well Hayley didn't follow guidelines. After all the coaxing, the fruit juice tea parties with "Betsy Wetsy", as well as having the doll sit on its very own little toilet, there was only one moment of triumph. I saw a dawning idea in Hayley's eyes. She rushed to the bathroom, dutifully went potty, and then smiled in satisfaction.

"Go pee-pee!"

Wow! It's a success! Shortly after, Hayley tired of the kitchen tea party with the wetting doll so before wrapping this up I reminded her it was time to go to the bathroom. She looked steely eyed, stamped her foot, and announced, "I no do." She promptly wet her pants. Point made. FYI: *That response is not in the book!* I gave up potty training lessons. Hayley began using the toilet on her own, when she wanted to!

David shrugged when I gave him the potty training report. "Well, how many kids in kindergarten are still wearing diapers?"

"I don't know, but I don't want Hayley to be one of them!"

"Don't worry!" David gave me a hug. "She is smarter than the Wetsy doll. She proved she got the lesson. This will work out." Oh, that man seems to skip to the end without all the work.

Later that night, I remembered Hayley had amazed me with a short sentence when she was six months old. It was my habit, when I picked her up, day or night, to always say, "I love you". One night, I heard her crying and rushed to her room. As I picked her up, she said "I love." I just didn't expect such a small baby to put two words together that soon. So why worry over potty training.

Susan A. Rader

Co-ed Backyard?

An alternative to eating out is, of course, an invitation to someone's home. But, we discovered it should be to a home where there is a child of similar age. There are safety-measures all ready in place, as well as age appropriate toys. It is also hard to take an only child to a friends' home when they do not have children because there is no way to sit after dinner and just talk. Little kids have to get up from the table and play.

At one dinner outing, our baby was sitting in a high chair next to a fruit bowl. Before I knew what happened, Hayely had taken bites out of each apple! Babies must be watched, which distracts from adult conversation! Why is it no one ever mentioned this? I should list this event in the column heading of "how to not be invited back to someone's home".

After discovering these truths, universally known by other parents who forget to share this information, we invited friends over for a dinner. Four children, age 3-7, would be able to play outside with all the toys, in a nice safe yard while all the grown ups had a chance to talk. At last, we were having a social occasion.

All the children got along famously. They ran in and out of the back door. David thoughtfully put the door handle down where all the little people could reach it and installed a very short hand rail. After awhile, my daughter ran inside with wide eyes.

"Hey, mom! You gotta' come see this."

I dutifully went with her to the back porch. "What is it, sweetie?"

Hayley looked around the yard but looked disappointed.

"Well, Bradley went pee-pee over there. It's gone now, but you should'a seen it!" This event is what we label as early sex education. Thankfully, she didn't ask me any questions, but Bradley's mother was mortified.

New Use for a Toothbrush

Since Hayley was growing more and more teeth, we had started a brushing routine. My dentist and his wife, the ones from the wedding, gave Hayley special treatment at her first dental visit, and it left quite an impression.

The next morning after breakfast, I was in the kitchen cleaning, with Hayley in the living room. Soon, I heard "Oooo, doggy," and then heard my old dog growl and snap. There would be a few moments of silence, then a growl and snap! Oh, if I only had a video camera! My old dog, rushing around the recliner just ahead of Hayley's short legs. In her hand was a toothbrush! Tana Man had no interest in dental hygiene!

"Brush doggies teeth, Mommy," Hayley said with a smile.

Tana Man ran for me and jumped up into my arms.

"Oh, hold doggy, Mommy. Doggy bad breath".

It was difficult to explain that Tana Man didn't need a tooth brush.

"Dogs chew bones to clean their teeth. Their teeth are special."

"Can I have bone, too?" Hayley was wide eyed with the thought.

"No, honey," I replied. "Little girls need to use a toothbrush like Dr. Cathy showed you. But, we could practice on Big Bear or dolly's teeth."

Hayley exited to play dentist, so it was off to her room for another adventure, much to the relief of the dog.

Baby, Pets and Toilets

As soon as Hayley could stand, she found the water in the toilet. I heard a "me-Ow," and then a very wet cat went rushing past me. Hayley toddled in with a big smile.

"Kitty, bath. Dolly bath." Since I saw what happened to the cat, I thought I'd better check the bathroom. Lined up on the edge of the tub were three dolls, and four stuffed toys, all dutifully bathed in the toilet. Thankfully, the dog was too heavy for her to pick up! It was at that moment I noticed the top of Hayley's head was wet.

I stood at the bathroom door, trying to think of what to do with this situation when Hayley rushed past me, flushed the toilet and said, "Lookey-lookey." The plumber couldn't retrieve what went down, but he didn't charge much to unclog the sewer line. In fact, the he thought it was funny. It reminded him of his son who had flushed an entire set of tiny toy metal boats down the toilet, to watch them float and spin. Now that's anything but cheap entertainment!

Infant of Days

When our daughter passed her 26 months, the doctor's office called me with the confirmation. We had baby number two on the way. We were ecstatic and this pregnancy was going better than my first. However things don't always go the way you dream.

At just about three months, I began to feel ill a great deal. The doctor had confirmed my pregnancy and we all ate healthy meals. The only thing added was watch my weight and take a vitamin. I expected things to go routinely, but there was an odd sensation, not at all like morning sickness.

Driving myself across town for the Doctor's appointment I felt preoccupied. Little did I know what this day would bring. How many times are there in life to wish for another treasure like our Hayley. The doctor set me up for an ultrasound.

"Hmm. That's not right." Dr. Motz said carefully.

"What's not right."

"Well, I thought..there is something wrong here."

My heart started a stampede. I whispered. "What's wrong?"

Doctor Motz sighed heavily.

"Your baby died. It was three weeks to 12 weeks along. I'm sorry."

I felt as if I suddenly didn't speak English. The Doctor's words made no sense. "My baby died? Did I do something? Is this my fault?"

"No, it's one of those things. You're beginning a miscarriage". There was no understanding this event.

"You are feeling sick because your baby was to be three months along by now so that hormones created for the baby take over. We will need to schedule a procedure that cleans the uterus. You may begin bleeding any time now. At this point in a pregnancy, the hormones from the baby should have started up, but they didn't. I'm sorry. I thought with your successful first pregnancy, you would have no problems. I'm sorry."

If the doctor said more, I don't think I comprehended it. I was stunned. I needed to pull myself together and call David. I needed David. I had to tell David. But what would I say?

The nurse came in and told me how sorry she was that the baby died.

"Susan. Listen to me. If you begin bleeding, or you begin feeling strange, like you aren't yourself, or you want to hurt yourself, you MUST call me. Here is the phone number day or night."

"Why would I do that?"

"It is a matter of the sudden loss of hormones. It's a huge hormone shift. You were feeling it and that is what led you to make an appointment.

This can be a condition called post postpartum depression. If you feel like you need to harm your baby, or harm yourself, you must call 911 immediately. I'm sending a prescription home with you, from our office. Now go call your husband."

This didn't make sense. Why would I hurt my baby? What am I supposed to do now? I did not realize I was already into postpartum depression. Across from the Doctor's office was fast food restaurant. I needed to find a phone. It seemed to take forever to get David on the line

"David." I gasped, chocking back tears.

"David, our baby is dead." I burst into tears.

"What?"

"David, the baby died. I..the baby died about two or three weeks ago but I didn't know. The baby died."

"I love you, Susan. You didn't do anything wrong. Stay there. I'm coming to get you and you can tell me all the doctor said. You stay there, all right?"

I can't remember if I answered him. I don't remember hanging up the phone. I felt strange. Time passed quickly. It seemed just moments ago that I called David, but suddenly he was there. I was missing 25 minutes. He guided me to the car but getting home was a blur. I didn't know was happening.

David had me lie down while he called our friends who were babysitting Hayley. They would bring Hayley home at nap time. David asked them for prayers.

I seemed to be in a partial dream. Lying on the bed I wasn't sure where I was but then Hayley came in. Part of me knew Hayley was my daughter, but there was a great distance between us. It was one of the strangest sensations I've ever had. I could touch her hand, and not feel it. Who was this beautiful little girl that I seemed to know?

I went to the phone, remembering the almost distant voice of the kindly nurse, saying *call me. Call me.* I dialed the number and the nurse answered.

"You know how we talked about my baby dying?"

"Susan, is this you? How are you feeling?"

"How am I feeling."

"Yes, dear. Tell me how you are feeling. Is your husband home?"

"Yes."

"Put your husband on the phone so I can ask him some questions."

"OK."

With help from the nurse, David gave me one of the pills to stop the effects of postpartum depression. I fell into an uneasy state, neither truly awake or truly asleep.

In the dream between consciousness and sleep, my feelings were of terrible loss and dread. I felt as if I were between life and death, if that place could be defined. There were shadows in the room, and dark places, frightening bright places next to the dark, as if in a hallucination. The falling sensation with these dramatic images in the room with me seemed to last for hours. I wasn't sure who I was.

It was past Hayley's bedtime and nearing the 10 p.m. news when I came out of the bedroom.

"Susan, how are you feeling?" David had jumped up off the couch to put his arms around me.

"Oh, feel like I've been taken for a ride on a roller coaster with strobe lights. I'm better. I just can't grasp what happened."

David took me to the couch to sit, cradling me in his arms.

"We don't know what happened, not in this life. Our baby is with the Lord Jesus, that is explained in the scriptures, and we believe God's Word". David hugged me tightly.

"We have an appointment at the hospital on Saturday morning, unless things go faster and we have to take you to the hospital sooner. Hayley will be safe and playing at Karenna's. We won't have to worry about her at all."

I began weeping again. "Did I do something? Did I NOT do something?"

"There was nothing you did or I did. This kind of thing happens. Maybe this baby needed to be with Jesus right now. We trust God with our lives everyday. We can trust Him with our unborn baby."

Then David wept with me.

Later that night around 4:00 a.m. July 12, 1992 the miscarriage began, with all the front contractions I thought should be the signal when Hayley was born. This was not back labor, but normal contractions as I understood them from the books we read. There was a great deal of blood and some tissue, but since David and I had read scriptures, and prayed together before he went to bed, I was calm now. No need for another one of those potent postpartum medications. I simply prayed as contractions and cramps seized me.

When I came home from the hospital, David's parents were there for support. I tentatively showed them the ultrasound image. That picture broke my heart.

They didn't understand what they were looking at.

"There's no baby in the photo," one of them said. I didn't realize they saw this ultrasound from a different perspective. They had lost no children. None of Mom's children had lost children. This was out of their range of thinking. I took back the grief I longed to share and snatched the ultrasound to hide it away in my dresser drawer.

It was the photo of my empty misshapen womb, because my baby had been fertilized and embedded to await growing, but it died somewhere after three weeks. By the time we reached the hospital at 6:00 a.m., the lining of the uterus was partially gone as I began to miscarry at home. My in-law's did not see that ultrasound photo as the saddest thing that ever happened to me, to David, and to Hayley who would have no brothers or sisters as playmates in this world.

As the weeks went by, David and I talked less and less. When he came home each night, there was no more talking about our baby. We held hands a great deal, went on walks as the summer evenings turned to fall.

"David, someone suggested we name our baby."

He hesitated before replying. "We don't know if it was a boy or girl."

"Well I've been thinking about how that is important to us, so how about two names?"

"All right. Do you have any ideas?"

"Yes. Let's do this using both our initials. Stephanie Alexis or Derick Ward, then when we see our baby in heaven, we will know."

We agreed. We couldn't abide the idea of a gender neutral name. As time passed, if I mentioned the baby, David seemed melancholy.

"What is it that makes you turn away when I mention our baby? Is it something you hold against me?"

"At least you got to hold the baby inside. I didn't have a chance to." Tears welled up in his eyes.

I put my arms around David and just then little Hayley came into the room. She rushed over to give us hugs. David reached down and snatched her up. We huddled together in silence except for Hayley's squeals of delight.

Providence reminded us of the jewel we have now, in Hayley who was ours for this world, and reminding us of the treasure He held in His Hands for the future.

Susan A. Rader

Infant of Days

Oh, empty arms, My heart cries out!
Baby, What would you be?
A son to teach us brand new ways,
To climb. And run and shout?
Or maybe a sister for our precious girl,
To teach her sharing in a selfish world!
God only knows our sleepless nights,
And thoughts. And tears. And dreams.
Someday, we'll see just who you were,
And you can meet us, too.
"Is it really you?"
And you can fill up brand new days
With joy *only you* could give,
When God calls and says to "Stand"
"And walk....and live".
Until *that Day*, we'll keep inside
Those precious little ways,
That you were planned for, Loved, and needed...
No more an infant of days.
July 11, 1992

Isaiah 65:20 "No more shall an **infant** from there *live but a few* days, Nor an old man who has not fulfilled his days; For the child shall die one hundred years old...

CHAPTER 10

A Date With "Kevin", Snowball Effect, Postmans Nightmare, Future Sight Of

A few years later, my mother began having health problems, and I volunteered to come to Atlanta. Hayley, age four and one half, took her first plane flight. She had her very own carry-on bag with her favorite toys, "Bunny, Becky Bear, and Kevin". Together, Hayley and I drove over all of the suburb outside Atlanta. I had a list a least a mile long of errands to run. However, the most memorable was the visit to a medical insurance office to pick up one copy of medical records.

After winding through a maze of offices and long hallways, I finally stopped to ask for directions at a Pediatricians office. It took several minutes to get the receptionist to stop looking for my name in the appointment book, but thankfully my daughter and I were only two doors away from our destination.

"Records: Employees Only. Knock for Service." It was another ten minutes before anyone came in answer to the knock. The clerk told us to wait, as it would take about 30 minutes to find and copy the records I needed.

It was approaching lunch hour, so the traffic at our end of the hallway dwindled to a trickle. Hayley was playing with her new "Kevin" doll, and I was pleased to see her so quietly busy using her imagination. I was concerned she would become as fussy as I felt about missing lunch.

I leaned against the wall across from the records door to wait, but failed to notice the sign next to me: "Psychological Services." On the other side of me was a small cubbyhole with three plastic potted trees, around which my daughter was playing.

I stood lost in thought, going over the list of things we still had to do, when a middle-aged woman came around the bend. She stopped suddenly to stare at me. She looked furtive, frowned, and then turned sideways, pressing herself against the wall as if to stay as far away from me as possible. *Well, what is her problem?* It was then I noticed my daughter had stopped making noises. Where could Hayley be? I wondered, especially since this woman was acting so strangely!

The woman moved uneasily past, glanced down beside me at the floor, then rushed out of sight around the corner. I looked to see what she saw. There, beside the "Psychological Services" doorway, standing on his own, *in a suit*, was the "Kevin" doll, and no child in sight! *It looked like "Kevin" and I were waiting for an appointment!* No wonder the woman ran.

Suddenly, Hayley popped out from behind the plastic tree and said, "Surprise!" When I asked what she was doing she replied, "Just a joke, Mommy." I guess she thought my standing in the hallway with a doll was very funny. This I classified as Hayley's first practical joke.

* * *

A Real Fixer-upper!

Constantly reminded of our very small house, we were in the habit of boxing things, rotating clothes, and rearranging furniture. Suddenly, we had the opportunity to buy the house next door. All we had to do was take over the payments. The new place boasted 1300 square feet, compared to our present, cramped 900 square feet. The elderly man who lived there was going to need full time health care, and offered to sell us his house. This was the answer to our space problems! We were ecstatic. That is, until we saw the interior.

Talk about your fixer-upper! This was straight out of the late night horror show—you know the kind that even the audience know *don't go in there!*

An old Christmas tree still decorated the corner of the living room, the decorative bulbs coated with a heavy layer of cobwebs and dust. It had been there eight years, the last Christmas before this man's wife died from cancer.

The elderly man and his pet dog lived in the large room at rear of the house, sealing off the main rooms with bedspreads. Cobwebs hung thickly from ceilings to the edges of furniture. Here and there were wasp nests, with evidence of mice. One bedroom had nine layers of carpeting on the floor. Apparently, he used very long nails, then cut off the bottom of the door so it could be closed!

Our insurance man said we could insure the house, if we put on a new roof. The Bank wouldn't loan us the money to purchase the house without a new roof. *But we can't put a roof on a house we don't yet own.*

So, from our savings, we paid for shingles and then invited some unsuspecting friends over to help us install the new roof. Of course, it was the hottest fall week on record, and it seemed that the shingling went on forever. The second afternoon, just before the heat became completely unbearable, David stood up, shaded his eyes and said, "Hey, that guy on the corner is putting up a 'For Sale' sign. I wonder how much he wants for it."

I started pounding with my hammer near his toes.

"You're delirious in this heat!" I shouted.

He just laughed. "We'll tell everyone we're playing monopoly. With three houses you get a hotel." Thankfully I realized he was teasing. The air felt like it must be 1,000 degrees.

Cleaning the inside of that dark house was a nightmare. Thankfully, my mother-in-law and my neighbor were not afraid of reaching back into the deep, dark recesses of the cabinets while I supervised. Curiosity got the better of them. I've seen too many scary movies to like dark places.

We found some treasures, like antique glass and useful kitchen items, but also a rat skeleton, a lighted neon beer sign, a stolen train signal, a sextant, and two telescopes. Other things we put in piles of "unknown objects" to be donated or tossed in the trash.

When the cleanup began, inside and out, it resulted in a daily trip to the City Dump. The first few weeks we hauled furniture, paneling, sheet rock, and yard junk. I knew every worker on each shift, and there was no longer need to show proof of residency. The workers would just say, "Oh, it's you again. Aren't you done yet?"

The sanitation team at the dump ramp wagered how many tries it would take this blonde to back a trailer up the hill between the two yellow lines! They should have been holding signs, like the Olympics! It didn't take me long to get a perfect "10"! It was frustrating to have them watching, doing nothing in the heat, while I backed the trailer up to the dump site. One could have at least directed me.

After cleaning the house and sorting out the "keepers," we had a sale to beat all garage sales. We used the driveways of both houses! At 6:15 a.m., when my husband opened the garage door to put the sign in the yard, there were three pickups parked along the curb.

"Susan, bring the cash box and the card table. We've got buyers!"

"All ready?" I shouted. "The sale isn't to start until 7! We made that clear."

"Too late," David replied. "Two men are fighting over the tires, and that antique, two-man tree saw blade. Hurry up!"

These "early bird" shoppers knew how to get a jump on both a garage sale, and a hot day. They turned on their headlights to start shopping!

For sale, there were boxes of old jars, a broken guitar, piles of old tires, and four lawn mowers, none of which worked! All of it gone in fifteen minutes! We even sold an antique mule harness with the mud still on it! In that first buying frenzy, using only headlights, one man said, "I don't know what this is, but I'll take it."

* * *

Remodeling "The Pit"

After the big commotion of the sale and finding restorable redwood floors underneath shag carpeting, the time began to drag. The more we worked, the worse it looked. Some days, when we became discouraged, David would take me through the house on a tour, reminding me of how it would look one day.

"You just have to visualize," he would say, reminding me of a line from one of our favorite old movies, *Mr. Blandings Builds His Dream House*. It's the part where the real estate agent sells Cary Grant and Myrna Loy a really dilapidated house. In the movie, a friend tells them, "You know, it's a good thing there's two of you: One to love it and one to hold it up!" We love that movie, but now those familiar phrases applied to us!

Squirrels and Geysers!

Looking into the attic spaces was as frightening as cave exploration! The attic area over the garage had fifteen bags of clothing, a drum set, and boxes of old books. In the space over the master bedroom, there were squirrel houses made from insulation and spit that had hardened into rock formations. Obviously, no one disturbed the squirrels for years, and they didn't take kindly to our cutting off their winter home. Squirrels screeched at us more than once, from inside the attic or while dangling menacingly from an eve. Have any of you seen an angry squirrel?

David had quite a time trying to find all the places along the edge of the house where a squirrel could enter. One afternoon, as we ate dinner David pointed to the power lines. "They're using the expressway again. Let's go!"

The "expressway" was the heavy power cable running under the telephone wires along the backside of the property. We had to rush next door and bang around on the eves of the house, and the base of a large tree out back to run them off! We considered this our after dinner workout. More than one neighbor asked why we suddenly ran next door and used brooms on the eaves of the house.

"It's squirrels!"

A week later, David heard little footsteps in the attic. He took a broom outside and banged along the overhang of the roof. As he approached the edge of the yard still looking up, one of David's legs sunk in a mud hole. When he pulled his foot out, a small geyser erupted. Great. It was the water main to the house. We called our plumber for instructions on where to dig and how deep. He told us we could lay the line and then he could check it with a simple tap into the city main for us. This would save us money. Sounded easy enough, so David rented a trencher.

Man In The Manhole

Someone should have set up the video camera. Things went well, after David remembered how to get the trencher to go forward instead of reverse. But the triumph was short lived when the machine came to the soaked ground near the wall of the house. Talk about bogged down!

With a little inspiration and rows of plywood, David made a path for the noisy thing. Every now and then he would stop and restart. The trench was like a jagged scar across the lawn.

David said, "Oh, that's straight enough!" Thankfully we were using plastic pipe which could bend a little in the "adjusted" trench.

At the manhole, near the street, David put plywood across the opening. "I'd better see if this can take the weight of the machine."

He bounced once and, without any warning sound, the wood gave way. My 6 foot one inch husband sunk to about 39 inches tall! The look on his face was priceless! After he realized he wasn't hurt, he just smiled.

"Well, scratch that idea!"

Since David wrestled the machine all over the yard, it was pretty muddy. We were to return it completely cleaned by closing time. That meant it was to be my pleasure to fill in the trench. This is an equal opportunity. David takes turns at the dishes and laundry occasionally, too. Several of our retired neighbors on their evening walks meandered by, and then groaned.

"Been there, done that. Never, again! I pay somebody else now!"

It didn't take long to get tired of explaining the gash across the yard. David came up with an exotic idea.

"That's where we buried our pet boa constrictor." It certainly cut down on more questions.

Varmints!

Every household has it varmints—the occasional mouse, a few spiders, granddaddy long legs, moths that fly into halogen lamps and stink up the room, plus odd looking, unidentifiable insects. That happens, but since this house was run down when we purchased it, we had some strange "creatures".

At the new, old blue house, as opposed to the Old red brick house, the varmints were discovered as we renovated. Hayley was five when we started, and exploring an old empty house with cobwebs and junk made it an adventure like her favorite cartoon "Scooby-Doo? Where Are You?"

"Mamma, look!" Hayley shouted. "In here under the stove."

I came in to be sure whatever she discovered wasn't moving.

"What did you find?" It was hard to see through the gray shadows in the windowless kitchen.

"It's a dinosaur!" Hayley's eyes widened with excitement.

We were looking at a complete set of white bones of what must have been a rat. It had died under the bottom drawer below a very old wall oven. *Who lived here before us—Dracula?*

"Well, Honey," I said as gently as possible. "These are the old bones of a big rat. It has to have been here a long time."

"It really IS a dinosaur!" Hayley said with great awe.

"Want to touch it?" I asked.

"No, but can you put it in a jar? You know, to show my friends?" This was just the beginning.

We called for estimates from termite and pest control, but only found three company's willing to crawl all over and under this very old house. Meanwhile, David was pulling down a stained piece of sheet rock from the ceiling in the main bathroom when he shouted, "Hey! Look at this!"

I ran in to be sure he was all right, with Hayley hiding behind me.

David pointed up. "Look what's dangling out of that hole."

A four-foot snake skin, thankfully unoccupied.

"Uh! How did that get up there?"

David answered, "Well, who knows where snakes go."

I looked around nervously. "I only saw snakes in trees in jungle movies. I didn't think they climbed into attics." A wave of horror swept over me. "Where do you suppose it went?"

"That's not the question," David said quietly. "If it was that big already, how much bigger is it now?"

Trying to lighten the mood I asked, "Haven't we seen this movie? You know, like Jurassic Park—the oh's and ah's, and then the running and screaming?" We laughed nervously, remembering that Hayley was watching.

"Ooh. Can we save it to take to school?"

"NO!" was our unanimous reply.

The first Pest Control man to arrive came in to our mostly bare house, glancing at framework for three walls we were tearing out.

"Looks like you'll have lots of room."

"Yes, eventually."

I pointed to the far wall and empty Closet which would eventually be the dining room wall.

"The crawl space is down there," I told him. "Be careful. This place hasn't been tended for a long time."

"No problem, lady," the man said. "I've seen a lot of stuff, and I don't mind spiders." The man easily fit down that small opening and disappeared.

I went on sweeping up sheet rock pieces, carpet padding, and loose boards. Suddenly out of the closet floor came the Pest Control man, white as a sheet, and covered in cobwebs.

"Hey, Lady! There's a six foot snake skin down there," he gasped. "Is the snake yours?...Never mind. I can't imagine how big the thing is now. I'll.....I'll send you an estimate," he shouted over his shoulder as he ran out the front door.

David looked at me thoughtfully. "Remember the four foot snake skin in the ceiling? Maybe that snake went under the house. I wonder how big it is now?"

"I don't want to find out," I replied. "If that seasoned pest control man runs away that fast, then I don't want something that big living under us." I shivered. "How can we be sure it isn't down there. You know, alive and waiting, like in the horror movies."

"Send the cat," David replied with a wicked grin. "She's been a real pain lately." He didn't really mean it, and thankfully, we never saw any size snake in the yard.

To be cautious, I closed up the floor crawl space and put a heavy box over it. Funny how all those boxes we moved served such useful purposes until they could be unpacked. We never solved the case of the disappearing snake, but I'm sure it moved on when the mice and rats left.

Part of the daily routine was finding strangely shaped bugs, dead or alive, as we cleared out debris, pulled up carpeting, and hauled off furniture and appliances. There was a large hole behind the refrigerator that puzzled us until we realized there was a matching hole in the wall above it. It was the size of the drain hose from the washer. Someone had run it straight down through the floor via the kitchen, since the garage had a concrete floor. I put a large, heavy box over it until David could repair that part of the floor. That area under the house is where the snake lived if I remember the trembling, pointing hand of the Pest Control man.

After seven months, we carted the last load of pulled out paneling and sheet rock. We could move into our new home. Of course, there was still the yard to clean up, but we had to move first.

The Snowball Effect

As time passed, we managed to get most of our "stuff" from the old red house and into our new blue house. Right away we noticed the 'snowball effect'. If I begin to clean the pile of "put away" things from the kitchen, it leads to boxes kept in the dining closet, which then leads to stacks in the living room closet, which leads to rearranging the linen closet. It reminded me of the game, musical chairs. Life keeps repeating itself.

One day, I was working in the kitchen for a long time, but stopped as the irony hit me. I started laughing, hysterically.

David came in from the garage, looked at the piles, stacks, and chaos of the living room and dining area with a puzzled expression.

"What happened in here?"

"Well, I tried to clean off the breakfast bar!"

"Oh, come on," he laughed. "Didn't we learn anything when we moved everything around to just to get the playpen in the living room? You forgot the plan."

"Go ahead, Plan Man," I smiled as I glanced at the chaotic mess in the garage.

"Let's see you do better in the garage!"

I winked. "We can compare notes after while, OK?"

He was about to find out it wasn't going to be easy when he moved his old work bench into the new garage. The new house would have more overall room, but NOT in the garage, and especially NOT for a workbench area.

From our old red house, it only took an hour to move shelves and the large workbench to the ready-made frame along the wall in the new garage. David thought it would keep going that fast. He discovered as he made more shelves, it required rearranging the boxes that were all ready in the garage. This led to locating boxes to move from the shed, and that led to sorting things for trash, future sale, or the attic.

It wasn't long before David came into the kitchen for a drink of water with a look of total exasperation! I glanced into the garage. There were so many piles, stacks, and boxes that it looked worse than when he started.

"Things going that well, huh?" I asked. He grimaced.

"Wanna try in here, and I'll try out there?" I offered.

"No!" he exclaimed. "There's some common principle here, but I can't pinpoint it."

"Well, it is a phenomenon called 'chaos'. Rearranging chaos produces chaos. It just means we got stuff and no place to put it!"

"One mess leads to another, right?"

"Right,' I replied. "Wanna' move back?"

We looked at each other and both shouted, "NO!"

He had a mischievous grin. "How about another garage sale?"

"NO!"

It is an amazing thing to own two homes and certainly a blessing. Regardless of the hard work to make our new home livable, and the other house ready to rent, this was just another of the adventures we shared together. I was glad to work along side David, and being part of the daily hard work we were teaching Hayley. Life lessons together are the best kind of memories.

Postman's Nightmare

The Postman, Chuck, was very confused with us living in two houses. I would see our Postman looking at the mail in his hands realizing he would be sorting for two different addresses. When I saw him drive to the blue house, then back up to the red house, I decided it was time to say something.

"Hi Chuck, can I help you?"

The mail carrier looked perplexed, then asked gently, "Did David move next door?"

"No," I laughed. "We just bought the house next door, and his name is listed first on the deed."

"Oh, good," He looked relieved. "Well then, just how many live here, besides "Occupant"? I've counted nine, this week!"

Looking back at the two houses, I smiled. "They don't look that big, do they?"

Chuck looked blank.

"Sorry! I was teasing," I added.

The explanation just became more complicated.

"Well, there'll be mail here for the former owner of the blue house and his son, maybe his daughter. Then there is my husband, our daughter, me, and mail that still comes in my maiden name. So, that would be former owners and family: A. J. Johnson, A Johnson, J. M. Johnson, B. K. Johnson and then us. D. Rader, D. W. Rader, S. A. Rader, S. Strawn Rader, H. Rader, H.E. Rader, Hayley Rader, Susan A. Rader, David W. Rader,...I think that's all."

Poor man. I assured him we'd make the official change at the post office as soon as possible to make his job easier.

"I'll mark things for those who don't live here anymore as 'moved or not at this address' so you can tell who actually lives at which house. Then, when we rent out the red house, we'll let you know to expect other names."

Chuck said, "Swell. The other guy who does this route and I are completely confused. You know we've been in this neighborhood for about twenty years. Neither of us has ever run in to so many names for two little houses."

Isn't it wonderful to give the U.S. Postal Service something new to consider?

* * *

Where do we live?

For a short time, we slept at the blue house, but continued to eat meals at the red house. It's like camping beside a restaurant. After the evening meal, Hayley would sigh and say, "I sure miss our old red house." At first we just laughed, but when I thought about it, I could understand her point.

My husband and I had moved so much as children, we never gave moving a thought! Hayley had known only one home, and our new one wasn't finished! I didn't realize that our partial move was so frustrating.

Hayley's pre-school teacher took me aside one day, and asked me where we lived, as they were putting gold stars on the board beside each child's name if they could say their address. My clever girl said, "1910 AND 1914 Ronald Street!" I explained that since we were eating at one house and sleeping at the other, my daughter was right! It was just temporarily confusing. Hayley got her gold star.

After a week of this nightly walk between houses, Hayley gave a dramatic sigh.

"Mamma, if we get another new house, could it all ready be pretty on the inside?"

I vote for that one!

We had chosen a private, half day Preschool for Hayley at age 5 based on their Bible based curriculum. Our concern over Hayley's introduction to school, good manners, and social surroundings led us to spend a great deal of time in prayer over our concern for acceptable education.

Our week day routine began with David being up first and fixing his breakfast. Then I would get up, prepare breakfast for Hayley and I before helping her get ready for school. If I made it out of bed before the alarm went off, I sometimes came out to find David still kneeling at the end of the couch in morning prayers. This is a wonderful way to start a day. What I didn't know was Hayley had observed this.

One day, I was sitting at the dining table going over a Bible lesson after David left for work and before Hayley was to go to pre-school. She came over and waited patiently for me to notice her.

"Mamma? You know how Daddy gets up early when it's still dark and makes the sun come up?"

She paused, and then whispered, "I saw him praying." I scooped her up in a hug.

What a precious moment! David's example was engraved in Hayley's heart. This made it simple for me to explain how important God is to our lives, and reminded her about the prayers we always said before going to sleep. This moment is so etched in my soul I can still hear her sweet whisper. Hayley thought her Daddy was so powerful he made the sun come up everyday, and yet he was kneeling to pray to God. She was curious what her Daddy, her hero, was praying.

Thinking back to when I was a child, there were no prayers at our house. So, David's priceless gift to me and Hayley, besides his excellent work ethic of leaving on time every work day, was 'putting God first'. This is faith in action. It was every day, not just Sunday. Those are the priceless, non-verbal lessons David taught our daughter. It only made me love him more.

***

Future Sights Of...

As we painted and remodeled our old red brick house to be ready for renting, we continued renovating our new "blue". It was all too soon, we ran out of energy, funds, and motivation. It was hard to remember what needed to be done at which house!

David's routine was to arrive home from work, eat dinner, go next door to work at our "blue" house, come back to spend the next four hours in the attic of the red house trying to re-wire for more outlets. Some evenings, he would get close to the goal, and have to stop for the night. With his humor intact, he'd leave a note beside a small hole in the wall:

"Future Site of Light Switch--Do Not Use."

When he moved to working in the kitchen, and removed part of a cabinet, the sign read:

"Future Site of Dishwasher--Insert Here."

Of course, this is funny now, but during all of this hard work on two houses, it reminded us of the Tom Hanks movie "Money Pit". For example, if I wanted to vacuum an area to clean up debris in a location it was NOT funny to be three feet short of the mess. All because the extension cord didn't reach the outlet. It made me want to get a straw to just suck it up and be done with it!

A closer outlet was needed, and when I looked down, I saw a hole in the wall, marked with a paper arrow and note: "Future site of outlet." Sometimes I would just stand there and perspire in disbelief, groan in agony, or start laughing because it meant I was done for the evening. My reasoning being that if I couldn't reach it, I couldn't clean it! That works for me! I could come back tomorrow, anyway, with another extension cord. Has anyone but me ever blown a kiss to a hole in the wall?

Meanwhile, I learned a great deal about remodeling, and had the wonderful opportunity to seal up a closet and straighten out a wall. I discovered the wonder of spackling compound. It's like very wet clay and slaps on like mud. All those mud pies as a child are now considered job training! Don't underestimate childhood experiences, as they may become a basis for tackling a new job, like wall patches, sheet rocking, or patching nail-holes. After a few hours on my latest project, I went to the mailbox before heading back to the "other" house, and waved to my neighbor.

"What's the stuff in your hair," my neighbor shouted.

Startled, I felt my hair and found hardened bits of spackling. "Oh, I've been fixing holes in sheet rock."

"Good, 'cuz it looks like bird do-do. Sort a like when you clean out a chicken coop."

"Thanks, Lulu!" After that, I wore a headscarf, hardly my most flattering hair cover. It's just another way to get a mud facial, and hair streaks all in one afternoon! Maybe as I grew older, I could use a little of this stuff for the cracks and lines appearing on my face!

* * *

How to Identify Cake

We were moving to the the 'blue house' now. I remembered I had very little furniture and just a few dozen boxes in my old red house. The place echoed when I listened to the radio or the television. Oh, how I longed for the days when there was plenty of room.

As David, Hayley and I encountered more and more varmints at the renovation site, it reminded me of my first week in my new home. Back then, I thought the small, half bathroom was haunted.

I awoke around midnight to a strange sound.

Thud. Splash. Silence. Thud, splash, thud!

What could that be? I went to the small bathroom door and looked inside. Nothing visible.

Thud. Splash. Thud.

It's in the toilet.

"OK," I said out loud. "I've seen this movie." *Who was I talking to?*

I went to the garage for the broom. Using the handle, I slowly lifted the toilet lid from the safety of the doorway.

Out jumped a huge bullfrog.

By now, my little dog was barking loudly, increasing the echo effect of the nearly empty house, and the big, wet, slimy frog was hopping toward me. *This is unreal. This isn't a monster movie, it's a frog.*

With the speed of a super hero, I scooped the frog with the dustpan, and threw him back into the toilet, slamming the lid in one swift movement.

"Uffh, Gross." One more trip to the garage for an old empty paint bucket and lid.

The Frog will live outside, and I won't be using this toilet again for a long time without first looking inside.

How could a frog get inside the house? My plumber gave me the explanation.

"This house has been vacant with all utilities shut off. I know you have an old clay section sewer line in this area. The poor frog just came up the sewer line until he encountered water in the toilet and decided to try to escape."

The poor frog gave himself a headache and me a panic attack. OK, we're even. I'll just consider that frog as house-warming gift in honor of my first mortgage. I think back to those days, alone at the red brick house, and I'm glad I'm married to David. Memories can be fun, but they aren't a place to live. If there is only the past, then the present is lost.

As all this moving, cleaning, remodeling went on now in both houses,

Hayley was growing faster and faster. Bugs and frogs, spiders and mice were becoming really 'cool' and exciting.

"Hey mom," Hayley shouted from the hallway near the sliding doors. "This spider has blue eyes...or *blue fangs*," she said as she bent closer.

"I don't care if it can sing and dance! Push it out the door. It belongs outside. Maybe Fred and Mary will like a snack."

Fred and Mary were the two new frogs that were in residency behind the air conditioning unit. Hayley liked to watch the clock around dinner to see what time of the evening Fred and Mary came onto the patio. Both frogs seemed to listen to her chatter about her day, as long as she sat on the steps and didn't come any closer.

None of us were fond of spiders. They certainly have never been one of my favorites. They're fine if they live outdoors or far away from where I am. When they crawl on the ceiling or around doors as the weather changes, it creeps me out. Hayley also began to pick up on "spider phobia", and anything that was a dark spot in a corner or on the ceiling, especially after nightfall was cause for alarm. Anyone looking up at the ceiling and then asking, "What's that?" captured everyone's attention.

One October afternoon, I saw a large black, hairy spider crawling along the kitchen ceiling. I swung a broom at it, sending it to the floor. Stomp. Get a tissue and put the flat spider into the trash. Problem solved.

October is also David's birthday, so we had chocolate cake set out on the newly completed kitchen breakfast bar. Anyone could come by during the day, take a slice and walk off. The dog could pick up scraps that fell to the floor. Anything on the counter top was still edible. Well, the dog was behind in his clean up. There was an odd black spot on the floor.

At five o'clock, David walked in from work, gave me a kiss and headed to the sink to dump out his lunch containers. I started to tell him about the day, but saw the black spot, and pointed.

"David! What is that?"

David stomped it with his shoe but with a strange expression on his face. He took off his shoe, closely examining his handy work, grossing me out and started laughing.

"It's cake."

"Cake?" I started laughing. We kept laughing.

"Wow, I really called that one!"

"Man, this is my best kill ever!" More laughter.

All the noise in the kitchen brought Hayley in to see what happened. She put her hands on her hips.

"Don't worry, Hayley, Daddy just killed some cake."

"Oooooooo—kay," Hayley said. "You two are crazy."

"Yes. *Here*, have some cake," David offered his shoe.

"Not when you have to step on it first," Hayley replied. More laughter.

Later that night, as we were getting ready for lights out, I saw a large spot on the bathroom door. David was standing by the sink brushing his teeth.

"David, look behind you. On the door. What is that?" *Spider-phobia!*

David swung at it and it flew off. "Well, it isn't cake!"

Around here, with our family sense of humor, it's an on going joke to tell *first, what something ISN'T*. Less panic. Hayley came down the hallway to say good night. David and I were still laughing.

"What happened?" Hayley asked.

"We just found out that the spot on the bathroom door isn't cake. It flew off," I added.

Hayley paused in thought. "Oh, well then, that makes it easy, 'cuz cake doesn't fly."

David and I started laughing again.

"If it WAS cake, you could lick it off your hand. OR have a really new flavor spot on the door! You know, like those flavor stickers," Hayley said.

David wiped toothpaste from his mouth. "All right. Here's the rule. IF it moves, it isn't cake."

"And if you hit it and mash it, be sure to look to see what it is before you lick it," I added.

"Unless it's on the bottom of your shoe or the flyswatter," Hayley said.

We love family conferences for sharing meaningful information!

***

CHAPTER 11

Introduction to Kindergarten, Daisies, Divine Directives

While we were finishing our move, it was time to enroll Hayley for Kindergarten. As I filled out the papers, I glanced over the list of things the teacher would be looking for in a 5 to 6 year old. I decided to "test" Hayley. Since I was a first time Mom, I may not have told her everything she needed to know. I didn't want her to be embarrassed or me to be worried about her starting school.

"Sweetie, let's go to lunch. We can come back and work on the house after a good lunch."

Hayley loved to play games with me, so I used my tea glass to make a mark on the table.

"Hayley? What's that?"

"A circle," she said, and clapped her hands together with excitement for a new game. I used some more water and drew a triangle. Hayley looked insulted and, in her patronizing voice said, "It's a triangle, Mom."

Suddenly, she perked up, and said, "Hey, I got one." She picked up her fortune cookie, broke off one end, then broke that piece in half. She laid the three pieces on the table in front of me.

"What's that?" she asked, with a twinkle in her eyes.

"Looks like three triangles," I replied.

She laughed. "No, Mom, it's a broken cookie!" Oh well, so much for kindergarten testing!

Within a week, it was the first day of school. How could Hayley be growing so fast? Out came the camera, and I took a posed picture of her carrying her school bag by the front door. It was three long blocks to the school crossing. There was a signal light so Hayley and I waited to be sure everyone stopped before crossing. I made her pose under the sign that read "Welcome Class of 2009". I think some of my joints groaned just then to remind me how old I'd be when she graduated.

At the classroom door, I gave her a hug and kiss. There she went, into the big world of kindergarten. I noticed I was the oldest mom there. One little boy looked up at me and asked, "Are you her Mom or Gramma?" His mother's face turned bright red. "Sorry 'bout that. He asks a lot of questions."

At the end of the week, the teacher took me aside.

"Mrs. Rader," the teacher said solemnly. "There seems to be a little problem with Hayley."

"Oh, no. What is it?" I couldn't imagine unless it was related to her being an only child.

"I didn't mean to alarm you," the teacher replied. "It's just at the end of the first day, one of the little boys came up and gave her a kiss on the cheek before leaving. Then, the next day, a few more boys lined up and gave her kisses, too. Now all the boys line up to kiss her goodbye."

"What in the world is that all about?" I asked.

"It's not something I wanted to draw attention to in class, but perhaps you could tell Hayley she can leave class when I dismiss everyone. You see, I lead a small parade to keep all the children together and we go to the front hall or just outside the school to wait until each child is claimed by a parent. All this kissing is holding up the parade."

We both laughed. "I've never heard of anything like this."

"In all my years of teaching, I have never had this problem." the teacher said.

On the walk home that day, I asked Hayley about getting kisses at the end of class.

"Oh, sure, mom," Hayley replied innocently. "Daddy and you always give me kisses when we're leaving."

"Well, honey," I said gently, "I think it would be best if you didn't do that at school. Just save your kisses for us. O. K.?"

"Why?" Hayley asked.

"Too many germs. Besides, it makes everyone late getting out front so their parents wonder where their little sweetie is," I added. "I would worry if you weren't right there at the front of the school when I came to get you."

Hayley nodded. "O.K."

Hayley looked up at me and added, "It was taking an awful long time, anyway."

Case closed.

＊＊

After the first few weeks of Kindergarten went by, and I survived half days at home without Hayley, I began volunteering to help at the school. It was such fun to work with the children's letter identification and reading, the odd jobs putting up bulletin board displays or working on various craft items for the teacher. This is when I met a woman young enough to have been my daughter. Christeena, a lovely petite brunette came to pick up her daughter who sported bright red hair, and another daughter two years younger.

"I'm interested in getting my daughter started in Girl Scouts," Christeena said shyly. "I wondered if your daughter would like to be in Girl Scouts."

"Sounds like fun," I replied. "What do we do?"

"Well, there is this meeting," Christeena said. "They'll give us training and a workbook. I thought it might be fun to help make friends."

This was to be the start of seven years of friendship, collaboration on everything, exhausting trips, "other people's kids", laughter, and fond memories. I didn't realize at the time, this journey along side of Hayley was also helping *me* mature. The friendships we developed, and the learning steps we took helped me redeem my lost childhood. Providence again, keeping promises from the scriptures.

Daisies

Kindergarten girls are officially named "Daisies", after Juliette Gordon Low, or "Daisy", the founder of Girl Scouts. Five and six year olds weren't interested in trivia, but they loved to play Rock, Bridge, Tree. It is a modern version of leapfrog. One girl gets down on her knees and folds herself into a 'rock'. The next is standing, legs apart as a bridge, and the last girl holds her arms out as the branches of a tree.

The laughs started with Christeena and I doing parts of the game. Nimble Christeena had no trouble, but my 48-year-old knees groaned.

Susan A. Rader

All I could think of was, this time with Hayley, playing as a child, would never come again. So—go all out!

Coordination left me years ago, but I wouldn't give up. To a few moms who never stayed and usually dropped their girls off at the meetings, it was a surprise to come back to riotous noise and see me tangled up in two sizes of hoops. Not very dignified, but dignity had nothing to do with it. Just playing, having fun, and enjoying the company. If nothing else, I considered it my exercise for the day. It certainly beat sweating to a video all by myself.

Christeena and I discovered that our girls were not the camping kind, unless there were cabins and proper toilet facilities. This suited us just fine. I camped enough in the Army. Our choices were Hampton Inn or Best Western. Even those brave moms who volunteered to caravan us to museums, nature parks, and scavenger hunts, had no trouble camping near a clean indoor pool, hot tubs, and continental breakfast.

We kept a busy schedule through those 7 years in Girl Scouts, visiting fun, odd, out of the way places, as well as historical sites. We made tombstone rubbings at the local cemetery, showing the girls tombs with special markers indicating early settlers from the first Oklahoma land run. Then, as we walked down main street to visit a mural of the Historic Chisholm Trail, we looked at old maps of the original town layout, showing the cattle routes and watering hole called Mulvey Pond.

On another outing we spent one half day behind the scenes at the Natural History Museum, learning about designing and setting up dioramas. Then how climate control cabinets now preserve some of many extinct plants and animals of Oklahoma. There were lots of 'oo's' and 'ah's', plus a "oh, that's gross!" when the museum guide pulled out a drawer full of dried bats.

Then there were Girl Scout cookies. We loved selling or eating them! With our living room furniture removed or pushed to the side, our house became the distribution point. I could use masking tape on the wooden floor to stack individual varieties that matched the order form. Then, a mother-daughter team could walk clockwise in the room to pick up the assigned cases. It helped keep order.

The mothers who volunteered to help us load and unload from the official Yukon cookie warehouse would always grab one box of their favorite kind of cookie, collapse on a stack of cookie cases, the floor or a chair if one was available, and enjoy eating half a box *before* the business of sorting cookie orders. It was tradition to have company while we ruining our diets.

Every year we set up a table in front of a busy store for cookie sales. We learned quickly which of our girls were too shy, and which girls would probably end up owning their own business. Christeena brought along her youngest daughter, pre-school, who would greet potential customers with a smile.

"Want some Skgirl Gout cookies?" Paige would shout. Her sister, Tiffani, would just laugh, and step right up to take orders. I think they'll both own businesses some day. Hayley didn't mind helping, but her shyness held her back from shouting "Get your Girl Scot cookies here!" She never complained about eating them.

Girl Scout cookie time became a way to measure the passing years. Another benchmark was moving up in the ranks of Girl Scouts to Brownies, Juniors, and finally Cadets. Time passed too quickly.

Our final Scout adventure, was a two day, over night trip exploring Western Oklahoma. Four hundred eighty six miles round trip but what sights to see! Digging for selenite crystals at the Great Salt Plains and then running for cover when a May thunderstorm took aim at our section of the Salt bed. After a stormy night at a motel, we visited Alabaster Caverns State Park to see a cave made of 'salt' and experience total darkness.

A Calling

As Hayley moved to 6th grade, she became more quiet. Stress and her asthma intensified. It was on a weeknight Hayley went to a Revival at our church tucked in with several friends. There would be a car full for the drive home, and I went to the church about the time it ended.

From the speaker on the television I could hear rousing applause and raucous shouting. It was a rally of enormous preportions. I was smiling and watching when the youth pastor made a call. Hayley came down front alone and she was followed by others. I stopped in shock. I watched with tears in my eyes as Hayley gave her life over to Jesus Christ. I really didn't hear much else that went on.

Oh, Lord, please let her be saved. When Hayley came out, she was with a group of people and it was hard to talk. So I held off until we dropped off the other girls and were on our way home.

Susan A. Rader

"Wow! You really gave your life to Christ tonight. How did it feel?"

"It was fine. I had put it off. I would have done this sooner but I thought it was harder to do."

"What?"

"Mom, it's alright. I was just shy."

"Well, I'm glad you are a Christian now. When will you be baptized?"

"This weekend. It's meant to be as soon as possibile. Jessi's coming over for it."

It was an amazing event. Here in the first of her life, she had given her self to Jesus Christ. It was an awe inspiring event. David was able to baptise her and I took the photo. It was awesome.

I shed some tears but it was expected. The funny thing was she waited so long.

A School Problem

By this time, all our girls were in 7th grade. Hayley had a rough time dealing with middle school social issues, gossip, and cliques. Shyness was her problem. One weekend, she spent more time than usual in her room. She seemed distant and we just chalked it up to her being a teenager.

Finally on Sunday night after neatly avoiding us all weekend she came out of her room in tears.

"I don't know what to do."

David and I sat down with her on the couch.

"Tell us, Hayley. Maybe we can help. You don't have to handle everything alone."

Hayley handed us a note. Scribbled on a crumpled half page were threats and list of members of her class that one young man was threatening to kill.

David and I exchanged startled glances. My heart rate went up.

"Oh Hayley, you have worried about this all weekend! You should have shared it with us."

She was weeping. "I knew I had to tell someone. I've been praying about it. I just don't know what to say. I'll have to tell who the note is from and where it was to go. It was passed to me, and I kept it."

We comforted Hayley, and together in our family huddle, prayed with her.

David spoke up. "Hayley, your Mom and I will go with you Monday to see the Principal before school. You won't be alone. It's the right thing to tell the Principal about this before school starts."

Hayley seemed calmer after sharing the load with us, and with the proof in her hands it was just a matter of getting to the school office as early as the teachers. She wouldn't be facing this alone. Why she felt she had to do this alone, we don't know.

The Principal knew the young man who wrote the death threat, and was surprised. He had transferred from another school for reasons not made known to us.

"He clearly has issues we weren't aware of," the Principal said as she put the note down on her desk. She looked at Hayley.

"You are exceptional student, not to have shown the note to anyone and then bring this matter to me privately. It must have concerned you all weekend. Thank you for coming to me first. I know his parents--his family are my friends. We will get this taken care of immediately."

Hayley took a deep breath. "Will he be in a lot of trouble?"

"Yes. This is serious, but he definitely needs help and we will get him the help he needs."

The Principal wrote a note for Hayley who was now late for her first class.

"You won't be marked as Tardy today. Go on to class and try not to worry about it. He won't be hurting anyone at school. Please continue to keep this to yourself."

Hayely agreed. When we went out of the office into the now vacant hallway, we huddled together with our arms around Hayley and David said a quick 'thank you' prayer. What could have been a school shooting and suicide was nipped in the bud. Providence answered our daily prayer to keep the local schools safe.

The young man missed a week of school, and during that time, not knowing what else might be going on, I felt it was prudent, as a safety-measure to meet Hayley after class. It was my helicopter Mom status—hovering near my daughter to protect her as long as I could.

The following Monday at the end of the last class, Hayley went to see a teacher about an assignment. While I waited in the outer hall, I saw the young man in question. Hayely was now out of my sight and I saw him enter the same class pod. He was hefty, and a foot taller next to my tiny daughter. Anxiously, I rushed to the doorway. The young man had his head down and was speaking quietly to Hayley. I was nervous wondering what was taking place, but just watched. Shortly, Hayley walked away and we headed toward the car. Hayely was sniffling.

"Are you alright? What did he say to you?"

She took a few minutes to compose herself.

"He thanked me."

Hayley's burst into tears.

"He said thank you for getting me some help. I'm sorry I wrote the note. You are a real friend not spreading this around, but going to the Principal. No one but us knows about it. I'm getting some help with my anger problem. Thanks. It won't happen again."

Not only is this amazing to me in today's cruel, selfish world, but miraculous. Hayley had prayed from Friday night until Monday about what to say because she knew what had to be done.

Knowing that you must do the right thing doesn't always follow that one has the courage to do it. When we prayed with her that Sunday evening, we asked for a peaceful solution and help for that young man. The young man accepted that he needed help. That was another miracle. God granted a gentle ending in contrast to the violence threatened in the note.

YOU DON'T HAVE TO MOVE THE WASHER TO MAKE TOAST

***

A Lion Cub For The Judge

As Hayley spent more and more time with her schooling, David and I found a place at Lions Club. Through this organization we volunteered for parades as well as service projects, and met a number of amazing people. One was a District Judge.

The Judge, a charter member of our club, could tell amazing stories for exercising brain cells. Some of his cases gave us pause to consider what it really meant being the one on the judge's bench.

Since he was a praying man, dedicated to justice, he also knew the value of prayers for wisdom. The Judge was a vital part of our club's activities. As happens, his schedule of cases would be heavy for weeks at a time, causing him to miss our regular club meeting.

The District Judge also belonged to several service clubs, keeping him busy. He had a great sense of community involvement and tried to attend every local club meeting. When he had missed several in a row I called his house to remind him of the next meeting and could only leave a message.

A few days later, I was overwhelmed thinking about going to visit the Judge at the court house in El Reno. Then, I thought I might just mail him a card. *No.* The more I resisted going, the more I was led to go, but I needed to make a "Missed You At the Meeting" card on the computer *and take a present.* I had to take a present and go today. *A present? What kind?*

I went to the store after getting the card made, and was looking for something that I couldn't identify that would be a present to go with the card when I came across an adorable stuffed lion. It was wearing a little hat and vest and holding a golf club.

Well, I bought it. It seemed to be a good gift item for him. I raced back to the house and altered the tiny little vest with a computer print out of the Lions Club International emblem to put on the vest. To get the vest on the lion, I had to cut away the strings holding the golf club. I didn't think the Judge played golf anyway, but the 4" tall stuffed lion was made to stand up, and his head was tilted back as if looking up at the sky. It would have to do.

I drove like crazy over to the courthouse in El Reno, got through security, and rushed upstairs. The Judge was coming from his court room.

187

It hadn't dawned on me that he might not be available or in court. I waved at him, and when I reached him I nodded in approval at his 'judgely robe' and said,

"Wow, Judge, you look good."

He smiled and continued on to his office with me following. In my exuberance, I began babbling. After all, how was I going to explain the real reason I came to visit when I didn't really know. That didn't make sense either!

"Hey, did they throw you off the bench?" my idiot voice asked.

The Judge's secretary gasped and looked wide eyed. The Judge turned to me and said, "I could hold you in contempt of the court for that and charge you with a felony."

I could have melted into the floor. I gasped and stuttered, "Oh, J-Judge, I was just k-kidding and I had no idea I shouldn't say anything like that."

He narrowed his eyes at me and then he sighed. There was long suffering in that sigh!

"Well, since I know you so well, I can let this pass. You say a lot of odd things. Just remember, we're not at club right now. Come into my office." *Oh, I thought I'd drop dead right there!* I followed meekly.

The Judge put up his robe and sat down at his desk with another sigh. "Well, what can I do for you today, Susan?"

"Oh, I just wanted to drop in to see how you were. I know you get really busy and you haven't been at several of our last meetings. I have some handouts and the club newspaper for you. And here are the tickets for the pancake breakfast, too."

The Judge took these items and seemed to thaw a little more. This seemed like a good time to give him the card and the toy lion. BUT I FELT STUPID.

"And, I made you a little card to go with this lion." I put the lion with the vest on his desk and he looked at me like I had three heads. What was this grown man, a District Judge going to do with a little toy lion wearing a Lion's vest? My heart was pounding very hard, *but I had to do this.*

"You see, this little guy thinks you've been working really hard and you need to come to club and let off some worries with friends."

At this point, like more of a moron, I tipped the lion onto all fours and since its little head was looking up with pleading eyes, I used a little play voice and asked, "Won't you come outside and play today?"

I can't tell you how stupid this is to describe, but God had a very good reason for me doing this idiot act. I just didn't know it yet.

The Judge just looked at me as if he was watching me loose my mind. It might fall out right there on his desk and fade away.

"Aaa. Thanks. I don't have one of these."

AWKWARD! I stood up and said, "Well, thanks for letting me make a fool out of myself, but at least I saw you smile once today. Please, come back to club soon. Everyone asks about you. Don't forget the pancake breakfast—if you can make it. Thanks again for not arresting me!"

I left feeling like I had made more of a complete fool of myself than I had in my entire life and then berated myself all the way home. Somehow, I couldn't shake the feeling that no matter how I messed up that meeting with the Judge, *I had been compelled to go and take the toy lion.* I could now relax, except for the concern that the Judge would never come back to our club!

When I reached home, I called David. "David, I lost my mind today. You know how I sometimes just have to go do something right now? Because it's God calling. I have to because somebody needs something."

David laughed. "Yes. Like that lady who came into Wendy's when we were in Illinois. She was so filled with sorrow over her daughter's death, you said you could hear her. Then you went over and got her talking then prayed with her."

"Yes, it was like that one. Well, I just had to go see the Judge today."

"OK. Tell me about it."

"Ugh, David, I don't think he'll ever come back to club. It began with him on my mind, and I wanted to be sure he was reminded of this week's meeting. I could have sent the newsletter, but then, I brought him a toy."

"A toy what?"

"Oh, it was a lion with a little vest. I cut off the golf club and put a Lions International symbol on the vest, and then....oh, I made a fool of myself. I tipped the lion over and asked if the Judge could come and play today, you know like I was talking to a little kid."

David laughed again. "I would have loved to have seen that! What did he say?"

"He just gave me a weak smile and said, thanks, I don't have one of these."

"Well, the Judge sees a lot of people and if nothing else, later today,

Susan A. Rader

he may just get a laugh out of this. I'm sure he'll come back to club when he can. He gets tied up with case loads. He knows you mean well."

"OK. It's just that I *had* to take a toy. That was as clear as if it were written in the sky. I don't know what this was about but I really wasn't acting like a Lions Club President."

Later that evening, the Judge called me around 8 p.m. David and I were reading magazines and talking. I saw his name on caller I.D.

"Oh, David, it's the Judge. I hope I can explain myself." I lifted the phone and said hello.

The Judge said something along these lines:

"Susan, I wanted to thank you for coming by my office today. I know I was a little sharp with you, but I wanted to call you to tell you something." He paused. "I had been praying about a case that was coming up this afternoon when you arrived. You picked up that little lion and showed me—no you *reminded me* that I have two sons, now grown. *I had forgotten how to play*. I used to know how to play with my sons. When you made the lion talk to me, you reminded me that kids need to be reached a certain way. I had a terrible decision to make today about the custody of two young boys. I can't give you any details, but I had to interview the youngest boy first. He saw the little lion and wanted to hold it. We played with it for a little while and he began talking to me. The older boy liked my autographed O.U. football, so we played catch and he talked to me."

"I believe God sent you as an answer to my prayer about how to decide their case. You reminded me to relax a little and play. It made all the difference. Thank you very much."

Believe me I was overwhelmed with relief and with thanks to God. "You're welcome, Judge. I just had to come today. I can't explain it, but I had to bring that lion and come up there and make a fool out of myself. I'm glad you don't think I'm as crazy as I thought I was all day."

"No, Susan. You are just you. Thank you."

David was as moved as I was.

"I'm so glad he called me. I've been wondering if I lost my mind, but couldn't come up with one reasonable explanation for taking a toy, but I just had to. It's amazing that God would use me."

"No, I don't think so. It's a gift you have. Remember, at Bible study we learned about the Holy Spirit giving us a gift when we are saved. Not a talent, but a gift. I think that's yours. You are easily moved and God doesn't explain. You just go and do it."

David took my hand and kissed it. "I think it's a great gift and I love the stories that come out of this."

It's a relief to know I can be used, when the results are a special gift God wants to give to someone who needs it.

* * *

Show Me

I think I should have been born in Missouri instead of Texas because I am a "show me" person. My prayers at this time had been heavily laden with agony over my being a prisoner at home due to poor health.

When I go in public, with my inner ear problem, I can stagger or have to hang onto someone else. Just a few days ago, it happened at a store, and I saw judgmental looks aimed at me, and pitying looks for my daughter Hayley. We casually entered a clothing store, and I promptly and quite suddenly staggered into a rack of clothing. I have pleaded in prayer, and maybe this day was just a reminder that Our Heavenly Father hears our prayers. This would be a little "wide place in the road" to give me hope in waiting patiently for him. Since He knows my stubbornness, as well as my joy at being able to laugh at myself, He decided to show me how quickly my health situation could change for the good. It was a nice thought. I could stay home until I returned to normal.

Laughs from the storm cellar

Tornado season can be year around in Oklahoma. There are huge weather swings that can shut down the city. So now, when it's time to change smoke alarm batteries and calendars in January, I schedule a complete check of the storm shelter from batteries, water, tools and testing the radio settings. I sit down there with pad and paper, imagining what might happen or what we might need—all those things we see in movies that happen once in a zillion times. This year, I stayed a little longer than I planned, but when I climbed out, I had a lot more ideas on contingencies.

My 'clean the storm shelter day' was foggy with cold rain. One of those days meant for cleaning out over looked places, reading a book,

Susan A. Rader

or taking a nap. I decided it was perfect for going down into the tornado shelter since the possibility of live bugs was slim to none.

We have a "Flat Safe"—one of those clever inventions. It sinks an eight person metal box into the floor of the garage so neatly it is hardly noticeable. There is a red 'stomp-on-it' button that releases the sliding top. With a push of my foot, a hole opens in the floor, and with flashlight in hand, I can climb down six wide steps, to disappear beneath the David's classic Mustang. It reminds me of Grandma's root cellar, cool and earthy.

A clever device used to pull the lid closed also doubles as a stair rail. It fits into a neatly imprinted hole in the concrete framework. Instant access to safety! As I descended the steps, I hit my head on something. Note: Duck head to avoid hitting license plate. Move David's Mustang up a foot.

Using my flashlight in the shadow of the car, I scanned the opening. Cobwebs hung loaded with sawdust and leaves. Using my trusty mini-vac, I soon cleared the opening, beginning a slow descent, vacuuming as I went. I switched on my husband's work light to see dead bugs and leaves on the floor. It reminded me of previews for horror movies. This wasn't going to be such a boring job after all. Cold, rainy days and imagination can be very entertaining.

When I reached the last step, I realized the acoustics in this long metal box were going to give me a headache. I shut off my hearing aids. Each noise I made reverberated as if I were inside a large bell, like shouting in an empty school hallway. Anything I hit with the mini-vac created new sound effects.

With some thought to counting all of this as aerobic exercise, I went up and down the steps, slowly removing the contents of the storm shelter from last year. There were sacks, bottled water jugs, a First Aid Kit, 3 Tool Boxes, hard hats, and a game box. On the bench was a storm radio with the batteries nearly dead. I poked my head up level with the garage floor, like a prairie dog, to place the radio by the back tire. *I think I'll completely empty the area.* Soon there would be just me, the trash sack, and a flashlight left. Time to reassess.

As I sat there in the cold hole in the garage floor I laughed. This was silly. My laughter caused an echo. What an absurd thing to do on a rainy afternoon with no thunderstorms in the forecast. Oh, well, I'm here and 'being prepared' is still a good motto.

I looked up at the opening in the garage floor and marveled again at this ingenious use of space and design. At the moment, the entire edge of the opening was cluttered with tools, electrical cords, and the supplies I removed from the shelter. What a mess to clean up when I was finish down here. Our storm shelter was just a little over four years old, and we were grateful for this expanded space—no longer having to depend upon a smaller reinforced closet.

As I looked at my list again, I was thinking of getting a new set of cards, a new pencil or two, even a dry erase board to add some fun if we were stuck down here during an actual disaster. If we were trapped by multiple storms and forced to stay for hours in the shelter, we might need distractions. Listening to the warnings over the radio, and praying for those in the paths of the storms, begins to wear on the nerves.

I turned my hearing aids back on. At present, all was calm. My husband was off to the store getting supplies for the week, and my daughter was in her room finishing college homework. The house was quiet enough for me to notice the cold north wind whistling around the garage door. I guess all that sound was covered up while I was vacuuming, sweeping, and moving supplies out of the shelter.

One more thing to check. I needed to remind myself of exactly how the door lid worked from inside. Using the flashlight, I saw the inside handle. Yes, just pull hard to slide the lid toward the latch until it locked. *Pull. Click.* There, I'm in the dark. Lock works. Good.

Now, to exit, I just pull down on the small "T" handle under the latch. O.K. *Pull down harder on the handle under the latch.* Try pushing on the latch. O.K. Try pulling the metal lock downward to help the "T" handle move. *Well, this is unexpected.* I sat back down. Who would have thought it! I can't get out.

What now? I laughed again and it echoed. This really isn't funny. *Yes, it is.* I think I saw this in some skit from a play. I began laughing again until my sides hurt. O.K., somebody will check on me after while. I hope soon. I'm not wearing a watch.

Try the whistle. Tweet, tweet, tweet. *Oh, shut off your hearing aids, Susan.* Three short, three long, three short—that's S.O.S. isn't it? I tried this several times and only managed to get an ear overload with the echo.

My daughter ought to hear me. After all, she calls me "Disaster Mom".

"Mom, the day you can't find something to worry about will be the day you die."

O.K. From under the garage floor, I decide to use the end of the winch as a gong. It seems heavy enough to make a pretty loud sound against the lid.

BONG BONG BONG! *Oh the reverberation!*

Perhaps, instead of S.O.S., I should try "Oh, Susannah!" *No!* Then the tune will be stuck in my head for the rest of the night. My husband should be back soon. After all, his list wasn't that long.

Was that a shadow I saw by the narrow opening at the edge of the shelter lid? I switched on one hearing aid.

"Mom?"

"Yes?"

"Are you O.K.?"

Now, I'm laughing, and it's really hard to talk."Oh, yeah. I tried S.O.S. I was going to play "Oh Susannah!" but you finally came out here to check on me."

"What's wrong?"

"The door won't open," I replied.

She laughed. "You're kidding, right?"

"Didn't you hear me blowing the whistle and banging on the lid?"

"Sure, but you've been making funny noises since you started cleaning down there."

"Well, before I lose my sense of humor, could you push down on that red button and let me out?"

My daughter laughed, again. "Sure, but now all I can think of is "Oh Susannah". It'll be stuck in my head all night."

"Well, I'm not going to play it with the lid closed," I answered. "The echo gives me a headache!"

Isn't it strange that my obsession with safety is no surprise to my family? But then again, I gained insight if we are ever trapped after a storm.

***

CHAPTER 12

4,500 square foot Mural

Most of our social life revolved around Hayley's school activities: Friday night football games when the marching band played, award's ceremonies, and school concerts. In her last two years of high school, Hayley enrolled in classes to earn college credit. She wanted to pursue an art degree by first taking two years of Graphic Art design. She loved the class, and her second year, took First Place at the SKILLS USA State level contest, to earn a place at the National Vocational Technical School. She competed against those who were already working full time as graphic artists. It was a great way to finish her certification as Graphic Designer.

Shortly after, Hayley started her college art classes. This is when an opportunity of a life time came her way. The children's area at our church needed a mural. Art departments from colleges in the area submitted designs but the cost was prohibitive. The task was a 4,500 square foot mural.

Being recommended by a church elder, Hayley placed a bid at a fair price for a beginning artist. Her largest painting that sold was 20 inch x 30 inch oil. This project was going to take a lot of prayer.

"The Safari room is huge." Hayley looked thoughtful.

"Well," I asked. "Do you want to do it?"

"Oh, I can paint realistic animals, it's the background details that could take forever."

"Well, I'm not bad at backgrounds, and we can use textured rollers, sponges,and even a rag to make vague looking trees and bushes. Then closer vines or trees can be painted over that background. A narrow roller on an extender pole, can draw lines with brown or dark green to look like shadows of trees further back. You're good at colors," I said.

Susan A. Rader

"Once you start, there will be no turning back," David added. "I won't be able to help much during the week, but I can start by showing you how to place a bid, figure cost estimate, a reasonable time frame and hourly wage. You won't make much depending on an hourly wage, but this is about painting God's Creation, and make the room colorful."

Hayley nodded. "It would be amazing to paint something that big. It's not the money. It's the idea of creating a piece of artwork that big. I already have an idea for the panels."

"Well, let's go over to the church with Dad and measure the room," I said.

David replied. "Yes, and when we get back, I'll show you how to figure square footage for the amount of paint you need, and approximately how long this will take. I'll dimension the room and with auto-CAD, make you a scale model. I work with these things all day long. You can tape the scale panels together to show doors, classrooms, and the actual mural areas. It will be part of submitting your bid."

After the measurements were taken, David drew the room to scale and printed several copies for Hayley to use for sketching. We prayed about it for a week. Hayley turned in her bid with a color pencil sketch that only took her 2 hours to draw. She really did have a vision in her mind of the finished mural. Her bid was accepted.

The 'Creation Theme' went well with the Safari sign marking the children's ministry wing. It also tied in with the stuffed animals on display, donated by a man who collected them on safari. This Adventure would change us all and have God's signature on every step of the four month process.

During a family brain storming session, we listed needed materials, types of brushes, buckets, pails, and roller pans. Hayley chose the color pallet of warm tones. We were all practiced wall painters. All of us spent time on our fixer-upper house. Of course, this was to be a gigantic painting, not just putting colors on walls. With God's help, we turned our newly purchased, but long neglected house into a home.

Then, Hayley repainted her room several times, and recently decided to paint the ceiling. I came in to watch, astounded at her artist's view.

"How do you know where to put the sky blue?"

"I see the clouds, Mom. I'm painting blue sky around them."

From her early days of pencil drawing while watching television, we were amazed at her ability. David and I never doubted Hayley had an artist's gift, from God, but when we stood inside the Safari children's wing, we wondered if this was too big a task for a 19 year old asthmatic, and her 62 year old mother with Menieres and Absence seizures. This was not only a big adventure, it would be a test of perseverance.

The East and West walls were 127 feet long with little grass hut facades around inset classrooms. The South wall was thirty feet wide, with large glass panels and exit doors from the floor to eight feet. It was a bright room, letting in lots of light, but desperately in need of warm colors.

On the original white walls, someone lovingly hand painted Savannah grass completely around the wall base. The hand painted detail was astounding, and blended with the 'grass hut' facades marking classroom areas. To Hayley and I, the idea of painting over this labor of love was heart breaking.

As we studied the room, David suggested we leave the walls alone in the classroom in-set, there by saving the hand painted grass. If we left the front of each class room its original white, the color background and mural animals would accentuate the 'grass hut and bamboo poles' facade. This idea was heaven ordained. We could cut out a large area that would not need painting. The mural would be on the flat wall panels between classrooms. The mural could be painted from the floor trim to the 18 foot mark, then go up and over each classroom.

Buying The Supplies

In the first few weeks, looking at this enormous room, we wondered if we were up to the task.

We needed to build stamina. Hayley's asthma flared immediately as we both adapted to the allergens in the area as well as the summer heat. We both felt very small and weak. Those were the stop and pray days. God is much bigger than any task He gives us. It was obvious at each open door, that He had given this job to Hayley. There would be no turning back. But isn't that what builds character? A challenge and then growing inside to greet the task, trusting God to provide the talent and energy to complete the job He wants done.

After going over the room several times to locate fire alarms, thermostats, emergency lighting, and room signs, we were off to buy supplies.

The day we purchased the paints, drop cloths and other equipment, we ran about one hundred dollars over budget. But at the cash register, we found a blessing. The paint Hayley chose was on sale that day. Within two weeks, we ended up returning some of the materials deemed not needed and broke even. All the materials piled in her Jeep Wrangler, once hauled inside, took up half of a class room.

We began with night work, using a projector to outline Hayley's design of the fourteen foot giraffe, six foot ibex, and the eight foot zebra. These animals would be painted about four to five feet from the floor to set them in specific scenes. Hayley wanted to be positive of the scale for these walls. Other than these three projected outlines, Hayley hand painted all the other animals from photos, estimating scale and adjusting as needed. I was definitely glad my job, at least at first, was masking off areas, putting down drop cloths, and rolling whatever background color she chose for each panel. I was totally intimidated by this room. Why? Each panel was really a canvas, and required uneven painting to create layers. That is a lot harder then painting a wall solid yellow or green.

Only by God's grace empowering the gifts He had given Hayley and I, could we have accomplished so much. However, those first few weeks did not go well.

The starter panel, the Giraffe Wall, seemed to have all the wrong colors. This was when Hayley discovered the plain 'white' wall paint had a subtle blue tint. That tiny bit of blue turned her lovely warm yellow color pallet into something resembling smashed peas. A change was needed in the color pallet.

A Change of Color

We were exhausted working 8 hours a day, and so far, the room looked like a careless mess. I had hand painted over the grass underpainting, going over these areas several times trying to get the 'grass' to disappear. The yellow background was greenish, and looked sickly.

As Hayley labored over creating dry savannah grass and the fourteen foot giraffe, I began the transition colors to the jungle. As I rolled the bright forest green I found it did not completely cover the wall with one coat. At first this alarmed me but then I remembered total coverage was not desirable! This was background for a gigantic painting, so those white patches showing through, as well as patches of overlap paint began to be the backdrop of jungle. At this stage, for those onlookers who brought their children to fall classes, the room just looked sloppy. People don't think of 'wall paintings' as gigantic canvas which requires layers, texture and a variety of colors to provide depth.

The area from the Giraffe Wall to mid room was Savannah gold and orange, then within a few feet changed to the lush green of jungle. All of it from the first wall to mid point looked streaked. Hayley was totally frustrated.

"This is a mess! This color pallet should be working."

"Well, you're the artist, go over and buy different paint. We pick up the tab if something doesn't work. In for a penny. In for a pound."

Hayley looked askance. "What?"

"Never give up, never surrender. Don't quit. Persevere. And, I'm now out of wise sayings."

"Thanks, Mom. Just keep thinking in terms of wise sayings," Hayley replied. "I'll be back in a while with something that works."

Hayley went back for two gallons of paint. She now knew to account for the blue green tint appearing in her first choice of paints.

In two hours, the Giraffe Wall was saved. I had the opportunity to 'mow' the grass down along the floor trim. Much easier to do with a paint roller than a mower! It would now be a matter of repainting the blades of grass with the new highlighter color.

'Viola! As Hayley pointed out, this first 18 x 18 foot panel with it's multi layers was the richest in texture. Her new color selection made the dried savannah grasses turn to deep gold and bronze. Thanks to the set back of this wall, the panel was getting rave reviews.

A Rowboat

As we continued to put layer upon layer on each of the panels, the background began to suggest depth. We were only at the beginning layers, and frankly, the room looked terrible by the time fall classes began. But this was a huge canvas, awaiting the colors God inspired. We kept wishing we could work on the under coat longer before the classes started, since it would have been more aesthetically pleasing for those who brought in their children. Oh, well, we put up with 'ugly'.

We didn't have to concern ourselves about all the attractive, detailed foliage needed as background for the jungle areas. God provided the hand painted grass which shone through the jungle green paint. Seeing the outline of the grass through the first rolled layer, Hayley mixed me a dark green.

"Here, outline the foliage for shape, then fill it in. This keeps the realistic blades of grass. And use this light frosted green as highlights. Don't use all the blades that show through. Cover over some so the grass looks natural. Not uniform like a copy. Use the base green to blot out some blades so it doesn't show through." This was my graduation from taping surfaces and rolling background to apprentice highlighter.

Near the front of the Safari by the check in desk, there was a large uncluttered area which set off the fenced playground. Right in the center of this area was a row boat named the S.S. Kid. Perfect for putting our lunch coolers, water bottles, purses, and jackets. Also, a great place to have lunch. We had been enjoying our 'boat breaks' for nearly a month when we started allowing our imagination to take flight.

I leaned over the edge of the low boat as if staring in to great depths.

"That looks like deep water."

"Hmm, better get your hand back in the boat, Mom. I think that's a shark." Hayley and I began laughing.

About this time Alan, the building manager, came in and gave us a strange look.

"Be careful, Alan, we think there's a shark near the boat." Hayley and I laughed again.

"Could be. We get spiders, crickets, and other things in here during the summer." Funny man leaving us with that encouraging thought.

True to his prediction a few days later when I moved a paint can, I saw something huge and black scurry out of sight to hide in our supply area. This was worse than when we fought varmints at home.

"Hayley! Come here." I rushed out of the classroom wide eyed.

"What?"

"Something really big, hairy, and moving fast just went behind the last row of paint cans. Are you up to a hunt?"

We gave each other wilting glances.

Hayley was grossed out. "Guess I am. We need the paint."

We armed ourselves with rubber mallets. Using roller extension poles, we took turns moving paint cans until the big black and brown spider came scrambling toward us. I don't think either of us squealed but our revulsion filled the room. With two of us hammering away, we finally landed a crippling blow. The spider kept moving. It was as large as a tarantula but didn't quite look like one.

As fall approached, more and more 'critters' filtered in from the field outside. We were constantly coming across an unwanted bug, so it wasn't surprising to see one of us stomping on something or jumping up from the floor where we were sitting.

"Okay down there?" I shouted.

"Could be. Not sure if I got it, but I'm not getting any closer to see."

"Want help?"

"No, Mom. I'm sure I'm bigger than this thing, but you can be back up!"

After a momentary scuffle, with retreat and then attack, I heard Hayley.

"Got it. Crickets are creepy. When they move slowly they creep like spiders, then they scare you by jumping. I'm telling you, the next time I see one *this big*, I'm going to give it a paint brush and put it to work!"

Hayley Picks the Perks

Hayley spent her evenings printing off more pictures of African flora and fauna, finding unusual animals, plants, flowers and butterflies. Then there were photos of waterfalls, rocks, trees, and the very strange Baobab tree. It looks as if it were tossed away only to land upside down, roots at the top. Her research was in depth, and every scene had elements of shapes, colors, and highlights to create depth. The animals and plants, flowers and butterflies were real enough to touch. I often thought they would step out of the scene to wander the room.

One of the most wonderful gifts God gave to me was this opportunity to work with Hayley and watch her mature. I was amazed as her talent grew, standing in wonder at animal paintings so realistic I expected them to turn and look at me. This was part of the transition of me letting go of 'my little girl', and learning to appreciate her on the adult level. What a gift Providence gave to me during this time. My mother and I never bonded like this nor did she ever see me as an adult. This time is still precious to me.

A few weeks into the project, one of the church members sent over a scissor lift. It's like a moving scaffold. Hayley could use it to safely stand

Susan A. Rader

to complete the sky, and a 30 foot wide by15 foot high Kilimanjaro at the south end. There was a breathtaking view of the room from there.

The hardest part of the scissor lift was learning to drive across stick on carpet tiles. It was my job to follow behind the machine, replacing pulled off carpet pieces, and sometimes weigh them down until they reattached themselves to the concrete floor beneath. Hayley was an excellent driver, with just a few slow motion collisions. I confined my use of the lift to 'up and down' only.

As the room progressed, and Hayley's artistic ability increased, we were able to enjoy the children's response to butterflies and flowers. With each panel filling up with multi-layered backgrounds for depth, the 'ugly room' began to come to life. The Tiger coming out from the bamboo grass was so real, it startled Alan, the building manager when he was working to clean classrooms one afternoon.

"Whoa!" Alan jumped back.

Hayley and I laughed.

"Gotcha!" I said, and Hayley was laughing.

"That's very realistic. I didn't know you finished it." Alan smiled. "But over there, I saw a paper sack taped to the wall with 'Baby Elephant' written on it. I don't know what art school you're going to, Hayley, but that's not the shape of a baby elephant!"

Alan paused at the yellow parrot in flight against the dark jungle green.

"Nice bird". Alan was a man of few words, but a constant help either with the temperature in the room, equipment we might borrow, or positive comments as the mural progressed.

*　*　*

The Wall of Contrasts

The 'Watering Hole' panel with waterfalls stubbornly refused to match Hayley's drawing. It put up as much of a challenge as the Giraffe Wall. No matter what colors we used on this 'wall of contrast', it looked flat.

We named it the 'wall of contrasts' because on one side of the watering hole stood a dry sandy mound with pale dusty ground and parched grass. On the other side of the watering hole there was a generous waterfall spilling from a hard granite outcrop into a pool. Side by side in the water was a baby elephant splashing in the shallows, and a bright white water bird at the edge of the waterfall.

Hayley drew the boundaries of the huge rock wall that covered half of two panels, going up and over a classroom. Above the grass hut facade was a granite textured rock with a reposing leopard. Using a texture sponge, my job was to make the rock outcrop on the wall match the color of the leopard's rock. But, the problem was, the rock looked two dimensional.

"Hayley, what are we to do about the cracks, crevices, and shadows on the granite? I can't get this to look like your drawing. Can you draw lines for me or what?"

"Oh, I don't know. I'm frustrated with this. I need to get back on schedule with animal details, and do final touches on the watering hole. Then there's the waterfalls. I have the base coats for the egret and the baby elephant. But, I can't think right now. I have to leave for my afternoon class. Let's pray about it."

Hayley and I spent some time in focused prayer. This was an important panel, very dramatic, and would be a favorite with the little kids. It was the closest wall to the fenced-in toddler safety playground.

The dynamics on this wall needed to be outstanding. At the base of the waterfall was a beautiful egret with white dry feathers and nearby, the leathery baby elephant, splashing in the water. So much had to be

Susan A. Rader

done with this wall, and we were behind schedule. God was listening and gave us the answer.

Being left alone, I ate my lunch in the boat while staring at this wall. Part way through my sandwich, I had the urge to try making a 'crack' using the texture sponge. It seemed to be an easy fix--if the crevice I painted looked awful, I could dab over it.

I moved the ladder to the wall and climbed half way up to be at the corner of the grass hut facade. The top of the waterfall was just above the classroom. This granite outcrop came up to and under the leopard rock continuing to the other side of the classroom. On the paint tray, I dipped my texture sponge into the black paint.

"Well, Lord, we could use some help."

Perched on the ladder thinking I could cover over a mistake, I drew a wide black line onto what could be a slight shade change in the texture pattern. It was curved at the end.

Scary. OK, this didn't look too bad, and so I feathered the light gray and white into the edges of my black streak. I climbed down the ladder. I did not have Hayley's ability to see the entire section without making myself dizzy.

Hmm. It looked pretty good and I decided to climb back up to deepen the lower curved area. Suddenly, I could see the next craggy split in the rock, *as if being led to see where the cracks and crevices went. This is amazing.* I think by now I was talking to myself. Then I saw another and another, working faster and faster, until I covered the area, blending, and shading, as if by Providence. I felt led to move from one spot to the next, like being shown outlines.

Since I suffer with vertigo, I always keep one hand clamped to a rail or in this case the ladder. My hand was nearly numb, but it was a good safety feature. When I realized I needed to move the ladder to the other side of the classroom, I was so focused on the location of the next crevice, I started to step off the ladder at five feet above the floor. When I took my eyes off the mural, I was surprised to still be on the ladder. There had been no sense of dizziness or fear of falling, but my heart was pounding from working so intensely. What a surprise. My focus was on what needed to be finished, not where I was.

I could see all the shadowed places, as if they were marked for me. And I never saw my hand move so fast. This is hard to explain, other than Guidance in answered prayer. God is able to give us the tools needed to accomplish things for Him, as well as give us knowledge or enhance skills we may possess. It was an exhilarating two hours on that ladder.

Once on the floor, I stepped away from the wall and couldn't believe what I saw. This was just like Hayley's sketch, with depth in the pool and shadows in weathered crevices. While painting for two hours, I had not once stepped back to see the over all look of the wall. *Thank you, Lord.* I snapped a photo with my camera phone, sending it to Hayley.

My phone chimed in reply.

"Mom, Did you do that?"

I replied with a text. "With God's help! I could *see* what it looked like!"

Hayley typed back. "It's just like I pictured. I can't wait to get there to put in the waterfall!"

As soon as Hayley finished class, she rushed back to see the wall.

"Wow, it's better in person."

"Oh, Hayley what an experience. It was like someone was right there encouraging me, showing me where to put the next crack. I couldn't seem to paint fast enough. But look around this room at all the amazing things *you have done*. Everyone's still talking about your 30 foot Kilimanjaro, and you couldn't see it all at once. God simply used me this time to answer your prayer, and get us back on schedule. Now, I want to see that beautiful waterfall come down across these stones."

I handed her a brush.

"Your turn!"

Susan A. Rader

***

Earthquake

As we finished rolling the larger areas, I was left with more time on my hands. Hayely had helped me buy a newer model phone so I could text her from anywhere in the Safari area or when she was at school. I was becoming proficient at texting. My hearing loss made it nearly impossible to understand something she shouted from the other end of the room. The echo in the large room didn't help. Texting was the answer.

We worked through July and August heat, being startled by sudden bangs and groans as the metal roof expanded from mid morning to cooling around four o'clock. Adding a hot summer wind that shifted the building, and the sounds blended in an odd sort of symphony. Hayley started wearing her head set to ignore the cacophony, choosing to hear her favorite music while she painted.

There were agonizingly long hours, and for each area finished, it seemed that a panel we just finished could use more work. When Hayley's fall college classes began, we would work in shifts. I started in the morning, going over areas where Hayley used chalk to highlight branches, leaves, or grass. There was always something on the list Hayley wanted me to do for background and I enjoyed the work.

One day, I was working in a classroom separating the cans of paint to keep at the church from those no longer being used. As I was moving paints to the flat rolling 'hooty' cart for transfer to my car, there was a huge jolt with a bang as if a monstrous truck had driven into the southeast wall of the church building. Startled, I stood in wonder as the floor rolled beneath me like a wave. An Earthquake. *Awesome!*

Having rarely felt earthquakes, I wasn't sure about that horrible jolt with a bang. This was not like the kind of earthquake I have experienced. Cautiously I went out through the classroom door into the Safari area. Everything was in place, but at the front of the room, the wall of glass was moving. *What a sight!*

The 20 foot by 30 foot wall of glass was undulating. It appeared to be liquid, like blowing soap bubbles, the glass panels bowed outward, moving in rhythm. The usually rigid glass was moving further than I'd ever seen glass bend without breaking. It was mesmerizing. Just past the glass wall, I saw Alan and his partner sitting in the Commons area. As the glass settled back into place, I went carefully to the door.

"OK, boys! You playing a little rough out here?"

Alan smiled. "Earthquake. In the 5 years I've been here, that is the biggest I've ever felt."

"Did you see that glass?"

"We did," Alan said. "I expected at least some of it to break. I've never seen glass extend out of a frame that far without breaking."

This was a record earthquake: 5.2. The jolt came from a slipping fault line, sending out shock waves. What an event! There was no damage at the church. Hayley, at home getting ready for class called me.

"Mom? Was that an earthquake?"

"Sure was. It hit the south east corner of the church. I thought a huge truck ran into the building."

"Oh, well, here at the house, it came like a huge bowling ball from the North."

"Wow, that's cool. No jolt. That's interesting," I replied.

Hayley sighed. "Well, it was interesting, but I don't think I like this."

Earthquakes have now become a regular topic since that day in 2010. Oklahoma has moved up to number five on the USGS list of most active states. California stays number one. We never thought we would see the day that Oklahoma was known for sheer numbers of earthquakes.

Being in the middle of the middle of the U.S., Oklahoma is best known for changing the Fajita scale with ever increasing tornado sizes. We would have our chance to take shelter for the largest tornado ever recorded in Oklahoma within the next three years, on May 31, 2013. A two and one half mile tornado that came within one mile of our home, then turned and lifted, saving the 11 people in our small storm shelter. It demolished the vocational school from which Hayley had just graduated.

***

A Plan of Attack

Back at the mural, during another boat break with lunch from a sandwich shop, Hayley and I were reviewing the wall across from us.

"You know, that wall needs a lot more background foliage, before I put in the butterflies."

"I didn't do well in botany class," I added.

"Very funny. You don't need botany to paint. I have so many details on the other walls to add, it would be great to have you take over the background. You're capable, Mom."

"Thanks. I don't feel it!"

We sat a little longer enjoying our companionable silence. Just about then the air conditioning came on with its usual wind up noises. I sat watching as a potted plastic fern began to wave shadows on the wall.

I jumped up, rummaged through the artist's case, and grabbed a piece of chalk.

"Oh, look at this!"

I pushed the potted fern closer to the wall then drew around the shadow of the largest fern leaf.

"What do you think?"

"That will work. Here, let me have the chalk." Hayley moved the fern closer as the air conditioner turned off, making the plastic plant easier to manage.

Hayley, excited, said "Now, if you move the plant across this panel. Pull it away for shorter ferns, then move it closer for a few bigger leaves. And, here's a small fern. Just copy it. Stagger the ferns with grass."

For the rest of our time with the mural, if I seemed to be without something to do and interrupted Hayley when she was in the painting zone, I would hear her say:

"Ferns, Mom. Go do ferns."

I would hang my head and look punished. A few years later, when David took me to Yellowstone National Park, I was not surprised to find lots of photos of ferns. I had memorized the shape. Ferns are hardy plants that look delicate. They can grow right next to an active geyser.

The final panel was postponed. The design was changed by the church staff. After a weekend with seminars on a Biblical worldview by Dr. Ken Ham, of 'Answers In Genesis', the staff changed the purpose of the Safari Mural. Instead of the giant Baobab tree and more jungle, the church Elder's wanted Noah's Ark.

This would not be some kiddie bathtub version, but the working, sea worthy vessel from Genesis. About that time, the staff had an invitation

YOU DON'T HAVE TO MOVE THE WASHER TO MAKE TOAST

from the Creation Museum, in northwestern Kentucky outside Cincinnati. They spent a weekend there, bringing back materials to teach all of the children's ministry. They also brought back a poster illustrating the type of design of the Ark, based on ancient sea going vessels, but using the dimensions from the Bible.

Hayley downloaded several views of this ship. Since the size of this vessel could easily take up a large panel wall, Hayley chose to sketch about three fourth's of the ship, set slightly at an angle. It was set into the scene about three feet from the floor, and stretching fifteen feet horizontally and ten feet vertically.

For the background, Hayley painted a volcano with mountains, and a rainbow. "Oh! This rainbow looks like a cartoon!"

"Only God makes rainbows. You'll have to ask Him."

Totally disgusted, Hayley climbed down from the ladder. I spoke up to diffuse the situation.

"Say, why don't you take yourself to lunch. Maybe the sandwich place. Better yet, buy me a sandwich and come back here to eat it. You need a break."

"OK. I'll eat there. What do you want?

I thought about it. "Usual. Turkey, cheese, spinach, green peppers, and a little bit of Ranch on Italian."

"See you later." Hayley paused at the door with a smile. "Ferns, Mom. Do more ferns."

"Wait a minute! You said there were enough ferns. There's not one spot without a fern!"

Hayley laughed on her way out. Then I remembered she had officially closed that panel, pronouncing it finished yesterday.

"Very funny! Next time YOU buy!"

After lunch, I began to roll the light blue over the rainbow so Hayley could repaint it. As I put down the first layer, I realized it was going to take several coats. The light blue was see through.

Hayley shouted. "Stop! That first coat dims the cartoon look. Here, let me take over the blue."

"OK, but I'm not doing ferns!"

Hayley laughed and pointed toward the corner. "Finish the sky, please."

"Bossy."

Within an hour, the rainbow looked natural. We left for the day noticing rain clouds gathering.

As we drove onto the highway, we could see a shower to the east of us, and a beautiful rainbow across the sky.

Hayley nodded. "God's got it right. Now I see I need to do a few more touch ups on mine. It still won't be as good, but at least it won't look like a cartoon."

* * *

Ark of Noah

Over the last month, with Hayley in classes each day, I went to work using a 'punch list' she provided me at the end of the previous day. That way, I could add highlights on vines, consolidate materials to start the transfer to home, or clean up on floor trim where a paint splat missed the tape. My last chore this day was to paint the flat brown base coat for the Ark. It was October 29, 2010. We had been working in this room since July 6.

At lunch time, Hayley arrived with a sack from the subway shop. As we ate lunch, she studied the flat brown shape.

"Well, that's the outline. It's not all there, but angled so the rest of the Ark is out of the panel frame. I'm not sure how this is going to look. The idea is there. There's time to do this. I just don't know..."

I put down my sandwich. "Let's pray about it first. Then I'll get water bottles and the camera. I'll need still-shots for the scrapbook."

Hayley began painting slowly, hesitantly. She moved lightly over the flat brown under coat, adding darker and darker highlights. She rarely stepped back to see the entire panel. I still don't know how she does that.

"Oh. Better than expected. Yes, I see more of it now." Hayley seemed to be talking to no one in particular.

I snapped a photo. It was amazing as the shape, shadows and highlights came to her. Soon, her hand was moving too fast for my camera.

"Hold the brush still a minute, right there, will you?"

It was as if she didn't hear me. The front shape of the Ark, with dark brown highlights with a touch of pale cream suddenly transformed

YOU DON'T HAVE TO MOVE THE WASHER TO MAKE TOAST

into a bulge. The hull was turning three dimensional as she painted. Brown-black, medium brown, reddish brown blended together as the Ark became crafted wood, perfectly fit together.

Before she climbed back onto the ladder, I shoved the water bottle at her.

"Here. Drink. It's been over an hour. Drink." I ordered.

"Thanks."

Hayley drank half a bottle and climbed back onto the ladder. Her hand started moving again at incredible speed. It was as if the vision would fade if she slowed down. The photos I snapped turned her hand into a blur. The Ark became realist wood on a flat wall in one hour and forty minutes.

When Hayley stepped back to look at this beautiful piece of artwork, she sighed. "That looks good. I think a few touch ups." She spotted the white wall switches. "Those white light switches have to go. We can't paint them—the paint will come off with use."

We purchased wooden light switches. After all, we couldn't leave white light switches on the side of the Ark. Alan agreed to install them.

The ship was breathtaking.

After a snack, Hayley climbed up beside the Ark to add the final touch on this Genesis account: a beautiful dove with an olive branch. Except for minor items on clean up, the only thing left was to write scriptures on each wall.

Within the week we completed the last verse and removed our equipment. The Safari Mural was finished. Hayley and I took a walk through the room, hardly grasping this colossal project was complete.

"What an adventure." Hayley said.

"What a lot of work. And a lot of God's blessings or we couldn't have done this."

"No kidding."

Hayley stopped beside a panel near the zebra. "I *SO* want to redo some of these animals and put in more background. I guess an artist's job is never finished."

"True. You are always learning something new with your art. It's a great gift." I smiled.

Hayley gave me a hug.

"Thanks, Mom."

We went out for a celebration dinner. There would be a formal dedication of the Safari Mural in a few weeks. David, Hayley and I were encouraged from this successful job of Artwork with God. What a list of blessings we could see and count! Little did we suspect on the heels of working daily with God's inspiration, we would face a family crisis.

Fifteen days after finishing the Mural, Hayley drove her Dad and I to the hospital. David's left leg, from the knee down had gone cold. What we thought was a pulled calf muscle turned out to be an aneurysm and large blood clot. God never promises freedom from trials. In fact Jesus said, "in this world you will have trouble. But be encouraged, I have overcome the world." God promises those who seek Him will find the help they need when the trial comes.

* * *

Emergency

Behind our home is a beautiful park and David, Hayley, and I have enjoyed walks as well as sliding down a huge hill in the snow. There are walking trails, historical markers for the Chisholm Trail, fountains and streams. It's also a great open space for flying kites and watching annual migrations of birds and butterflies. Since David works at a desk all day, he enjoys long walks. His idea of a long walk is over a mile, and with his long stride, there is no keeping up with him.

One evening he came home limping. "I think I pulled a muscle in my calf."

"Chasing dogs in the park again?" I quipped. "Let me get something to rub on the muscle."

"Man this hurts. I stretched before I started out." David said rubbing his left leg.

"Well, you'll have to take it easy for awhile. So if you go walking tomorrow night, do more stretches but walk your normal pace. Don't try that fast walk you do."

The deep heating cream and massage seemed to help a little with the cramping sensation in David's leg, but it persisted on into the next week. Each day it seemed he limped more. I already knew he wasn't sleeping soundly. The tossing and turning was the pain building in his leg.

David sat down. "I think this is getting worse. My left foot is cold."

"What do you mean?"

"The heart doctor says I don't have a lot of circulation in my lower legs or feet. Anyway, my foot is cold." David looked concerned. "I think we'd better go over and make sure this is really a pulled muscle."

It was one of those evenings where I was enduring dizzy spells, due to my Meniere's. I wasn't going to be capable of driving. My frustration level went up. I'm helpless to help him. With a prayer before they left, Hayley drove David to a Med Care Clinic. It was the Doc-In-The-Box we usually used, only a few miles away. I waited impatiently at home for their return.

The phone rang.

"The doc in the box says this isn't a pulled muscle. Maybe a blood clot and I'd better get to St. Anthony's right away. Hayely will take us. We'll be there to get you in about ten minutes. Take your Dramamine. I love you."

I grabbed a cloth bag for tissue, bottles of water, and two nutrition bars. Hayley's driving was excellent and it really didn't take much time to reach the hospital, but with my dizzy spell getting worse, plus my worry over what could be wrong with David's leg, it was a long seventeen miles.

From the Triage Technician, Mike said, "You have no pulse in your left ankle. We've called your heart doctor. He just got back in town from

Susan A. Rader

a conference, and he's called a surgical team. They'll meet here shortly. You just have to lay here and don't get up or move around."

Hayley and I were startled. *No circulation in his foot?* I was feeling alarmed. Hayley gave me a knowing look. David and I exchanged glances. Things were serious. True to family tradition, it was time for us to lighten the mood.

"Well, while we wait for the Doctor to get here," I teased, "tell me, did we update your life insurance?"

Hayley smiled, taking her cue. "Hey, Dad. Can I have your classic Mustang?"

ER Tech Mike surveyed us through half closed eyes, searching our expressions. We sounded mercenary. Thinking about the startled look on his face, I thought I'd better explain.

"Oh, don't mind us. We do this all the time. It's our way of coping with serious situations."

"Riii—ght," Mike said. He didn't believe us.

David added his comment. "I changed my will. No coffin. I want to be *buried INSIDE* my car!"

* * *

At that moment a lab tech arrived with a wheel chair to whisk David off to the ultrasound lab. There was a huge blood clot from David's left knee to his ankle. While the technician transferred the information to the Doctor, David and I held hands, with Hayley next to me.

"The Adventure continues," David said. "I love you. You may have to make some decisions."

"Yes. I'll do my best. I love you." My heart was aching for what he was about to go through.

"David, you can't die because I'm just getting used to you."

"I love you, Dad." Hayley added and gave him a hug.

As he moved his leg, pain registered on his face. David smiled. "Well, we know this is serious. I wish it was a pulled muscle. So, let's pray. God knows what's going on and He will decide the outcome. No matter what it is, I love you, Susan. I love you, Hayley. We've had a good life and you know where I'll be if..."

I put my fingers on his lips. "Nope. No dying tonight. If you're thinking that way, I'll auction off your car."

David smiled. "No you won't. My car makes you dizzy just standing beside it."

We laughed lightly.

David said a quick prayer. "Heavenly Father, You alone are in control. Please guide the doctor's hands. Give all of the staff, technicians and nurses insight. Increase their skill. Help Susan and Hayley be calm, waiting on Your answers for tonight. In Jesus name we pray." We kissed him goodbye.

Two large technicians arrived with a gurney to move David from the ultrasound lab table. After kissing me and Hayley, David allowed himself to be rushed to surgery. Angioplasty.

Left without David, we followed a nurse to a waiting area across from the radiology-surgery unit in the basement of the hospital. Hayley and I went into the family seating area which was pitch black, but we had to hunt for the lights. The seating area was filled with old fashioned Victorian furniture, in dark red with walnut trim. We sat together on a small sofa.

"It's nearly ten o'clock. I'll call Denise. She should still be up. I'd better let the family know this could be something really bad pretty soon."

Hayley just nodded. "I know Mom."

After the call to David's sister, we sat in silence. A woman from registration bustled in.

"Are you Mrs. Rader?" She pushed her glasses down her nose to see me better.

"Yes."

Pushing her glasses up, she read from yellow highlighted pages on a clipboard. "I need David's insurance card, social security number, driver's license, donor card, and you'll need to sign this paper in case they need to amputate some or all of his left leg." *O, Lord, protect him.*

About this time, we saw a Doctor run past the waiting area toward surgery. Hayley and I exchanged glances. *Oh, Lord, help David. Comfort us as we wait on Your answer.*

My eyebrows went up. I couldn't even confer with David right now, since he was rushed into surgery. *How do I make a decision like this?* His leg or his life. Two possibilities. It's amazing when life's motion comes to a halt, and there is nothing more important than the decisions and outcomes of the next few minutes or the next few hours. Hayley watched me fill out the papers as she began sending text messages on her phone.

When the woman with the papers left, Hayley said, "I've sent texts to my friends who stay up late and to Pastor Scott."

"Good idea. I'll send one to Facebook."

There was no conversation for about thirty minutes, just the tap-tapping of cell phone keypads. Texting everyone we knew.

"You know, God knew this was coming. He doesn't cause things like this." I sighed.

"I know Mom." Hayley replied.

Silence stretched between us again. It wasn't awkward or stilted. We were both assured by a peace that didn't make sense, except as a Believer. My husband, Hayley's Dad, was in that surgery across the hall, enduring who knew what and we were calm. *God promised us this peace, if we call on Him, trust Him, and wait on the answer.* We were aware that everything was out of our control.

"We've just been through the Mural with God every step of the way."

"I know Mom."

"We know that if this blood clot breaks off, your Daddy could die. Or he could lose his leg."

"I know Mom. I understand what's going on. But God knows we want Dad around. God has answered a lot of our prayers." *I keep forgetting how much we had been through together and how much Hayley had matured.*

"That's right. Since He cared to help the two of us create a 4,500 square foot mural for the church, He's listening to us now."

I looked around the room. "It's really weird sitting here. I feel that everything is out of our hands. Of course it is, we're just not used to *understanding things are out of our control*. We make choices every day, all day, and they deal with what we are experiencing. But those things are our routine, and at some point we have choices. This is different. We aren't doctors, we don't know what's going on in that room, and we don't have any say over it. But I'm not anxious like I usually am. Maybe that's why the Mural took longer than we expected, so we would be fresh from the miracles that took place there. God knew that clot was forming and prepared us."

"I know, Mom."

I smiled at Hayley. "I just want to say these things out loud, so we can both hear them."

Hayley gave me a hug. "I know, Mom."

Hayley and I prayed again, as we waited. We heard footsteps. David's sister arrived with two take out bags full of tacos, and three drinks.

"I'm guessing you haven't had any dinner," Denise said. She looked tired. Working as a mail carrier, walking 6 miles a day, plus a driving route, she was exhausted at the end of her shift. She would be up and leaving for work at 4:00 a.m. It was now 11:30 p.m.

We both got up to give Denise a hug, for her company, her concern for her brother, and for the food.

Denise chuckled. "You two look lost down here in the basement, sitting together. You look really small."

"We're glad you came." I smiled.

Hayley and I both smelled Mexican food.

Wise Denise said, "I figured you hadn't thought of eating, and I remember we all like Mexican food. So I just grabbed some. I hope it's stuff you like."

"Oh, God bless you! We've been busy since six. Mexican food is perfect."

Hayley gratefully took a bag. "Until I smelled that food, I didn't know how hungry I was. Thanks Aunt Denise."

With little conversation, Hayley devoured two tacos, and a burrito, while I filled Denise in on what few details we knew. Before she could ask questions, a Doctor came into the room.

"Hello, are you with David Rader?"

"Yes," both Denise, Hayley, and I answered.

"I'm Doctor Hahn. If you'll come with me, I'll show you what's going on."

The Doppler X-ray screen showed blood flow and then a gray blob from near David's left knee completely to his ankle.

"As you can see on the screen, the clot re-forms as fast as the doctor can remove it. David has remarkable clotting factor."

We watched the monitor wondering how this could turn out.

"We already had one of these this year. It's an aneurysm just above the knee. A bulge in the blood vessel slows the blood flow causing it to clot. This is a rare aneurysm. About six months ago, I just happened to be on duty when a man came in like David did tonight. That's why we knew right away what this was. Twice in the same year. Very rare."

He pointed to the screen showing the arteries of David's leg. "Look at these shriveled up blood vessels on either side of the artery. This is a birth defect. The blood vessel, that artery starting at the knee, is supposed to divide into three blood vessels to carry the blood uniformly to the foot. These blood vessels would all be smaller—more narrow to keep up pressure so the foot has a supply of blood. Without them, the circulation is poor from the knee down. An aneurysm in the leg is *very* rare."

Dr. Hahn looked thoughtful.

"You know, the technician in ultrasound was on duty that night, too. This is Providential, if you know what I mean. On the other man's leg, it took a while to diagnose. His aneurysm wasn't nearly this big, or the clot for that matter. But we saw the same symptoms tonight, that's why we caught the problem right away. Otherwise, it could have been considered non-emergency, like an injury. David could have waited until morning to be seen, and it could have been too late."

"Thank you for being here." I said softly.

Dr. Hahn just smiled and pointed in God's direction with a nod. We were to go back to the waiting area to learn what the next step would be, just as David's heart specialist came out of surgery.

"I don't know how we can save his leg," the doctor said to the room. He ran his fingers through his thick hair. "I can't see how it can be saved."

As if remembering there were three other people in the room, the doctor turned to face us.

"We have David on a very high level of blood thinner. We have the aneurysm isolated, in a way, but we will have to finish the surgery tomorrow. We're moving hims to ICU and we will keep him sedated to keep movement to a minimum. You can say good night to him upstairs in about fifteen minutes. Then tomorrow morning, come back to see him before his surgery at 11:00 am. We can keep him stable until Dr. Henry is available. He is the best blood vessel surgeon in the state. This will give you time to get more family here."

It was 2:00 a.m. when Hayley, Denise and I left the hospital. For a fall night in November, it was only slightly chilly.

"I'll be calling in for leave so I can be here for the surgery." Denise gave us each a hug and we left for home.

Hayley and I were so tired, we just dropped into our beds, with the alarm set for 7:00 a.m. We would have breakfast, and then Hayley could call her college art professor to be excused from class. David's parents and a handful of our friends from the church arrived to wait on the outcome. Surgery would last from 4 to 6 hours.

Our associate pastor Scott arrived and gathered us all for prayers. Then more friends from church arrived at regular intervals, with bags of snacks to share with the crowd. Junk snacks, the universal comfort food, gave us more to talk about. Dividing up what arrived in bags, under categories of 'I can't eat this', 'allergic to that', and 'oh look, home made chocolate chip cookies', kept conversation flowing and filled the time. It was comforting having family and friends, with lots of conversation, or silence if we chose.

After six hours, Dr. Henry, the blood vessel surgeon came into the room.

"David's leg is going to be fine. There was no need to amputate any part of it. We removed the artery from above the knee, sutured it to promote better blood flow, and put it back. He will have to be out of bed tomorrow to start walking. He'll stay all week so we can keep his wound clean and make sure he gets up several times a day. He's been moved to a private room. We ask just a few at a time to visit him."

All of us thanked Dr. Henry.

Pastor Scott said, "Let's close with prayer and give thanks for God's intervention. That's amazing the blood vessel can be taken out, fixed and put back."

After a group prayer, Denise, and David's parents followed Hayley and I to David's room.

I rushed over to his beside, with Hayley right behind me.

"So, no wooden leg. That's a break!" David smiled. He seemed so pale.

"Well, how can I drive my Mustang with one leg?"

Hayley came up to the bedside. "I'm glad you're alright, Daddy." David put his arms around us.

"You'll have to wait a while before you inherit the Mustang."

Hayley sighed. "Oh, Dad, I don't want your Mustang. I love my jeep."

Susan A. Rader

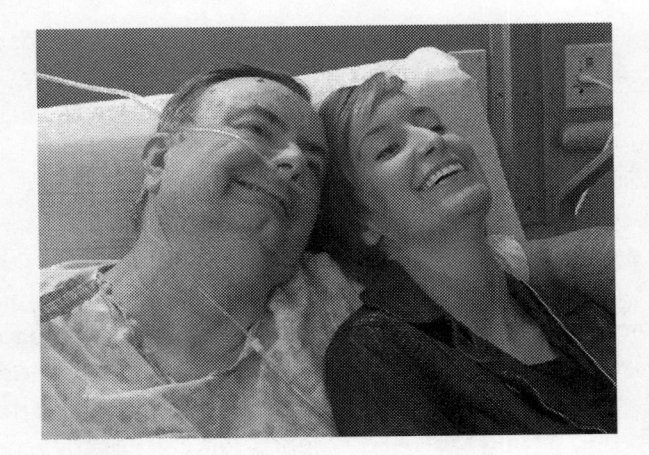

***

CHAPTER 13

Our Daughter Moves Out, The 'Plane' difference between MS & WY

After David's three week recovery, he was back at work, all of us still amazed that a blood vessel could be removed, repaired outside the body, and put back again. In a few months, Hayley graduated with her Associates in Art, mentioning again and again those dreaded words: "when I get my own place". *Panic. My little girl out on her own in an apartment complex. I can't breathe. Is this that Empty Nest thing?*

Yes, David and I knew she had to finish growing up and that meant moving into her own place. We had talked to Hayley about that inevitability since before high school. But to me, those words were simple: Parenting 101. I had not honestly thought about what it would mean *to me* when our only child moved out—and on.

Whoa! This is staggering. What would my job be? How does our relationship work? My totally dysfunctional background created hard questions. *If I'm not in her daily life, what am I supposed to do with myself? Will I see her again?* When she moved out, how could I watch her grow as she gained confidence in her job and routines of her personal life? How can I finish growing up?

Well, the 'moving out' was getting to be fact, no longer an abstract idea. Since I left home in a hurry to get away from violence and knowing only a few who left home peaceably, I was confused. Right now, I knew two families who couldn't wait for their kids to move out, stomping mad or otherwise, as long as they moved. That was just as strange a concept to me as the peaceful parting we had in mind for Hayley.

I tried to imagine how I could be involved in this process so it was a transition, not an escape. Also, participate without taking control away from her. I needed to be involved, but Hayley didn't need me taking charge. Help moving her things and packing them so they didn't break, was one thing I could offer. Hayley had her own ideas, so that made me the 'dependent one' in this scenario!

After praying about my fears and control issues, I decided to look at this as a practical exercise. I looked through drawers and cubby holes in the kitchen, unpacked boxes of little kitchen things I couldn't bear to throw away, finding extra flatware, measuring spoons, and other odds and ends.

It helped me to cope to collect, box, and label these possibilities. Before long I had an entire cabinet full plus more boxes in the shed. My intention was to be prepared by the time Hayley started apartment hunting. This way, I could adapt by acknowledging the fact of her moving. As I packed, I remembered stories to tell from living on my own. This was a way to share her adventure. David had stories too about his bachelor days. We could share her experience, aid her enthusiasm for this adventure, guide her with wise advice, and help her where needed.

When her classes were finished and her certification as an I.T.—Information Technologist, Hayley brought up the topic at dinner.

"I really want an apartment of my own."

"Well, do you have some ideas?" David asked. "You have some friends living in apartments. Have you been to see them?"

"Yes. But I don't know how much they cost. I never asked my friends."

"Well, then, how about you and me go apartment hunting this weekend?"

"Really? That's great." Hayley heaved a sigh. "Where do we look?"

David replied, "Make a list of all the apartment complexes in the area, then call their offices to find out if there is a deposit. Ask about how much rent is per month, and how long their lease is."

While this conversation was going on, I was having difficulty breathing. I was comforting myself that her moving was normal and a part of her maturing process. *Right, Susan, keep telling yourself that.* I gave serious thought to my 'separation anxiety' and wondered how to deal with it.

My first solution was to work harder on the 'stack of things she might need' and the pile of boxes in the hallway grew. Ice cube trays, sponges, towels, kitchen utensils, and disposable plastic dishes for making her own lunches or storing food in the frig. Even a box of baking soda to absorb odors. It calmed me that I could provide help with this list, trusting her to use them as she needed or wanted them, or not at all. It would be her choice to go through and sort, saving much needed 'start up money'.

While I was considering things for the 'apartment check list', I would have flash backs. My mother's reactions to a change of plans. The memory finally surfaced with such vivid detail, I began to relive it. With my post traumatic stress disorder, there was no stopping the surrealistic reliving a nightmare. All I could do was go through it again, hoping for a break in this altered state, so I could grab onto where I was right now. No luck this time.

What Happened To Me

I remember I drove six hours to see my mother and my step father to have a talk about changing to another college. My geology classes had run out at the private Christian college I was attending. It was going to be easy, and two years was nothing.

My arrival met a chilly reception. I was told, flatly, I could not change colleges, because my mother supported it. This college was connected to her church, giving her status that I would ruin. *This was news to me.* Somehow, my changing schools would 'hurt her', and shame her reputation. The illogical discussion suddenly blew out of proportion. There was yelling and shouting, so my step father slugged me. My chair went over as I crashed to the floor.

"Well, hitting women must give you some kind of thrill," I remarked, unable to let this brutish act pass in silence. He kicked me in the ribs for good measure. This wasn't the first time. Saying something or keeping silent—his response was always the same. If I wasn't beaten by one parent it would be the other one. That scenario was my entire past. My mother had picked the same kind of man as my father--only fat, rich and twenty five years older.

I got up from the floor, my ribs aching.

"I'm out of here. I'm out of college. Keep your tuition. I'll find a way to finish college."

My mother laughed. "If you leave this house, with *MY CAR*, I'll call the police."

"YOUR CAR?" I was stunned. "You signed the loan but I've made all the payments. What are you talking about?"

"That car is listed on the company insurance as a fleet vehicle."

"You told me I didn't have to have insurance in Oklahoma. That you'd take care of it." I stood firm on the floor. "Well, that doesn't matter. I can get insurance and pay for it myself."

"Don't even think of leaving in that car." Her voice changed, as it did many times to the low, threatening growl of an animal. Her madness filling the room with an aura of over powering evil. In a matter of moments she was upon me, slapping and clawing me.

That was my cue. I grabbed my purse. Shoving the toppled chair in the direction of my over weight step father to prevent him reaching me, I flew out of the house, speeding away, with my Ford Fairlane leaving tire marks on the driveway.

It was two days later when I found out there was a felony arrest warrant against me—Interstate Transportation of stolen vehicle. *How could my mother have done this?* Easy enough, when you have money, prestige, and know a judge.

I turned myself in to the Kingfisher County Sheriff. My friends, Jean and her mother Reba accompanied me. Reba was a friend of the Sheriff, having been the attending nurse at the delivery of the Sheriff's three children. Since Reba knew Sheriff Ben, he allowed us to come in voluntarily.

"Ben, you need to hear this story first. This is a false charge."

Sheriff Ben led the way to his office.

"Yes. I saw the warrant. A man and wife came to this office two days ago to try to file charges against you, Reba. As a nurse, you have access to drugs. They had a story about you giving drugs to your daughter and her friend, Susan. I didn't believe it and they had no proof."

Reba, Jean, and I exchanged glances. This sounded like my mother's M.O.

"Let see the proof you have," Sheriff Ben sat down with authority.

I presented my canceled checks from the bank that held the loan. There was proof of my ownership. My mother's name had changed with her remarriage, and I worked summers for her company so I was listed as an employee. The warrant explained I was an ex-employee who stole a company vehicle, crossing a state line.

The Sheriff gave me an puzzled look.

"Why would your mother do this?"

"I wanted to change colleges. She said "no", so I said, 'I'll get another job and pay for my own classes'. That sent her over the edge. She screamed and hit me, then my step father hit me and kicked me for 'upsetting my mother'. I took off in the car thinking she just might call the police like she said, but not imagining being accused of stealing my own car. I've made all the payments. I guessed that if she called the police she'd have to make up something. Well, she did."

The Sheriff put his hands over his face, pushing his glasses up onto his forehead. He seemed to be weighing this insane discussion of changing colleges with my mother's response. The silence in the room was broken only by the ticking of a clock on his desk. I could feel my stomach churning and the fear rising.

The Sheriff's voice was weary.

"If I arrest you now, which I'm supposed to do, you'll have to stay in the Kingfisher County jail until sometime next week. I'll have to wait for prisoner transfer paperwork and a prisoner escort car from Kansas City to pick you up. Then you'll have to wait for a hearing. That is a long time in jail."

The Sheriff ran his hand through his thinning hair, took off his glasses and wiped his face.

"I've heard a lot of family reactions, but this takes the cake." He took a sip of his coffee, made a face at the dregs in the cup, put his chin down and chewed on the end of a pencil.

"Here's what I can do. First. *You didn't come in here.* You get yourself to the Johnson County Jail within the next 24 hours or I *will* have to arrest you. Do I have your word?"

"Yes, sir."

The Sheriff remanded me to the custody of my friend, Reba, who promised to drive me to Kansas City. Reba was as good a her word, and the Sheriff knew it.

My friends drove me to a suburb of Kansas City. There wasn't much talk, but Reba did offer a prayer before we went into the Johnson County Court House. At that time, it was like my life was the same kind of mess my parents lived. The same violence, selfishness, and vindictiveness that continued when my mother remarried. I could have spent a week in jail in Oklahoma before going to jail in Kansas. Then, there was the gentle way I was treated at the Johnson County Jail, in stark contrast.

Susan A. Rader

When I reported to the front desk, the large police officer on duty looked up from his paperwork in surprise.

"Well, young lady, what can I do for you today?"

"Uh, there is a felony arrest warrant for my arrest."

He laughed. When I didn't laugh, his smile died.

"What? You don't look like the kind of people that usually come in here. What'd you do? Pick flowers from the neighbor's yard?"

"No. I am accused of stealing my own car."

The officer frowned.

"You're serious."

"Yes, sir."

Officer M. Howard went to the stack of warrants.

"Well, I'll be." He looked up at me with a shocked expression. "Oo---Kay. Do you have identification? How old are you?"

"I'll be nineteen next month."

"Do you have any other names you go by? Any alias?"

"Well, I blush easily. My friends nicknamed me "Strawberry"."

"Oof! I feel like I'm arresting Little Red Riding Hood. Come this way."

I said goodbye to Reba and Jean. It was a lonely walk to face what would come next. I was trembling, whether from lack of food or terror, I never knew.

After submitting to finger printing, and a police photo, I was ushered into the the Sheriff's Office. By now, the entire jail staff had heard all or part of my story.

Sheriff Jim interviewed me, called the bank loan officer to verify payments were current and my signature, and listened carefully to my story.

"Well, I wish you would have shown up on Monday. Then we could go straight down to the legal department and you'd be out of here in a few hours. Now, I have to lock you up."

With an escort, I was taken to third floor of the Police Department. The jailer came from behind his desk, jangling keys.

"Well, two great big police officers to escort 100 pounds of teenager? What'd you do, skip school?"

"It's a mistake but I can't fix it until Monday."

"Ah. Too bad. You're the one I heard about. Arrested for stealing your own car."

"Yes. Nothing I can do about it now."

A female officer brought me faded purple overalls with pink stripes and checked me for weapons. I could keep my underwear and tennis shoes without the laces. I looked around the jail entry way. There were rows of solid steel walls, with doors interrupting the box shapes. In the doors were tiny little barred windows, and off to the side, close to the floor, a slot to pass food trays. *Oh, great. Like a dog in a cage.*

The jailer indicated where I was to sign the log book, and the matron left.

"I'm sorry. You'll be in the 'female tank' with a drug case. The other woman shouldn't bother you. She's coming down off a high. I'll try to keep watch in case she's hostile. It's not her first time."

Druggy

The night passed slowly. I had a bottom bunk with no pillow or blanket. I finally fell asleep around midnight, my mind rehearsing the sequence of events that landed me here. It was a night of evaluations. Suddenly, I was awakened by someone grabbing the front of my over sized outfit.

"Wake up!"

My eyes flew open and I held perfectly still. I'd been grabbed like this in the night all my life.

In the dim light I saw a woman in her late twenties, with hard, blood shot eyes, and foul breath.

Her face was just inches from mine.

"Tell the Guard you want an aspirin, *now*! My head's killing me. Got it? Tell him you got a headache. *Now!*"

I dutifully went to the door and called out to the jailer.

"Uh, sir, excuse me. I have a headache. Could I have an aspirin?"

"Sure thing. Give me a minute."

The jailer brought the aspirin to the narrow, 'dog food flap' in the side of the wall.

"Here you go. And I brought a paper cup of water."

"Thanks. I appreciate it."

My jail mate came over to the metal table in the center of the room.

"Don't say nothin'. I'm gonna need more aspirin." Her threat was implied.

At this point, threats didn't bother me. I resigned myself long ago that my life would always be filled with threats, injustice, and violence.

The jailer waited until my cell mate returned to her bed and then called me to the door on the pretense of having a phone call. He let me out of the jail cell, locking the door behind me.

"No phone call. I know your cell mate and she'll be restless and irritable for the next few hours. How about a round of cards? You can tell me your story. I've heard part of it, but I don't understand how someone could do this to their kid. How about a coffee or cola? What do you like?"

"Pepsi, thanks."

The jailer, named Harry, was in his forties with a family. His kindness will always be remembered. We played rummy for about an hour when the bell for the elevator sounded. There were two police officers escorting a prisoner.

As the doors slid open, one policeman jumped up onto the bars like an ape, shaking them violently.

"Open up! It's the cops!"

My jailer laughed. "Like I haven't heard that one before."

When the officers with a belligerent prisoner came to the sign in desk, they spotted me.

"Oh, entertaining, huh?"

Harry snapped. "This girl doesn't belong here. She's a guest until Monday. If it was up to the Sheriff, she wouldn't be here now."

After watching these officers handle a rough drunk, who refused to cooperate, I was glad I didn't put up any resistance. They were fair, but it was hard to stay composed having so little sleep. In a short while, Harry the jailer checked the surveillance video from the cell.

"Your Roomy is asleep. I think she'll keep 'til breakfast. You'll be all right if you want to go to sleep now. I go off duty at 5. I wish you luck with legal on Monday. I hope you get off by noon."

Monday morning in the elevator, I stood between two six foot police officers to be escorted to the Legal Department. I looked dangerous. I certainly didn't feel dangerous. When the elevator doors opened onto the lobby, everyone stepped back out of our way. I blushed. That's incongruous with prisoner overalls. The County Courthouse was busy with business as usual. There were a lot of raised eyebrows looking at me. I had no comb and in that outfit, well lets say my appearance had not improved over the weekend.

When I finished explaining my predicament, showing my canceled checks and a copy of the loan agreement to the fifteenth 'assistant' county attorney, I was declared unjustly jailed. This young attorney left me in his office as he went for a release paper. A female officer escorted me to a hard bench out side a judge's office. While I was waiting, I heard my mother's voice behind me.

"Oh, my poor daughter." She sighed dramatically. "Always in trouble. But I've come to help her, again." *She should get an academy award for this performance. Her expression appeared genuinely surprised to see me in a jail outfit. It wasn't my color choice!*

My rage boiled to the surface and my face turned red. For once, I said nothing, but my expression elicited a smile from her. *Sheer satisfaction on her face. This was a no win situation.*

The silent female officer asked, "Was that your mother?"

"Yup."

"Man, that's one cold woman. She looks so respectable. Good luck."

The result of my 'doom boggle' was convoluted. I was interrogated by the judge for distressing my mother and questioned about having trouble with college room mates. *And what did that have to do with being falsely arrested?* I didn't know.

My mother's performance had to have been detailed and convincing with the judge to still be on her side. Her diversionary tactics made a successful campaign of throwing the judge off the track. Her reason for filing a false report on a stolen car was her 'desperation over my mental condition'. It didn't matter that I was an 'A' student, and held a job on campus.

I ended up being in a psychiatrist's office, and being cleared, so that I wouldn't have to come back to Kansas. My mother wanted me admitted for psychiatric assessment. Since I was no longer living in Kansas, and over 18, I was allowed to leave.

This is how I left home. Any belongings I had at home were kept by my mother, forfeit as she claimed them. Not a pretty tale. Remembering my own split with family, I could understand why I was confused about dealing with Hayley's leaving home. I had to rewrite myself. I didn't want to react badly to her move. There were simply a lot of bad memories for me to sort through, as well as handle the range of emotions from sadness, to rage, to terror, to wanting revenge. Hayley and David didn't deserve fallout from my unsorted past.

***

David and Hayley spent two weekends going to different apartment complexes. After traipsing all over town, they went out to lunch to talk over positive and negative points. David discussed managing finances on her own, and helped her understand the risks of a young woman coming and going from work by herself. They were fine but I was a wreak, losing sleep and having panic attacks again. But I didn't want Hayley to know how her much needed next step in adulthood was affecting me. It was hard to keep my mouth shut. Fear is a monster I've lived with most of my life.

My life had not been as sheltered as Hayley's. I know I over compensated. For a long time I was sure sheltering Hayley was a good thing. At least she knew she was loved by both parents, she had been protected, and we would come to her aid if she needed us. This wasn't some family blow up because she wanted to live on her own, but, I was terrified for her safety. I rarely felt safe and I projected my fears to her circumstances. I felt my prayers were ineffective, and couldn't seem to control my emotions.

Every news broadcast the next few months featured some woman assaulted in a mall parking lot, or pumping gas, or washing her car. Hayley wasn't careless. She could take care of herself. *The terror was inside me.* Had she been prepared for this? Had I told her the things she needed? *Let her go.*

In order to handle my panic, I did a lot of praying. It was another transition time on this adventure with Hayley and David. I was suffering from my own unreconciled fears. As I thought back on the dumps I lived in, the ratty neighborhoods, going hungry, losing jobs, and then being in dangerous places, God reminded me of His intervention. I *had* been looked after. This was a matter of letting God know I could trust Him, as well as letting Hayley grow. She had good judgment. My life experiences on my own were a combination of insecure upbringing and a *lack* of good judgment. *Take a deep breath, Susan, and let Hayley live her life.* Easy to say, but not to do.

Another Step In Time

While Hayley was working or apartment hunting with her Dad, I perused garage sales. Unlike David and I, Hayley likes old fashioned furniture. We like modern style with clean lines. Ugh. All I could think of was my mother's and her mother's solid old country furniture with curly cue swirls that took forever to dust. I saw a likely candidate to dust at a yard sale.

"Haze, I found the cutest love seat. Old fashioned just two blocks away. There's a lamp and end table comes with it. $40. What do you think?"

Hayley said, "Gotta work. Send me phone pic."

The garage sale was experiencing a lull in the early June afternoon heat. The family running the sale let me hang around long enough for Hayley to text back.

"That looks good. I can re-cover it!"

When I mentioned it was for my daughter's new apartment (which she didn't have yet), the man was so happy to get rid of it, he put everything in the back of his truck and drove it the two blocks to our home—free delivery!

"These are still good pieces of furniture. The lamp I just threw in, no charge. It works, it just needs the top glued back on."

After we unloaded the two pieces of furniture, I handed him $40.

"Thanks. I'm glad to get rid of it. Wish your daughter good luck."

Next on her furniture list was a dining table and chairs. David and Hayley hunted through second hand furniture places, and found a heavy pedestal table with the top in good shape, plus a set of old fashioned wooden chairs. Hayley decided to repaint her furniture and selected a bright neon green spray, for color. For over a month, our living room was the extra storage unit, while she boxed and stacked items she wasn't using in anticipation of her new address.

In the meantime, Hayley had secured a position as an Information Technologist with a nearby school system. Our prayers as she was going through school were focused on a place for Hayley to be employed and happy—not be just a numbered employee in a large corporation. A place where she could enjoy the people she worked with and having enough variety in her job to prevent burnout completing repetitious job orders. Prayers above and beyond what we asked were answered. She had a fun staff to work with, and was responsible for job order repairs and computer maintenance for three schools. She now had her own office and responsibilities.

To say I am proud of her would be an understatement. With my backwards upbringing, I had to work harder not to be like my parents. With God's grace and Biblical understanding, I could teach Hayley using lessons from my past. My family did not live according to God's laws or wisdom.

My parents demonstrated family as a way of taking, using, manipulating and being self serving. Or just too drunk to work.

But a job with responsibility, accountability, loyalty, dedication, and honor should never be underestimated. Working just enough to get by, paycheck to paycheck, just for self, and just for the money misses all the benefits of a job. It defies Natural Law. I know I lived that way for years, until I began to see the futility of those 'sink hole' goals. Just before I volunteered for the Army, I had begun to see a new perspective. Right now, I was delighted that Hayley wouldn't waste good years of her life seeking sink holes.

All along Hayley demonstrated her maturity and good sense. She followed David's budgeting examples. Even as a child, she would look at the money she had and after carrying a toy with her for a while, would put it back. Like her Dad would say, "I think I'll wait a little while on this".

Hayley saved her higher education allowance, received as a supplement for being a child of a Veteran, and lived at home. She used small amounts for her Jeep maintenance and fuel, but clothes were usually from second hand shops. She was slender enough to fit into the 'designer labels' donated to thrift shops. When she received her first pay check she was ecstatic.

"Wow, I feel rich!" Then she laughed. "But, I'm going to eat here and save it!"

Concern over her moving out grew when she filled out the paperwork for an apartment, awaiting a background check, and the other tenant moving out. The date was a little uncertain, so she had to bide her time. For me, it became daily conversations with myself.

"She has to take this step of independence. She'll do fine." My normal thinking self was confident. Then my worried Smother, Insecure Side would reply, "But remember some of those run down apartments where you lived. How a fire started from some kid playing with a lighter?"

Those times were good for my prayer life. I'm glad God is patience with me. I had a lot of 'night watches', praying about the kinds of things she might encounter, as they passed through my mind. I prayed David and I would arm Hayley with the knowledge she needed.

Protecting our daughter, is a great illusion. We can only marginally protect ourselves or our daughter, for it is the Lord watching over everything, knowing what is to come. We aren't promised safety in this life from trouble. The world unwinds according to His Natural laws. It's good to remember that on any given day. We are, after all, "to fully rely upon Him".

Alternate Plan

The apartment complex she chose was less than one mile from our home. But to me, it felt like the distance to Mars. Every day for weeks, each of us brought home empty boxes so Hayley could pack the emptying closets, book shelves, and miscellaneous items. It would be August before the other tenant moved out and the place ready for Hayley. It was too far away for Hayley but all too fast for me.

David and I were anxious for our vacation to Yellowstone National Park and the Grand Tetons in August, when word came *six days before we were to leave*: Hayley's new apartment was ready!   Panic set in for me. I wasn't ready to send her off to her new apartment, or seeing that it was clean enough for her, or to help see all of her things moved and arranged. I wasn't even packed for vacation! Quick, rent a truck, reserve it for Thursday and Friday. *Eek! We were to leave for vacation on Saturday morning. No time to adapt. Breathe, Susan. Young adults move away from home all the time. This isn't your situation!*

This was when I realized this timing was answered prayer. *Make me face it all at once, and trust Him to watch over her.* Then I thought how this coincided so exactly with our trip. This was God's help for me not to hover. No mistaking answered prayer. This gave me confidence, seeing so completely that this was God's timing.

We prayed about the apartment complex. It had a rather run down appearance, but with the best safety record in town. Of course, her apartment would be upstairs, which meant lifting and carrying a great many boxes. David went with her to sign her apartment agreement, and then went to the hardware store to purchase brand a new door handle lock and deadbolt.

Returning to the house, Hayley was excited.

"Good news, it's already been cleaned. Bad news, we'll be moving everything up a steep flight of stairs, but it's ready for me to move in." She waved the rental agreement.

"I've seen the apartment and other than smelling like left over smoke, it looks pretty clean. I didn't look too closely, but it probably won't take us as long as I originally thought to get it ready."

After Hayley began moving boxes, I went with her to do touch up on paint. The kitchen needed deep cleaning, and the shelves all needed fresh paint inside and out. I went over during the day with our home vacuum cleaner to use on the dingy carpeting. Unbelievable! It was clogging my sweeper with screws, nails, tooth picks, cat litter, and the list went on. No way that carpet been cleaned, as stated in the lease.

David came to the rescue by renting and wrestling a carpet steam cleaner. He was disgusted at the heavy smoker scent as well as grungy color, so he cleaned the carpet two days in a row. At least the floor looked a shade lighter, and the cigarette smell was less noticeable. It worried us about the ever present nicotine odor, as Hayley battled asthma and allergies.

As it became increasingly obvious with my nagging, I was being over bearing. I kept handing Hayley lists of what should be done and what to look out for. Hayley was as patient as she could be with me, and quite often left on errands when I was at my most 'smothering'. Helicopter Mom strikes again.

My mother never wanted me back. *And don't let the door hit you on the way out!* I wasn't missed. I set out to do things differently with Hayley. My idea when I found out I was pregnant with Hayley was to be as opposite of my mother as I could be. That didn't exactly work out since good intentions are not enough to over come bad training. At least I had the benefit of mentors among church friends. Those women who cared for their children with logic, rules of fairness, and were not verbally abusive. Bookstores had some reliable sources on defusing parent-child situations, and of course, the Bible is filled with wisdom. Who would know what we are made of and how we respond better than the Creator?

Since Hayley was getting her own space, I thought about how our parting was certainly better than my own experience. There was a lot of daily prayer about my letting Hayley 'go to grow'. Part of me was trying to hang on, and part of me proud of her independence. It was a constant struggle. The apartment was ready, and Hayley's best friend, Tennyson, was going to help her move.

Providence timed Hayley's move to coincide exactly with our vacation trip to Yellowstone National Park. *Oh, no! We would be gone her first full weekend at her new apartment! What if she needed something?* I should apply for a job as a hover craft.

Since I was at home during the day, while David and Hayley were at work, I rented a small truck, just large enough for me to handle. I had lots of truck driving experience working summers and holidays at my mother's moving business.

It was unbelievable, how much furniture and 'stuff' Hayley managed to arrange in her 9 x 11 room at our home. Then it was surprising how much of the truck space it took to put all those boxes of books, clothes, art tables, book cases, collectible action figures, dressers, chairs, and finally, Alfred, her metal Knight in Shining Armor. Oh, don't forget the Celtic Broad Sword and stand. This was like those Circus Clown Cars where fifteen clowns get out of a car that holds four people. Well the boxes and furniture and bags just kept coming out of Hayley's room. We all made jokes about the *Dr. Who* television show: It's bigger on the inside.

The truck was nearly full! No wonder she wanted her own place. There wasn't a spot left to use in that room. If I hadn't seen it with my own eyes, I would never have believed so much could be in such a small place and still be able to walk through the room! She certainly had a gift for 'economy of space'!

After her bed was put into place at her new apartment along with the night stand, and the last of the boxes of kitchen items were brought upstairs, Hayley dropped onto a kitchen chair, delighted but exhausted. This would be her first night in her own apartment. *Don't panic, Susan. You can call her tomorrow before we catch the plane for Wyoming. Breathe. She will be fine.*

I couldn't think of anything else to make her come home for one more night since her bed was now in her apartment, so I was going to have to get used to this. She noticed me standing by her pantry with tears in my eyes.

"It's OK, Mom. I'll be fine." I hugged her tight.

"OK, well you have friends in town to help you. We leave tomorrow for Wyoming. You must text me every day. Or I'll call you."

"OK. I will." Hayley was looking sadly at me.

Sniffling again, I said, "Well, you can go over to the house and eat or raid the frig. Just be safe."

My daughter hugged me again and held onto my shoulders. She smiled at me.

"I will, Mom. I'll be fine. You and Dad have a great trip."

God knew I needed to be gone to remove the temptation to meddle as well as let me see Hayley was fine on her own. The one thing I did NOT want to do was give Hayley the feeling she was not capable of caring for herself. I just didn't want to let her go. The problem was me. Sometimes, when God shows me things about myself, it isn't something I want to see. Sometimes it's a problem I don't know how to handle. *What if Hayley needed something over the weekend?* Well, she didn't need a thing. I would have been on 'stand by' all weekend for nothing!

* * *

Off to Vacation

After a quick call to Hayley to see how she felt about her first night in her apartment and being assured it was great, we headed for the airport. *Jackson, Wyoming here we come!*

We planned this trip for a year. Yellowstone was the topic of one of my research papers in college. My love of volcanoes, rocks, maps, and National Parks was about to be satisfied. While I researched the geology and climate conditions, David memorized the map of the park. He was very interested in the architecture used in the Old Faithful Inn, made of huge timbers from the area.

We were also looking forward to visiting parts of the Park mentioned in a family Journal, written in 1912—Buffalo Bill Cody's niece, was by marriage a relative of mine. She and my father's Grandmother went by wagon from Grasshopper Falls, Kansas (now named Valley Falls, Kansas) to California, by following part of the Oregon Trail through Cody, Wyoming. There, they stayed at the Cody Ranch to visit with relatives, before continuing on to Yellowstone. On their trip they stopped to visit friends who had moved north and west, as well as family members.

With references in Nellie's Journal, there were lots of people from the Grasshopper Falls that had moved north.

Most of Great-Great Aunt Nellie's Journal notes dealt with conditions in 1912, traveling by mule pulled wagon, as well as her observations of conditions at Yellowstone National Park. Word had spread of the wonders of Yellowstone's volcanic landscape after it became a park in 1872 and tourists started visiting. Aunt Nellie's Uncle, Buffalo Bill Cody, built a famous inn opened in Cody, Wyoming in 1903 and it was on her list to visit. It is also on my list now that I've seen the south east entry to the Park, where Nellie's wagon almost toppled off the narrow road into the canyon below. There was less than one foot clearance on the trail for their wagon. Everyone walked those miles along the canyon.

David and I could travel in our rented, air conditioned SUV to visit the exact places my ancestor walked 101 years before. It was exciting to read her cryptic notes.

"Bought a bull dog for $2.50. Crossed Blue River (Nebraska). Drove out to old school house to camp. Jim sold Gray Bell and the mule for mares from a horse trader. Can't get enough to eat. Went to a farmhouse to trade for milk."

That bull dog, not named in the Journal, ended up saving the lives of Nellie's three children at a camp site near Lake Yellowstone when a grizzly bear attacked them. Her comment in the journal was "Dog worth $2.50."

It was fascinating reading her descriptions of the rocky terrain, cliffs with narrow wagon trails, the harsh conditions for finding clean water and safe campsites, the violent high plains storms with hail, and the fatigues of the journey.

Great Great Uncle Jim and Great Great Aunt Nellie traveled with a young couple, newly married, and one other wagon. It was safer in groups. Nellie mentions in her journal that the very young bride was not used to traveling or using a fancy camp stove. The young bride set their own wagon on fire twice. Those journal entries put a new perspective on the word 'travel'.

David let me read to him from the journal as our plane took off. We weren't concerned that we were to fly from Oklahoma City to Houston to catch a connecting flight to Jackson, Wyoming. But, we should have paid more attention this time to our flight plans. It was a little odd that we were routed south when we needed to go North and west. In the Houston airport, we located the electronic board display of flight

Susan A. Rader

schedules, listing times and gates for flights leaving Houston. On the board was Jackson, MS.

For a few minutes, David and I continued to search for our flight to Jackson, Wyoming. We became alarmed as our schedule showed little time to catch our connecting flight. We hurried to the airline counter.

David pulled out our itinerary.

"Excuse me, can you tell us what has happened? We're on our way to Jackson, *Wyoming*."

A very bored, 'heard everything', grumpy, sullen airline woman took the papers and began working at her monitor.

"There are no flights from Houston to Jackson, Wyoming." The never smiling woman began looking at the three pages David handed her.

"You are booked from Oklahoma City, Oklahoma to Jackson, Mississippi, with a return flight in 6 days."

David and I just looked at one another in stunned silence.

"Where does it say Jackson, Mississippi? This itinerary shows Jackson, Wyoming. We have a car rental waiting for us late this afternoon in Jackson, Wyoming."

By now another woman wearing airline insignia and the male supervisor were studying our paper work.

"Here. In very small print, on the third page is reads: Jackson, MS. Every where else in this document, it just reads: Jackson."

"What do we do?"

David and I exchanged glances.

"Well, we could go back to Oklahoma City and start over." David shook his head. "No. I have these days off for vacation. There has to be a way to get to Jackson, Wyoming tonight." He turned back to the airline desk.

"How much is a flight from Houston to Jackson, Wyoming, so we can get there tonight?"

"$3,500.00, there and back to Oklahoma City. But, it looks like we can get you from Houston to Cody, Wyoming tonight."

Stunned. Angry. Frustrated.

"How could this have happened? We talked to our travel agent about the geysers, the volcanos and the Grand Tetons side trip, plus our reservations are in West Yellowstone, Montana! *Tonight*."

The airline clerk just shrugged.

David and I went for a walk. We guessed it had been an oversight, the kind of mistake where the computer anticipated Jackson and added Mississippi. It should have been written out as Jackson Hole, Wyoming. It was clearly the travel agent's fault. But, what now? The travel agent was gone for the weekend, and what would we say if we could call her?

"Well, we had a great trip to Houston."

David smiled. "I think everyone should fly to Houston, just to see the airport."

I laughed. "Well, honey, I'll go with you anywhere. Why not Houston?"

David pulled me over to a quiet corner for prayer. The price was not in our budget, and it meant straightening out the finances when we returned. This was a lot of money to replace from savings, not knowing what part of our trip might be reimbursed by the Travel Agency. The next problem was getting to our hotel reservation tonight, when that was four states away. Providence took a hand.

The airline desk clerk began routing us through Cody, Wyoming, arriving at 9 p.m. 'Miss Angry At Everyone' had almost finished setting us up with an impossible schedule when her computer went down. All information was lost. *There is no mistaking divine intervention when it happens!*

The desk supervisor called another reservation desk. While our unfriendly airline clerk was still being grouchy, the man she talked to set us up with an incoming flight with stop over in Houston. There were two seats available to Denver in time to catch the last flight of the day to Jackson, Wyoming. *Thank you, Lord.*

We arrived in Jackson Hole, Wyoming, only three hours later than we planned. There was just enough daylight to see the southern part of the large geyser field on our journey through Yellowstone. The stands of tall even trees, the hills, towering mountains, and the alien landscape near the geysers were breathtaking.

At sunset, we drove near Old Faithful with a full moon on the rise. Darkness fell quickly as we continued on to the North. The giant geyser fields smoked eerily in the moonlight, wisps of vapor creating changing, shifting shapes that disappeared, then producing more. Stands of dead trees killed by proximity to the active geyser fields stood in rows, like bleached sentries. The ground near the geysers glowed in the moonlight, with distorted markings around them caused by chemical deposits. It was mystical and awe inspiring.

When the road turned west away from the geyser fields, we began driving along side a river flowing from the heavily wooded area ahead of us. The trees began closing in, covering the road like a tunnel, shutting out the moonlight. As a curve approached, I saw something move at the edge of the headlights, like a huge shadow.

"David. Slow down! Animals. Large. In the road or crossing it." *I was suddenly grateful for having had the job as a child to watch for deer or other animals when my father was so drunk he could barely see to drive.* It was an odd time to thank God for training under such distasteful circumstances, but now I was thankful. Some things in your life might be miserable to live through, but there is usually at least one lesson to be learned.

David slowed as we entered the curve, and our headlights picked up three large elk. One raced on across the road, and two stopped to look at us. There were no cars behind us, just darkness, so the two female elk began to graze again.

David dimmed the headlights, moving the SUV very slowly until we were within 15 feet of two elk. One looked up from the tender grass she was munching and stared at us. The other ignored us. We couldn't believe the size of these animals! The top of the SUV was the height of their backs. It was like parking beside a Clydesdale. We were awe struck. Of course, we've been to natural history museums with their wildlife displays but these were living, beautiful, moving animals, powerfully built and amazing to watch.

David smiled. "Welcome to Yellowstone."

I laughed. "We've been officially greeted!"

The two elk became alarmed, turned and vanished into the dark forest. What a trip! With that as a sample of our five days to see the wonders of Yellowstone this was enough to keep me so occupied, I only called our daughter twice. I sent photos and texts everyday, but knowing we were being looked after, assured me that Providence was watching Hayley too.

Little did we know that as soon as we changed our travel agent's schedule, an automated message went to her desk in Oklahoma City. The poor woman discovered her mistake on Monday while our vacation continued. She worried and stewed all week, concerned over our plight as well as our reaction to her mistake. When we returned, David called her. As soon as he gave his name, she burst out with an apology, explaining what happened. She also told David we would receive the $3,500 back,

YOU DON'T HAVE TO MOVE THE WASHER TO MAKE TOAST

and told us how guilty she felt receiving an officially stamped Yellowstone postcard. We accepted her apology. After all, we had promised her a post card from the place she wanted to visit most: Mammoth Hot Springs.

* * *

CHAPTER 14

A Wedding for Hayley and gown for Mother of the Bride

Over the next year, we shared another adventure when David experienced his first kidney stone, and a flare up of the pain in his left leg near the site of the aneurysm. Thankfully the kidney stone was small and a change of medication corrected the pain in his leg. Life was letting us know that time was marching on, and we weren't getting any younger.

Hayley was enjoying her job, learning new things, and spending much more time with her boyfriend, Tennyson. They went on periodic dates, picnics, and game night with Tennyson's friends at his house. It was looking serious. I was concerned as we didn't really know him very well. He had been over a few times but appeared awkward around us. It might have been us being our scary selves.

Tennyson seemed to be a nice guy, a little younger than Hayley, but with an old soul. His family lived in town. Hayley and Tennyson shared their information technologist work, both being 'computer geeks' and video game addicts. We didn't see much of him and when he came over for a dinner or a movie with Hayley, he rarely talked. It seems he wasn't much for family games like 'Racko' cards or pick up sticks. I was concerned she hadn't dated much and was just settling for the first guy to give her some attention. My paranoia and suspicions were from the hard life I led. Tennyson was handsome and they shared many interests, but I couldn't get Hayley to open up. Our daughter kept information on her beau strictly to herself.

One day I asked her bluntly about Tennyson.

"So, do you think he's the one for you?" I believe in directness. No need to beat around a bush.

Hayley looked at me for a long minute. "I have never met anyone like him. He's the closest thing to a soul mate I believe I could ever find."

This was stunning. *Was this a good thing? How should I know! I'm blessed to have been pursued by David. What did I know about this?* I just wanted Hayley to be safe with the man she chose, and then happily married.

The following February, on a Sunday evening, David and I were sitting in the living room quietly reading. The phone rang.

"Hello, Mrs. Rader. This is Tennyson. How are you?"

"Fine, Tennyson. How are you?" *Awkward conversation.*

"Could I speak with Mr. Rader?"

"Certainly. Just a moment."

I handed the phone to David.

"Hello, this is David."

I watched David listening to a short conversation with no facial expression. He said goodbye and hung up.

"Well?"

"Tennyson made an appointment with me for tomorrow evening. Just me."

Silence as we stared at each other.

"Is this about Hayley?"

"I believe it is."

"Oh, David. They're so young. Neither of them have been working for very long. I know they met four years ago and have been slowly spending more time together. Is he going to ask to marry Hayley?" *Here I am, not breathing again. My heart was pounding in my ears.*

I sighed. "Well, 'head of household', get a notepad and start writing questions to ask Tennyson. I'll make a list of things I want to know, and you check them against your list." We spent the next hour scribbling on notepaper.

As I wrote out questions and thought of Hayley being bound by a covenant to a young man, I couldn't breathe. I knew my past was weighing heavily on the negative side. So many times in my life, I had been tricked into believing someone could be trusted. Then I thought of how many people married young, before having set a 'life path'--continuing to change away from old fashioned values in the face of the realities of today's world. Walking a godly path was harder when difficulties arose. I began experiencing panic.

"David, we need to pray about this. You need discernment. I need to not panic."

"We both need discernment."

"I can't make this decision. I have to follow your lead. David, my background is a handicap. I'm struggling with paranoid thoughts, remembering the cruelty, and deceit in my family. Hayley is an innocent person. Tennyson probably is too. She has always been able to trust us."

"No need to panic. You told me what Hayley said about him being her soul mate. Her heart is set on Tennyson. She's not a foolish girl. They've attended church together and church activities, and most often are in a group. I think they've abided by the rules she learned at home. She told us Tennyson is a believer, not just someone who says they're Christian."

When I put my list next to David's, there were a lot of duplicates, so David divided them into categories. Everything required Biblically based answers from Tennyson. This is how we lived our lives so this would be how to make this determination. It was obviously a positive point in favor of Tennyson, since he wanted our blessing on their marrige.

The list of questions covered Personal Priorities, Church attendance, the Essentials of the Faith, Finances, Personal Salvation, Marriage Questions, and Future Plans. Thinking about the questions and what his answers might be, I didn't sleep a wink. If only I could have had their starting point when I met David.

I was going to have to live in suspense for the two hours during David and Tennyson's interview. Working on the computer was taking a great deal of time so I'd be busy enough waiting for David to call me into the dining table. Then, I could ask Tennyson any question I wanted. I trusted David's decision making skills. After all, he didn't have a past filled with family divorces, generation after generation, due to violence and alcoholism.

I loved David's first question.

"Why do you want to marry my daughter?"

Tennyson answered: "She's spiritual. She's down to earth. She's talented. She's beautiful. And I can't imagine living my life without her."

When it was my turn to join the interview, I looked to David for some signal. *Yes or No?*

I sat across the table from Tennyson.

David said, "Well, it is on the subject we thought."

"And, how did he do on those questions?" *As if Tennyson wasn't there in the room.*

"He answered both pages of questions with sound answers."

I was quiet for a moment, trying to absorb this information. I looked at Tennyson and asked,

"So, what did Hayley say, when you asked her to marry you?"

Tennyson looked startled and offended. "I haven't asked her yet."

Startling answer but what a lovely reply in this culture of 'anything goes'. I smiled. Tennyson was old fashioned and Biblical. I decided he was going to be a great son.

"So, did you think you would be approved?"

Tennyson laughed nervously. "That's what I came to find out!" He smiled. "My phone is buzzing in my pocket and I know it's Hayley wondering if you killed me yet."

We all laughed as the suspense wound down. Then in what was the best move we could have imagined, Tennyson reached into his jacket.

"Just in case it came to violence, I brought my Authentic Star Trek Klingon Phaser Blaster."

He pulled it out of his pocket, pointed it between us as a light beam came out. We laughed again, delighted with his sense of fun. I jumped up from my chair, reached across the table to shake his hand.

"Welcome to our weird family! Let me get my Star Trek TV Remote!" I rushed out of the room.

David said, "I thought about sitting during our interview while I cleaned my shot gun. But I don't have one!" Tennyson looked blank and then relieved. I came back with a variety of Star Trek items that blinked and beeped. We talked a short while about fun sci-fi shows including Dr. Who.

Tennyson rose to leave. "I'd better answer Hayley or she'll think I died."

We gave Tennyson genuine hugs, both of us at once. He seemed over whelmed.

"Goodnight. I'm sure I will be seeing you again." His eyes twinkled.

After he left, David and I talked about his answers to our questions. "He has a sound mind. He's good not only with scriptures but with applying them to budgeting and financial restraints. He mentioned possibly having a wedding in July or August."

"That soon? Oh, David. There will be so much to do."

"Well, let *them* plan the wedding."

Oops. Meddling and Smothering again. *Right. Let it go. But, you can make suggestions!* David and I spent time in prayer asking God for the right date for them, the right time, the finances to provide a wedding for Hayley, and God's blessings on their relationship. It was a long prayer, and detailed. We had adapted as parents, but how did you handle a son-in-law? In partial answer to the prayers, David received a bonus from his boss.

"Weddings cost a lot," his boss said as he handed him an envelope. This was just another reminder that God approved, and that He provided this job for David. When David's job of 12 years ended due to the business closing, it had taken him nearly three months to find a new position. At the time, being three months without a job and pounding the pavement five days a week seemed a long hard trial. David's new boss had exceptional leadership skill plus kindness and concern for his employees. It didn't take long for his boss to see David's architectural skill, especially with handicapped codes and engineering details. This was Divine Intervention.

A Full Length Gown

Thinking back to our wedding, I remembered we had a wedding plan and a list of what photos we wanted. It was an old fashioned idea, but it would be a place to start. I pulled the wedding diagrams and planning sheet from our wedding album to make a copy for Hayley. She was less than thrilled. My thoughts swirled around, trying to deal with the idea of my daughter turning 23. At least she wasn't 40 and getting married.

Thoughts and flash backs and planning ideas swirled in my head. I was so distracted with 'what do I do', I managed to lock myself out of the house twice and once out of my car. I just stood in the driveway wondering what happened. *No concentration. Mind wondering.* Then, I remembered my friend Artie Martin. She helped me plan for my wedding night and took me lingerie shopping. *Yes! I could do this for Hayley.*

Hayley chose her wedding colors, and told me she wanted to make herself a butterfly bouquet instead of flowers to carry. "My bridesmaids can carry my favorites. Bunches of Tiger Lily, Sunflowers, and Red Roses."

Armed with this information, I volunteered to shop for her and rushed to Hobby Lobby. There was a sale on their expensive, realistic single long stemmed flowers, some with drops of water, as if fresh from the florist. The perfect day to shop. The mad race was on to find out the details, and help where ever I could. Then, suddenly, there was the idea of me in a gown. *All stop. I'll be M.O.B! Mother of the bride. Oh, no!* I will be mistaken for her grandmother.

A full length gown? I haven't worn a formal gown since my wedding! I rushed to search the internet for 'Plus Size Styles' for a short, wide, round woman. My favorite color, sapphire blue, was available in any number of styles. Hayley helped me pick one to order online. *What did I know about styles? Ugh!* When it arrived, all I had to do was hold it up to see it needed four inches off the hem. *How do you hem taffeta? I only sew buttons on shirts.* This started me thinking of old fashioned girdles, and I realized there were probably better body shaping materials available now. My wedding was 26 years ago. I held up the beautiful sapphire blue shimmering gown in front of me to look in the mirror. Well, this will need a strapless bra....*I don't even want to go there!*

I tried the dress on, and it was two out of three rounds before I got it on my sagging body. I went around and around trying to pull the zipper all the way up from the back. It reminded my of a dog chasing his tale. The short jacket which I wished were big and baggy, was barely big enough to cover my flapping arms and ugly Army tattoo. *Whew!* That was close. Time to lose some weight and go find a body shaper.

In a local store, I found the lingerie department to hunt for 'slimming' devices. One rack after another of body suits. *Aw, yes, the three quarter body slimmer.* The tag read: *EASY ON.* False advertising. Easy had nothing to do with this! I picked a black strapless bra, the ¾ body slimmer spandex, and headed for the fitting rooms. The strapless bra made me feel like my front now had a perfect escape route—just bend over. *Ugh.* My *decolletage'* would be all over the place.

So, I scanned the picture on the tag of the body slimmer, re-reading hopeful words: "Slim your thighs, narrow-your waist-and hips, plus firm your sides-all in one body shaper. Easy On-Pull Up."

This torture device should have had instructions with 'how to' photos.

IF I can wrestle this body squishing portable torture device past my knees, I'll be trapped! Suddenly, it would go up or down!

There I was, alone in the small fitting room. *This is good.* I was too embarrassed to yell for help. I pulled harder, staggering against the sides of the fitting room. Thankfully there was no one in the next fitting area, or they would have thought this was an earthquake! Obviously, I got it on, then somehow got if off. Mostly by peeling as I wrestled once more around the fitting room. I was exhausted and sat there for a while to recover my strength. *This is going to take a lot of work.*

At home, thoroughly determined to wear this body shaping monstrosity, I put it on and off and on again to master some semblance of a technique. Of course, I needed the space of an *entire room,* a bed to fall on, and managed a complete gymnastic-aerobic workout to help me look slimmer and firmer. Actually I just looked like a really old lady in an outfit that was 'not really a good fashion choice'. Or I could be described as a really 'unfortunate view for the eyes' in this spandex black shapeless mass. Note: when you take it off, it crumples. It lays like some abandoned material on the floor. If you don't pick it up to put it away, you'll come across it, be confused and ask 'what IS that'?

After spending the afternoon fussing with this contraption, I finally put the dress, over the 'never seen anything like it torture device' underclothing. David was home from work and heard my gymnastic routine.

"Did that hurt?" He shouted from the dining room.

I shouted back before presenting myself. "Oh, not any more. I have a routine!"

"Sounds painful."

"Not anymore. Just a minute. I'll show you the dress." I took a deep breath then entered the hallway toward the dining room, practicing being regal.

"Wow! You are gorgeous!" David gave me a passionate kiss.

Hmm. Maybe this wasn't as much of a wasted afternoon as I thought!

***

Planning The Day

The wedding day was swiftly approaching. We learned from Hayley that Tennyson's grandfather, a retired missionary and pastor was to perform the ceremony. How wonderful! Since his grandfather attended a large church, he made it possible for us to rent the services of his church wedding planner. The church was reserved for July 12, 2014.

Hayley's personally designed and printed invitations dutifully mailed, returned in stacks, until they counted over 235 people wanting to attend. We hired a professional photographer from our church who knew how to plan the needed photos. Our photographer, Tracey Montgomery, had great ideas to coax smiles out of the stuffiest, stressed or stiffest crowd! David was a hard sell on smiling in photographs.

Hayley's custom made dress, size two and one half arrived in the mail. I called her at work and she rushed home. After pulling out the dress and unfolding it, I picked up the camera to take photos of her expressions as she examined the details of the beaded bodice and drape back. Finally she decided to model it.

When she called me to see her in her wedding dress, she looked so beautiful, I cried.

"Mom, what's the matter?"

"Not a thing. You are so beautiful."

Hayley gave me a hug. She twirled to see the low back of the dress in the full length mirrors. "Oh, this looks elegant. Just like the photos. And I look bony. Malnourished."

"No, you look young and slim." Just then I noticed how the train of the dress had wrapped itself around her feet. "Oh, that's a good sign. You are very graceful, and just turning to see the back, you are posed for an excellent photo. Hold it, while I get the camera."

After a few poses with her dress, it was time to hang it up. "I won't use the steamer on this lace material. Only the satin underneath needs pressing. I know what setting to use on the iron. The top doesn't need anything."

"Thanks, Mom. It scares me to think about touching this with an iron."

"Oh, I know what you mean. I've already tested the iron on my taffeta gown. When I had it right, I used a permanent marker on the dial, so I won't forget the setting. It's not hot enough to scorch any material. That's too much money to ruin with an iron!"

"I'm so proud of you and Tennyson. You have kept your virtue and fought against the tide of just living together."

I considered my background and paused for a moment. "There were so many times in my life when the people around me had more influence than God's principles—His outline for a blessed life. Over the years I heard the philosophy of 'if it feels good, do it', or 'if you aren't with the one you love, love the one you're with'. There is no value in that way of life, but I went along. I found out for myself there are too many regrets." I turned back to Hayley.

"Your Dad and I made a covenant with God first. Our covenant with each other was always second to that. Don't forget this. God is first, and everything else has order after that."

"I know, Mom."

"Of course you do. I so wish my family had these values when I was young. But that's past.

Now, your Dad and I will get to witness your covenant with God. You're giving us a wonderful gift. It's answered prayer from when you were anointed shortly after you were born."

"I don't think you ever told me about that." Hayley looked puzzled.

"Well, it was a ceremony to ask the elder's blessing on your life and health. Then your Dad and I made a covenant with God to raise you according to God's commands. We were to speak of God's laws as we lie down, or when we got up or going through the day, so you would learn the laws of truth, honor, valor, and righteousness. It doesn't make us perfect, but following God's rules has advantages no other way can offer."

I wiped my eyes. "This is how you fulfill 'Honor your father and mother' command. Now, we will see this blessing fulfilled in your marriage covenant to a young man you love, who loves God. How awesome is this?"

Hayley gave me a hug. "Thanks, Mom. I love you."

***

Meeting an In-Law

A few weeks before the wedding, I went to the fabric store looking for glass candy dishes to display in the reception area. I wandered around the shop finally settling on two stemmed eight inch dishes with hand painted butterflies. Pleased they were on sale, I took my place at the counter, and began talking to the cashier about my daughter's upcoming wedding. I purchased thread for my brave friend, Patsy, who volunteered to hem my taffeta gown. I was so glad I wouldn't have to use scissors and glue to get the four inches off the dress! I could only imagine how that would look, based on my experience with tape and staples when appearing before the Promotion Board in Europe. To the cashier, I was explaining how it was 26 years since I'd worn a gown. I then added, "And my daughter's wedding bouquet will be made of butterflies."

The woman stopped, wide eyed, and asked, "Are you...are you Hayley's mother?" She was probably trying to guess my age. This cashier was Tennyson's Grandmother. I honestly think I'm older than she is...*oh, tolling bell sounds.*

I actually was old enough to be Hayley's grandmother when she was born. I was 42. I was certainly old enough to be Tennyson's grandmother, too. *Good gravy! What a way to meet a future in law!* Small town America. Hayley told us Tennyson had a great many relatives who would be attending the wedding. We knew that many of David's family would be coming too. What a crowd!

All I wanted to do was not fall down, trip, or otherwise embarrass myself or embarrass Hayley. Me in a gown, walking regally, gracefully! *Ha! I've never done that in my life.* I'm more apt to arrive like Carol Barnett swinging on a rope or tripping over nothing. Better add *calm* and *regal* to my prayer list.

Tennyson gave Hayley an heirloom wedding ring set from his Great Grandmother. The stones were European cut. Hayley wanted Tennyson to have a ring designed by her. Since I still had the European cut diamond belonging to my Uncle, we offered it. Hayley and I went to look at ring designs at our local jewelry shop where Hayley picked a design. The jeweler said it could be done. We traded the weight in yellow gold from our college rings, and a ring of my Uncle's for the purchase of white gold to be used for Tennyson's ring. They would both have family history in their promise rings.

During the ceremony, Tennyson would remove Hayley's Purity Ring, worn since she was thirteen, and replace it with her white gold wedding band. Their rings would be kept on stage in a small three by four inch silver jewelry box which belonged to Hayley's Great Grandmother Genevieve—*something old*. Hayley and Tennyson did not miss one opportunity to put their family history, family heritage, and personalities into the ceremony.

The church was beautifully designed. A simple yet efficient sanctuary, classrooms, meeting rooms, and an open two story reception area complete with kitchen. Lots of July sunshine to light up their special day. There was a long hallway with a dozen white archways and more summer sun pouring in to set the background for most of the wedding photos.

The ceremony would be in the sanctuary, then everyone would follow the crowd through a few hallways to the reception area. Hayley and Tennyson would leave the stage by the back stairs to reach the upper balcony in the reception hall, high above the crowd. Once there, they would be introduced formally as Mr. and Mrs. Tennyson Boothe to the applause of family and friends. Several generations of both families would be in attendance. The long hallway requiring the guests to turn in order to end up in the reception area gave me pause for thought.

"Hayley, what about a sign post? We can make one that has an arrow on it to show people where to turn at that hallway junction."

Hayley was delighted. She added a thought. "What if several signs pointed to places like "The Shire" from the Hobbit. And I'll give you names of places from our favorite video games. The ones Tennyson and I love to play. But the one on top can point to Reception!" Good collaboration!

David, on his evening walk, brought back a wonderfully aged six foot fallen limb. With some quick saw cuts, a unique sign post appeared. David brought a weathered section of plywood to the garage, and in less than an hour, he presented me with several sign posts cut into varying size arrows. The arrow pieces simply required hand painted titles by Hayley. With a plastic vine wound around the branch, and just for fun, a pair of white Love Birds, the sign post was finished.

* * *

Guys at the Mall

Tennyson made a reservation at an exquisite tuxedo shop. David met him and his groom's party at the mall. It was great that David brought a camera. There were plenty of strange looks on the faces of customers seeing this crowd of young men arriving in baggy saggy clothes with flip-flops or tennis shoes. They stood looking at displays of elegant tuxedos, with vacant expressions. David snapped photos as each took turns being measured by a petite female wedding expert. It was good that another wedding party wasn't waiting. This event of finding head to toe elegant attire for four young men and my husband took several hours. It was worth the trip.

In the mean time, Hayley and I went shopping for lingerie. Since Hayley knew the story of my friend Artie taking me shopping, she only needed encouragement to keep shopping. It seemed we were having trouble finding classic lingerie in colors that flattered her. Perhaps the idea of an old fashioned, modest, trousseau was out of style. So many of the items at popular lingerie shops were tacky combinations seen in burlesque—bad mixtures of colors. Hayley and I both were wearing out.

"Oh, if I find a style I like, it only comes in a dumpy color. Some of those color combinations look like they're from melting a box of crayons."

"Well, there are a lot more stores. We don't have to do this in one day."

Hayley sighed. "Usually I like shopping, but trying to find so many things the same day seems impossible."

"OK. Lunch break. *Then* we go back to the trenches!"

It actually turned into a lovely afternoon when we hit a jackpot of feminine colors and modest lingerie at Dillard's.

"Oh, this is more like it!" Hayley exclaimed as she flipped through racks of nearly sheer lacy pastels. When Hayley took an arm load of lacy clothing in the direction of a fitting room, I cautioned her.

"Just don't get any with pajamas's feet in them!"

Hayley rolled her eyes. "I know, Mom." Then she paused and turned with a twinkle in her eyes.

"What about T-shirts?" We both laughed as she disappeared into the dressing room. Comic Kid.

* * *

Wedding Day

The day of the wedding, I was a guinea pig. A hairdresser who knew how to make my corn silk thin hair look good worked on me for an hour, then I raced home to meet my Mary Kay Make Up friend, Sherry who was able to fill in cracks and crevices on my face. I had tried practicing my make up but the only thing I did consistently was erase and redraw my nonexistent eyebrows, poke myself in the eye with eyeliner, and draw on lopsided lips. *Ugh!* I am so thankful for Sherry Rogers.

When I think of that day, I think of how it only took ten minutes to get into the torture device and then the dress. So basically it took four women to get me to look good. One fixed my hair. One put on my makeup. One ironed my dress. And one knew to soften the focus on her professional camera!

After getting ready, I reminded myself I could breathe, and there was only one thing left—enjoy Hayley's wedding.

In the dressing room at the church, we waited, wondering how many photos could be taken before the ceremony. Hayley and Tennyson did not want the guests to wait around for pieces of their four specialty cakes. Hayley took out a gift box and handed it to me.

"Oh, what's this?" I asked.

"I wanted to give you something special. It's not much," Hayley replied. "I think you'll like it."

I opened the box and saw a silver bracelet. "Look inside, Mom. It's inscribed. I saw this and it was just what I wanted to say."

My eyes began to tear up. Inside, in script were these words:

"Today a bride, tomorrow a wife, always your daughter."

Well, I lost my self control and grabbed Hayley in a hug. Both of us were crying.

Our photographer, Tracey, snapped a series of pictures during this, and I treasure the moment.

Pretty soon, Hayley and I were trying to find tissues to wipe our faces, but keep our carefully applied makeup. We started laughing. Surrounded by friends and family, it was a blessing moment as well as a reminder that even though Hayley was to be a wife now, I wasn't losing my best girl friend.

Hayley's gift to David caused him to tear up, too. Then we thought he would crush Hayley in a bear hug. It was Batman key bob inscribed: *My Dad, My Super Hero.*

The specialty cakes looked great on an exotic cake stand designed by David. It was painted neon green. Using initialed glasses, a bottle of cream soda for a toast, silver engraved cake cutter and a Knight's helmet ice bucket on the neon green table cloth, turned the cake display into a dramatic center piece for the reception.

Their gift table was decorated with miniature rose garlands, and a handmade leather book purchased at a Medieval Fair was set for guests to sign. With a little help from the internet, we made inkwells to hold feathered quill pens, one red and one neon green. Every detail added to their personal touch on every aspect of their special day.

As mother of the bride, I was to take note of the music before the bridal party was to enter. The song was *"Close to You"* by the Carpenters. As it began to play, I stood up early since the doors to the sanctuary weren't even open yet, but I couldn't help it. I would have stood for the entire ceremony, I was so happy for them. It took a new in-law from across the aisle motioning me to sit, to remind me everyone was watching for the signal to sit down. I wondered what she was waving at!! *Oops. Too focused. Sit down, Susan.*

The reception area was filled with happy relatives and a great many people I'd never seen before. Of course I recognized our family, and many long time friends.

Tennyson led Hayley down the stairs of the balcony to the applause of family and friends. The wedding planner introduced them as Mr. and Mrs. Tennyson Boothe. As the applause grew louder, Tennyson leaned over and gave Hayley a big kiss. The crowd below whooped and whistled. *What a day!*

Before they drove away two hours later in Hayley's black Jeep, most of the family had left. The church wedding planners had cleaned up and gathered all the things we brought for decoration. It was time to go home.

Our little girl was all grown up and happily married. Now what in the world was I supposed to do with myself?

My wise sister in law, Brenda from Oregon said, "Don't worry. In about two years she'll start coming back around to talk."

Two years. Oh, my, I hadn't realized how much I was going to miss our daily conversation. But, David was still there. It was time for me to change focus. My job for this part of Hayley's life was finished. It was all right to give thanks that evening, and feel as if our prayer was answered with a 'Well done'.

* * *

Susan A. Rader

Photographer, Tracey Montgomery

CHAPTER 15

Meeting Faith

As my birthday approached, I was dreading it. I would turn 66. That meant so far I'd outlived my father, my uncles and aunts, and of course grandparents. I never could have believed I would have lived this long, given the dangerous events in my life.

My birthday was planned as a steak dinner at our favorite restaurant. I fell into an uneasy sleep, as day and night seemed to blend together over the last week. No energy, pain head to toe. Pressure in my chest, heart burn, and strange numbness on my left side. There had been a few odd jolts, like electricity going from my neck to my right jaw, almost as if the dentist hit a nerve. Sleep was not possible for more than a few hours at a time. Then about every five days, I slept in exhaustion.

My prayers were repetitious, begging for relief. I wondered why things were happening to me that couldn't be explained.

At 3:00 a m, on a Monday morning, I woke David from his sound sleep because of the pain in my chest. This felt worse than acid re-flux or simple heart burn. My chest felt heavy and it was hard to breathe. One place I never wanted to go was to a hospital. I didn't feel well enough to deal with what might happen. Hospitals have always stressed me out, unless I'm visiting someone else.

We arrived at the emergency room, and I was frightened. My heart was pounding which made it harder to get a deep breath. It felt like there was an elephant sitting on me. Or, maybe on the inside of me, a huge over inflated football.

When I'm under stress and anxious, I make lame jokes. That's how I cope. This time, I kept gagging, the need to vomit nearly over whelming me. The male nurse gave me a green plastic emesis bag. Since nothing would come up, I put it on for a hat at about the time the ER doctor arrived. She frowned.

"Well, what seems to be the problem, Mrs. Rader?"

"Oh, it's probably gall bladder and acid re-flux but it seems different. I was getting panicky so I thought we'd better come see what this was. Besides, it's my birthday and we really didn't have a party planned. This seemed like a good place."

Who knows what this doctor thought, but her mannerism reflected total impatience. I could tell because I gave flip answers, trying to play down the problem. I didn't want this to be a case of staying all night. I could see I was relegated to the 'non-emergency'. So often I've seen that reaction because I don't whine, or cry, but keep trying to lighten the mood. I hate it when I go into that 'nothing is wrong' act. I learned it at an early age and it was the wrong thing to do.

A Car Wreck

Going to a hospital was the last thing I ever wanted in my childhood. The abuse could be spotted. If we had to go, we had to have a story that was about an 'accident' or it was just a clumsy moment. The irritation on this doctor's face reminded me of another emergency room visit, four hours after a car wreck when two of my sisters and I were suffering shock from our injuries. The nurses and doctor on duty were angry then, too. We just didn't know why. They treated us kindly, but we didn't miss the angry frustrated looks passing between them as we were treated. How could we know the anger was not toward us, but in our defense.

It was a Sunday afternoon when I was 15. We older three hated Sundays. Our baby sister didn't have to go on a court enforced visit with our father. It was always the same with him. He would have been drinking before he arrived to pick us up, and then keep drinking after we made it to his dark, dank garage apartment.

That particular Sunday I wasn't going to put up with this anymore. Instead of the waiting around while he picked one of us, I asked if we could go for a ride in the country, or wading in the shallow river just outside of town.

Sick of the smell of liquor in the car, tired of his lewd remarks and innuendos, I suggested he let us ride on the hood down a nice country road. He said yes. It was my bad idea and all of us would pay for it. Afterwards, the guilt ate away at me until I had another ulcer.

We were enjoying the ride, but noticed Dad was going faster. Ahead of us, we saw a jeep going slowly as it approached a driveway leading to a farmhouse on the left. At that moment, Dad began to pass on the left, but obviously didn't see the jeep turning into our path.

My sisters looked at me, wide eyed. They were 14 and 9.

"We'll be all right. Pray. Hold hands. This could hurt, but I don't see us dying."

I'll never know why I said that last part as it came from certainty. At this point, we saw the wreck happen in slow motion.

We heard the crunch of metal on metal, and the next thing I remember was a view of the car and jeep locked together at the front wheels, and not far from me. They were skidding, grinding and gouging gravel from the road into a drift at the front of the tires, heading toward me. I saw all this upside down as I skidded along the road on the left side of my head. Then blackness engulfed me.

I heard a voice far away. It was my father's voice. I hurt so badly that I wasn't even frightened that I was disobeying him.

"Susan. Wake up. Susan, say something."

I hurt and didn't care what he did to me if he'd just let me die. Then I heard my two sisters crying and it startled me awake. The pain in my neck and back made me sick to my stomach.

My father was shaking me.

"Stop. Don't touch me," was all I could say and my voice seemed small and far away.

I must have blacked out again, as the next thing I remember, I'm sitting in the back of Dad's car with my sisters. We were covered with dirt, cuts and scraps. When I moved my head to look over at our younger sister who was crying, my neck seemed stiff, and pain shot down my back. I tried to get her to hush.

"Shh. It's going to be all right. We gotta keep quiet. The people in the jeep don't want police here but we can't say anything. Don't let on that something hurts."

My younger sister by 13 months showed me the palms of her hands. Tears were coursing down her face, but she made no sound. I stared in disbelief. There was no skin. Red, raw flesh with muscle, dirt and rocks. She sighed heavily.

Susan A. Rader

"I'm sorry. I shouldn't have asked for us to ride on the hood."

She shrugged and then pointed to my left ankle. My sock looked odd so I pulled it away from my leg. *Gross*. The car ornament was the difference between me being delayed at the point of impact, saving me from being crushed as the two vehicles locked together in the skid. By being held a few seconds behind the crash, I was also kept from being run over.

We returned to his apartment while he drank coffee. He alternately cursed or cried. We had to wait until he sobered up before going to the hospital and we were threatened. Over and over again, he went over the rules for when we got to the hospital. Refuse to answer questions. Don't say anything about how this happened. We had a car wreck but he was to do all the talking.

At the emergency room, it was established we had no insurance, and all three of us girls were separated for questioning. It would have been obvious to anyone that the lie my father told didn't begin to answer what happened to us. I kept seeing looks of anger on the faces of the hospital staff. It was of course, my fault. I refused to go first. When it was my turn, two nurses helped me get up on exam bed. As I lay down on the clean white sheet, rocks and sand came out of my hair and ears.

The nurse asked me where I hurt. I refused to speak. I wanted to appear rude in case my father heard me volunteer any information. There would be consequences when we left, if any of us said anything.

"Well, young lady, let's see what kind of injuries you might have." The kindness in the doctor's eyes made me trust him enough to mention my ankle. I wasn't going too, but it hurt really badly, and I was dealing with guilt because of the cries from my two sisters. One sister had to have her hands numbed and scrapped, and wrapped, and the other endured broken bones in both feet. My ankle required a burning injection at the site to numb it, then a tetanus shot, and three stitches. I felt I deserved the pain.

Other than saying thank you when we left the hospital, we said nothing. I didn't realize how this spoke volumes about parental neglect and child endangerment. Our Dad took us away, unchallenged.

Hospitals still make me feel nervous and sick.

Back To ER

Suddenly back in the present, I sat up on the gurney expecting to vomit. But it passed.

David, trying to lighten the mood, said, "Hey, don't ruin your party hat!"

We both smiled.

"I'll get you for trying to cheer me up. This is getting worse."

The male nurse put on the leads for an EKG.

"Going to get a baseline of your heart to make sure this is acid re-flux. This won't hurt. We will have to wait on the lab results."

I leaned back against the bed, pretending to study the ceiling.

"You know, you have room over there for a rug by that window."

The male nurse looked up at the ceiling, frowned, and asked, "Why would we want a rug on the ceiling?"

"Oh, great conversation starter. Besides, look at all the wasted space. Down here, this room is really crowded."

He smiled. "OK. I get it. Just wait here while I get your blood sample to the lab."

David came over to hold me. "I'm not going anywhere until we find out what's going on. Don't worry about my job."

"I'm sorry to wake you up."

"It's all right. I'm glad you did. I have to have you when I need to get medical help. I'm here for you. I love you."

By then, the lack of sleep, held over from only two hours sleep the night before, began catching up to me. My heart was pounding so loudly I could barely hear, and it seemed I was struggling for every breath. I just wanted to be asleep or unconscious. I just want someone to knock me out.

The formerly irritated Doctor returned but was suddenly very kind.

"We've checked your heart enzymes and that plus the EKG indicates you've had a heart attack." She paused to let that sink in and watched my eyes widen.

"Just relax, we're going to keep you over night and put you in a room upstairs with a monitor. It's nearly five o'clock now. You won't have long to wait for tests. It will be around 7:30 a.m. before the heart doctor can see you. Upstairs, we can help make you feel more comfortable."

I looked helplessly at David. I didn't want a long slow death. If death came, I wanted it fast.

David came over to me as the Doctor left and took my hands for prayer. I didn't know what to ask. Thinking about this, I realized David and I had made a good life, and now our daughter had her own life. Perhaps my time was up.

The hours passed slowly. Fatigue, complete body pain, and difficulty breathing seemed to make time stand still. I was so dehydrated there was difficulty putting in an I.V. I was feeling despair. At 7:15, a technician arrived to push me through the corridors for a stress test, echo cardiogram, CT and ultrasound.

A New Life

Everywhere I went, I saw people on gurney's who must have looked as pale and frightened as I did. At first it was hard to smile, to give them a funny remark or a 'hope you get well soon', because all I could think was to ask God, "Why now? Why this?"

As I lay in ER and then in hallways waiting on a procedure, I continued the discouraging thoughts I'd had all week long. I was tired of being sick, with no answers. I wearied of life.

I thought about how many times I nearly died. One memory came to mind that I hadn't thought about in years. I was saved from certain death by a warning dream while I was in college. All I had to do was move one step backwards to save my life. A heavy metal light protector fell from the top of the gymnasium while I was standing on a volleyball court directly below. Because I stepped back at the right time, it punched a three inch hole in the wooden floor. Why was I saved then?

How many times should I have died due to someone trying to kill me, beginning with my parents; two intruders where I lived; two tornadoes one night that went right past me on highway I was driving on or the hurricane in England. Maybe, since Hayley was taken care of with her new life, it meant my time was up.

Why had I been spared then and why just now was I feeling as if life was over. There would be no saving me from this long terrible trial. There is no guarantee in scripture that I won't suffer a long painful death. My thoughts were jumbled. It was as if I never had faith at all.

I asked God to tell me the significance of why I lived through so many things when I had NOT asked to be kept safe, and now, when it looked really bad, I felt He would say no. What was the message? He would give me the answer the next day, in the form of a person.

As I went through the day I was becoming more discouraged in my thoughts. The more I listened to the heart doctor's long list of surgery procedures and possible multiple surgeries, the more depressed I felt. Yet, I kept meeting kind, compassionate people with peaceful aura's. Always a "God bless you" or a reference to faith. It became harder to stay discouraged.

When I was alone, I remembered a Bible Study that explained how praising God can cure a heavy heart. I began thanking God for the new life he gave me in 1982. I began listing my blessing, as praise. I have a loving, kind, faithful husband, and godly daughter and now a son in law.

It was time for another trip to another clinic. The man who pushed my gurney joked with me about not having a license to drive. I kept meeting people with kind words, a 'thank God', a smile and words of comfort....a very sick man in the hall who smiled a 'hello'; one lady on a gurney waiting on a test who looked like death warmed over, gave a weak smile and a nod....that kind of "God is with you" moment to help you hold on a little longer.

Prayers went out.

I spent the day going from test to test and clinic to clinic, when all I wanted was sleep. I finally dozed off, but I was awakened again by nurses checking my I. V. and giving me a blood thinner to prevent clots.

When I was allowed to have food, I used the phone in my room to call the kitchen. Whoever answered, said, "Happy Birthday". My information came up on their monitor so they saw my date of birth matched with today's date. One of the kitchen managers who was ending her shift brought up my tray. She had added a huge piece of chocolate cake with chocolate frosting. Too rich, but I had a bite. Even the ticket that came with my food had 'Happy Birthday" printed on it.

I once again started to list blessings given to me. David didn't lose his leg with that aneurysm. We have traveled widely and our daughter was able to go on a European trip. We were blessed with trips of shared time together as a family. So much to be thankful for, and then I dosed off until David came to my room after work.

Susan A. Rader

Isatu

We were sitting in my hospital room talking, waiting for me to be taken for one last test late Monday afternoon. A beautiful black woman from Liberia came in. She was Janitorial. We greeted her, which seemed to surprise her. She had a beautiful smile with that lovely dark brown coloring and bright white teeth. She bustled around us as we continued to talk. She left for supplies and came back in, then stopped just inside the room. She looked at me as if for the first time.

She said, in her heavy accent, "I thinks you bes Chreesh-john!" I smiled back at her and replied, in like manner, "I think you are Chreesh-ton, too, Yes?"

She laughed and came over to grab my hand with both of hers and said, "Praise God".

Then suddenly remembering David, she turned hurriedly and said, "Excuse me, Sur, I forgeet my place".

David said as he stood to extend his hand, "Hello, my name is David". This amazed her and she took it with both hands and said, "Praise to God". Then with a big smile, and a nod went back to work.

She came back with more cleaning materials, and bags to collect trash, then stopped to put her name on the wall chart.

From where I lay on the bed, I couldn't make out her name.

"Excuse me? How do you say your name?"

"E-saw-tu," she replied and smiled.

"What does your name mean?"

She looked puzzled. It took a bit for us to communicate. She spoke English, but the main language was Congolese Creole, then two other Liberian dialects.

I told her I was interested in languages. I asked her how to say 'Hello" in Congolese Creole.

She laughed.

"To say 'hal-o. You say HAL-lo, MAHN, how you bees?"

We laughed with her.

I tried it and she laughed.

"Tell me, what does Isatu mean?"

She frowned, not understanding.

"Oh, like my name, Susan. Susan means, Lily. That is a delicate flower that grows under harsh conditions."

Isatu nodded her head. "My name is Isatu Nom-May."

"So what does each name mean?"

She stopped to give it some thought. "Isatu (ee-saw-too) was my father's mother's name. She was Chrissht-jun. Nom-May"....she paused. It was difficult to translate to English so we could understand. She selected her words carefully.

"My mother, she did not want to have baby. Me. She tried to get baby out so baby die. But that not be. I was born, and my father took me. He named me Nom-May. Means: *The one who was to die (or be killed), God saved*. My father is Chrissht-jun, too!"

The meaning of her name hit me like a rock slide. Over the past year, I kept asking God questions, and especially when I arrived in the E.R. I kept reminding myself of how many times I nearly died. I have lived through things I can't explain, even before dedicating my life to the Lord. Then there were more times that defy explanation, except for Divine Intervention, which occurred when I chose to let God change me from the inside out.

I begged God to answer me while I waited on the first EKG during the wee hours. How is it after so many miracles that now I felt the weight of despair itself would kill me? I had just become aware of how to be more involved to serve at church, yet one health problem on top of another stopped me at every turn.

I believe God sent Isatu Nom-May, with the message. "The one who was to die, God saved," and I needed to think about what that meant.

First, this was proof of God's calling for me. Since I have been saved over and over, to live, that means I am still growing spiritually. And God has more plans for me—another Adventure to tackle, for His Glory.

Second, it is reason enough to Praise God for the hours, the days, the years He has given me. He is not finished with me. Looking back, I can see see more and more of those turning points, and God's Merciful saving power. Should I be afraid now?

Sometime in the evening I fell into a deep, exhausted sleep. Near dawn, a lab technician arrived to draw blood. Instead of the usual struggle to find a blood vessel that didn't collapse, he was able to draw three vials in less than a minute. He was done and I fell back to sleep.

The first blood tests taken in the E.R. showed a massive body wide bacterial infection, severely depleted potassium levels, tell tale heart enzymes, and all the signs of a 'silent heart attack'. Now, the blood tests revealed NO system wide bacterial infection, normal electrolytes, and the pain in my chest, arm, and neck was gone. Amazing.

The signs of the 'silent heart attack' were minimal. I had what is called Left Bundle Branch Block, mild nerve damage. As to when that happened, there was no clue. I felt healthier than I had in years. There was no heart muscle damage.

The heart specialist scratched her head. "You had a heart attack, but I don't know when. Now it seems, you didn't have a heart attack. There is no explaining this."

The on call Doctor for E.R who admitted me, dropped in to say I was too healthy to be in the hospital. When I asked him what happened to me, he waved his hand, without answering my question, and changed the subject.

"How would you like to go home around noon? You look too healthy to stay any longer."

"Sure. I really want out of here. But tell me. What happened?"

He just shook his head, waved his hand, again without answering and replied, "I'll have the paper work finished so you can call for someone to come take you home." And he left.

Isn't it odd when Doctor's can't explain miracles?

After a good night's sleep at home, I went to visit a few friends here in town as I ran errands, telling them what God had done. He saved me. I have an occasional extra heartbeat and a mild nerve anomaly that can appear and disappear. It may be related to various kinds of heart disease in my family background, but I have been given notice and time to do what I can to take better care of myself. God gave me the time. I can't undo the damage, but I can accept the days that God has numbered.

Whatever His plans are for me, they will include situations where I must trust Him. That is NOT a 'downer', that's encouragement. Faith tested builds Trust and makes me stronger. I will wait to see how God presents the next challenge. And His solution.

I will *Trust Him!* This doesn't mean I won't be attacked by fear, but as the list of God's intervention in my life grows longer, there will be more to recite. When I remind myself or tell others what He has done for me, I will be praising Him, giving Him the glory because I could not do these things of myself.

Jesus Calling

In *"Jesus Calling"* by Sarah Young, the page marked September 8, is especially poignant.

"Your assignment is to trust Me absolutely, resting in My sovereignty and faithfulness. On some days, your circumstances and your physical condition feel out of balance: The demands on you seem far greater than your strength. Days like that present a choice between two alternatives—giving up or relying on Me." (Psalm 42:5; 2 Corinthians 13:4; Jeremiah 31:25)

My song when going through trials comes from Psalm 66:16.

"Come and listen! All you who fear God so that I may tell you what the Lord has done for me."

I have wanted to write about these things so everyone will know God is Alive. God gives life, and redeems the time. For those reasons, I want to praise Him for the life I have and for renewing my life, on the anniversary of my birth. During that 24 hours everything changed. As if the clock were turned back and I was given more time. I know my spirit soared.

Lessons from this? I am not to concern myself with my short comings and physical weaknesses. Whatever work God has for me to do will be accomplished. I just have the privilege of being one of the workers. I must do what I can when He directs me, and He will supply what I need to finish the work.

The Lord knew that within the next six months, I would face more pain, sleep deprivation, and two surgical procedures. I was going to need to remember meeting Isatu, and how everything indicating a heart attack, including heart enzymes, disappeared overnight. That reassurance was going to be needed.

Doctor Dyer

My body had been malnourished as a child, abused, poisoned, and badly treated over the years. It finally caught up with me. The next problem was surgery for a malfunctioning gallbladder. While I was healing from this surgery, glad that the pressure in my chest was gone, I began experiencing worse acid re-flux. Something was causing this, but was over looked by three different stomach doctors and four endoscopic surgeries. Clearly, an answer to multiple medical problems needed Divine insight.

David and I asked for prayers at church. It seemed every week there was something new. The acid had eroded areas of my teeth near the gums, and damaged them, but especially the permanent bridge in the front. I was going to have to see a specialist to decide how to save them.

In the meantime, I was experiencing more problems with my ears. Infections in my ears began to cause pressure build up in my eyes resulting in visual problems. There were longer periods of severe pain in my ears and the infection created continuous problems in my digestive tract. Obviously, some clear course of action was needed.

It was during a visit to a new ear doctor that Providence intervened with an answer based on another test and the doctor's personal family medical experience. The doctor wanted to see inside my middles ears and the mastoid bones. He ordered a CT scan. This was normal for chronic ear infections especially with Meniere's Disease.

When I arrived at the follow up appointment to see if the X ray of the inside of my head revealed anything, I joked that it was my brain leaking out of my ears, making more 'air space' to account for my being such an air head.

Doctor Dyer was to meet me in a room with a huge screen showing two views of the inside of my head. Creepy looking angle of the skull, and lot's of gray places. While I was waiting for the doctor, I was reading the day's entry in "Jesus Calling".

Dr. Dyer rushed in with two student doctors. He shook my hand and then saw the brown leather book lying on the seat next to me. He picked it up and turned it over.

"Ah, *Jesus Calling.*" And he smiled at me, knowingly. He was obviously a believer.

"Yes, HE is. I love this book."

Dr Dyer nodded. "It's a great book."

I was introduced to his students and allowed them to examine my ears as Dr. Dyer explained my condition, speaking in 'doctor-ese'--that language they use when they want to communicate in front of someone without them understanding a word they say. It's like being an exhibit at a museum while the tour guide drones on about historical events.

"Susan, all these places on your CT scan should be black. Those places in your middle ear and all the holes in the mastoid bones should be showing black. They're gray, because they're filled with fluid and infection."

"How do we get it out of there? Cut it open."

Dr. Dyer cringed. "That would be a procedure. I'd like to try ear tubes again. They are less invasive."

I sat for a few minutes thinking about the less invasive version.

"The problem is if my ears are draining, I can't wear my hearing aides. Then I can't socialize because I won't have speech recognition. I'd be home, alone, for the rest of my life."

Dr. Dyer's expression changed. He was thoughtful for a moment and then, as if he had a revelation, he asked me, excitedly.

"Do you happen to have acid re-flux?"

"Yes. Really bad. It comes out my nose sometimes."

"That's it!" The Doctor seemed ecstatic. Personally, I've never been than enthusiastic about re-flux.

"My two children had stomach surgery and so did I. Too much acid coming up into the throat and sinuses. Then it goes up the Eustachian tubes and infects the middle ear. My second child also had pneumonia from aspirating the acid. The stomach surgery stopped this from happening."

"Do I have your permission to show these CT scans to a surgeon friend of mine? He performed our surgeries. He is a specialist in this area. I can make the referral for you. It's laproscopic. Faster recovery."

Finally, after all the years of unexplained infections, an ear doctor made the connection between my constant sinus problems and the source of incurable middle ear infections. Finding what was causing the problems throughout my digestive track had always been too complicated, and not treatable by medication. But who could imagine that my chronic ear infections were related? This was answered prayer.

The new doctor sent me for a simple test. Drink barium so I glow in the dark. Actually, it just shows what happens on an X-ray. It's my sense of the ironic that affects my humor. Drinking an X Ray liquid was less invasive but that thick past wasn't easy to swallow. This was the most effective way to show that ¼ of my stomach was up inside my esophagus. The opening to my stomach was nearly 6 inches across. This is called a diaphragmatic hernia. No wonder, medication did nothing.

Surgery was scheduled, and I had high hopes. Being medication sensitive, a problem arose with the pain medication when I awoke from surgery. After taking the first dose of the pain medication, I began hearing words from the machine controlling my I.V. Each time it monitored the flow of fluids, I heard the monotone words: "The Code". I was getting really irritated. I asked the nurse to listen to the machine talking to me and she insisted there were no words. She said it was the machine cycling the I.V. *Oh, great. I've finally lost my mind.*

I stopped mentioning it, but then the wall outlet turned in to double smiling faces and the design on my tulips kept changing. My heart rate went up as I saw more and more strange things. I wasn't able to sleep, so except for being under anesthesia, I had been without sleep for 36 hours.

This was no longer a one day surgery with one overnight stay. My prayers became repetitious again. *Please, God help me! Will this never end? When can I have my health back?*

Those questions reminded me that I needed to thank God and recite all He has done for me. A calming verse from Psalms, used in a hymn came to mind. *My help comes from the Lord.* I reminded myself, it was another time to wait. Take a deep breath and ask for the patient endurance I needed.

Sink Hole

When I came home from the hospital, it was a week before I was able to give up sleeping in the living room recliner. Regardless of where I was sleeping, the acid re-flux would choke me in the night and I'd wake up gasping and coughing. Quite often, flashbacks or night terrors accompanied the re-flux, and my heart pounded in my ears. It's an odd sensation to hear nothing but my heart beat. It is like being completely alone.

Thinking about these illnesses, and recovery times, I understood why it is so easy to give up planning, or socializing, or attempting to leave the house to physically attend church. I've been a 'shut-in' over and over in my life. I know how easy it is to become self centered, and then, complacent with isolation, hiding in reading books or watching movies. I believe this is a way of giving up.

This is 'sink hole' thinking. A sink hole forms when everything that supports the ground is removed from underneath. From the human perspective, your life falls apart by being undercut. This amounts to spiritual warfare.

It comes in many forms, and the solution is in scripture. Unless a person has been in this sink hole, with health problems or family problems weighing more than a person can handle, it is hard to understand. In that sink hole, there seems to be no way out, and the desire to try is gone. It becomes tough to imagine anything harder to rise above. This *can't* be overcome without God's help.

While I was at the bottom of this familiar sink hole, David asked me to go out to a restaurant for dinner. I gave him one of my withering looks.

"What if I start choking and everything comes up? That would be really gross. It's one thing to deal with this at home, and another in public."

David took my hands. "Let's pray about it. You have been doing so much better. I really believe you can go slowly, and do just fine. How about some soup? That usually works."

I sighed. "Well, I could try. And we could always bring my soup home as 'take out'."

David laughed. "That's your favorite kind of food group!"

At the restaurant, we saw a couple from church, an elder and his wife. When they spotted us, they stopped to say hello, asking how I was recovering.

Gary said, "Well, fancy meeting you here. It's a good place to eat."

Gloria added, "That soup is a great choice. So, you are doing better swallowing?"

"Yes, thank you. It's been a real adventure trying not to hurry through my food when I'm so hungry. But, the weight loss is great."

This reminded me that I was at a restaurant with my husband, out of the house, actually eating and not choking. This IS progress.

I smiled at David. "Thanks for taking me out to dinner. It's been a long time. I think I was a little nervous about being in public again."

"Well, so far, you haven't embarrassed me!" As David smiled, part of his deli sandwich fell onto the front of his shirt, leaving a trail of mustard.

I started laughing. "Hmm. You need a bib."

David looked down at the mustard on his shirt.

"Looks like a I missed a spot. Next time, I'll ask for more mustard."

Susan A. Rader

Airing A Tire

When we pulled into our driveway after dinner, I noticed the driver's side front tire on my car was very low.

David said, "Well, if you are feeling better tomorrow, you might go over to the 7-11 and use their air pump. Just check it with the gauge."

This gave me pause to think about how 'home bound' I had become. I had not driven my car in several months. The tire had enough air to get me to the pump but that meant being in traffic. *What's the matter with me? I'm trembling.*

I felt as if I had to learn to drive all over again. I waited for the rush hour traffic to subside, then took a long way around, the less traveled route to the store. I arrived at the gas station and pulled behind a car already in line. I watched the man exit his car, start up the air pump and fill two of his tires. *Thank you, Lord, for the reminder.*

Here I was trembling at the idea of using an air pump to fill my tire. How is it possible to be afraid of doing this? My independence, my confidence, my life experiences were suddenly all in question.

I spoke to myself out loud. "Well, Susan, just take yourself home and let David do it."

NO! Not only was this unnecessary wear on the tire, but it was foolish to be sitting at the air pump right now, trying to decide to drive back home. I just had a demonstration on using the air pump. *I can do this.* Actually, I needed to do this. *It was like getting back on a horse after being thrown.* I am capable of doing this job.

If I planned on doing more and more as I recovered from this last surgery, isn't it a good thing that I start small, with something that needed doing? This was a new view of how much I stopped participating in life as I sat despairing, and complaining.

This was a prayer matter, requiring repentance, and requiring relying upon God's help. I do the part I am capable of doing, like shutting off the television, getting off the couch, and setting my heart on restoring my relationship with God. How long has it been since opening my Bible? Then thinking about the past six months, I saw Isatu's smiling face again. I remembered God's message. *The one who was to die, God saved.*

There is a benefit to going through helplessness. The mindset of *"Thank you Lord for the opportunity to trust you more"*, isn't my normal state of mind in a crises. I like *my* independence, *my* strength, *my* vitality, not dependence. But Hope doesn't come to me in that condition! Waiting for God to work in my situation connects me to heaven. I may know I am helpless at that point, so the best thing I can do is read His Word, which tells me God loves to reveal Himself to me. I like that part.

Being wrapped up in anxiety, panic attacks, fear, and physical weakness robs me of Joy. This is me turning away from God, and into myself. I don't like that part. I become very sick of my complaints and then I turn those complaints into conversation that does NOT uplift family or friends. It is me turning away the joy, laughter, and hope I have already learned from other adversities. That means I'm losing ground trying to save myself. *The one who was to die, God saved.* That is what I should remember. God saved me. I didn't save myself.

Deaf

At this point, reminding myself I am dealing with a fallen world and aging body, I remembered another frightening event. Early in the morning on February 14, 2012, I was startled awake by utter and complete silence. Then I realized both my ears were ringing loudly as if I were standing in a bell tower, with multiple peeling bells overlapping. I heard my heart pounding, but there was no other sound. Not my feet on the floor, the bathroom door opening, or the water running in the sink. I stuck my hands into the water to be sure I was seeing what I could no longer hear.

There's no sound! No sound!

I didn't want to wake David, although I wanted him to hold me. I was frightened. I rushed out to the living room, turning on lights as I went. *There is no sound.* No switch noise. No floor creaking as I moved around the room to turn on lights.

I grabbed my Bible and turned to Psalms. I began to read and then I could *hear the words I've read out loud.* I could hear words in my head, as if they were spoken. The more I read, the more relaxed I felt. At least my pounding heart slowed to a plain steady beat.

I may be totally deaf today, not knowing how long this will last, but I can hear God's Voice.

Oh, the relief! God's Word read the same whether I could hear or not.

When David came out of the bedroom dressed and ready for breakfast, I rushed to him.

"David. I'm deaf. There is no sound."

He looked startled and held me for a moment. He must have been talking because he pushed me away to look at my face. I saw his lips moving. *Oh, Lord Jesus, I can't hear my husband's voice.* I cried.

David held me once again, then steered me over to the couch to sit down. He hugged me tighter.

When I stopped sobbing, he handed me some Kleenex.

There was no sound, but he mouthed the words, "I love you. God loves you."

He pulled me against him and rubbed my back, which started me crying again.

I looked up into his face and said, "You know the saddest thing of all? I can't hear your heart beat anymore." Whenever I had a panic attack, David did his best to comfort me, and one of those comforts had been hearing his heart beating, slow and steady. It helped me to take slow even breaths and try to slow my heart beat to match his. Now that comfort was gone.

The total absence of any sound stayed with me for three complete days, then I could hear random sounds but not identify them or know from what direction they came. I kept having panic attacks trying to adapt. There is no where to run to find sound, and I can't escape myself.

Thankfully, we had been to the Oklahoma Hearing Association the last time my hearing suddenly diminished. At that time, I needed a vibrating alarm clock, as well as a volume controlled phone. It was a comfort to know we could go back now to see what else they might have available.

My trip to the Veteran's Administration audiology officially verified sudden, profound hearing loss in both ears. I would need special hearing aids to help me with speech recognition, for whatever sound I may be able to hear. They are like 'smart phones' for the ears.

While waiting on the hearing aids would take three months, I used a Pocket Talker. I called my Pocket Talker, 'Susan Talk Radio". This was a headset connected to a portable microphone. Weird but effective. Of course, in crowds the sounds rushed together and it was impossible to clearly identify one voice. It reminded me how hard it is to live in a 'hearing world' and interaction would have to be different. My world keeps getting smaller.

The frustration was compounded when David would walk in the door from work in the evening. Of course, I couldn't hear the kitchen door open or noises from the garage entry. When we were in different rooms, he might walk in and I'd see movement, become frightened.

My world was soundless. I was alone in the house even with David here. Fears were reawakened, from my past helplessness as a child, being suddenly grabbed for punishment, or being shaken awake. Nightmares moved into the day hours. I needed help.

David installed *"Clarity* Alert Master" boxes and motion detectors which use flashing light as an alert. We plug a lamp into the back of the Alter Master Box, which has a set of 6 icon pictures. When a sensor trips, from the motion detector in the garage, or someone uses the doorbell, the lamp flashes.

I was furious with these confusing things! What sound is the box indicating? I'm supposed to adapt to a blinking light? *I've turned into a moth!* Now, the light means sound? *Susan, look at the icon on the box!* Is it the automatic garage door going up? Is it the picture of the door? Is it the picture of the telephone? *What is it?*

Try it sometime. It's amazing how long it took me to connect a blinking light to a sound. So, I worked on not being frustrated or startled by David or Hayley coming into the house. I couldn't seem to understand why the light was blinking. Usually, that meant a power fluctuation due to high winds or storms. I didn't think I'd ever get this right. Poor David startled me all the time. He was having to adapt too. He began flipping the overhead light off and on several times before entering a room. It seemed the forced 'adaptations' narrowed my life down to watching for a light.

Then, with this thought, I started laughing. How many times in my life have I used the phrase,"well, the light in my head finally came on!" Understanding an idea has always been pictured as a 'light bulb'. This helped me be grateful for a light to tell me something important is happening.

* * * *

Weight Loss

Considering the last few months, the surgeries limited all my food choices. *But this is not the way I wanted to lose weight.* What good is it to have money to buy anything my heart desired for breakfast, lunch or dinner, and not be able to swallow it or digest it? When I accepted my food limitations, I learned to appreciate the food I used to gobble.

Junk food lost its appeal. An interesting result of this hard lesson of recovering from body repairs is now I can go through the narrow aisle at a check out register, seeing all the chips and junk snack foods without wanting any of them. All I have to do is remember how any of them taste, then think of how many ways my stomach could create agony over the next few hours if I ate one of them. That mental exercise is better than my microwave-bowl-splitting-ooze-test on oatmeal. Portion control but with nothing to clean up. Through all of this, I've learned patience. I can add that I have more experience trusting God and His timing.

Perhaps God is working all my brokenness, physically and emotionally, so He can send me on the path of another great Adventure.

THE END

Psalm 42: 5 Why am I discouraged? Why is my heart so sad? I will put my hope in God! I will praise Him again, my Savior and my God!

Printed in the United States
By Bookmasters